Theatre of power

By the same author

International Politics:
The rules of the game

THEATRE OF POWER:
THE ART OF
DIPLOMATIC SIGNALLING

Raymond Cohen

LONGMAN
London and New York

LONGMAN GROUP UK LIMITED
Longman House, Burnt Mill, Harlow,
Essex CM20 2JE, England
and Associated Companies throughout the world.

*Published in the United States of America
by Longman Inc., New York*

© Longman Group UK Limited 1987

First published 1987

BRITISH LIBRARY CATALOGUING IN PUBLICATION DATA
Cohen, Raymond
  Theatre of power: the art of diplomatic
  signalling.
  1. Diplomacy
  I. Title
  327.2   JX1662

ISBN 0-582-49476-1

LIBRARY OF CONGRESS CATALOGING IN PUBLICATION DATA
Cohen, Raymond, 1947–
  Theatre of power.

  Bibliography: p.
  Includes index.
  1. Diplomacy — Language. 2. Nonverbal communication
(Psychology) 3. Soviet Union — Foreign relations —
1945– . I. Title.
JX1677.C64 1987   327.2'0147   86-15300
ISBN 0-582-49476-1

Set in AM Comp/Edit 10/11pt Plantin

Produced by Longman Group (FE) Limited
Printed in Hong Kong

CONTENTS

INTRODUCTION

This is a book about the tacit ways in which states communicate with each other – by using nonverbal signals rather than words. However, it is certainly not meant to be an esoteric or abstract treatise. On the contrary, it is concerned with what states *do* and is therefore fully illustrated with concrete examples. The intention is both to sustain the interest of the reader and to avoid obscurity in the presentation of the argument.

It may seem odd to call a study of international politics 'Theatre of power'. Is not theatre about appearances and power about substance? There are three justifications for the title. The first is that the term 'theatre' is being used as a metaphor for the repertoire of visual and symbolic tools used by statesmen and diplomats when they communicate on international issues. In fact, as the book goes on to argue, the comparison of diplomacy with theatre is a not inappropriate way of looking at how settings, performances and appearances are used to carry political messages.

All servants of the state must be sensitive to the impression they make on observers. For those engaged in the conduct of foreign affairs this is true not only in a public relations sense, but because what they say and do is taken as a guide to official policy. Anyone who follows international relations in the press cannot fail to be struck by the scrutiny to which every detail of state behaviour is subjected. Alexander Haig, former secretary of state of the United States, amusingly and aptly likened the diplomatic community to a vast monastery whose inmates spend their time patiently poring over the smallest item of evidence in search of meaning – whether overt or hidden.[1]

Once their every action and gesture is perceived to be significant, leaders' appearances are bound to become self-conscious and purposeful. As such they can surely be subject to the same sort of 'dramatic', if not aesthetic, criticism as other kinds of public performances. Extending the metaphor, we can view the foreign policy leadership as dramatists or theatrical directors, providing an overall political conception to the performance. There is a script, a basically prearranged text. The setting, consisting of props and backdrop, is meticulously prepared. Not even costume and gesture can be left to chance when the length of a handshake or the warmth of an embrace may be carefully noted. (If this all seems far-fetched, recall the attention every facial twitch of the leaders of the superpowers receives whenever they meet.)

A second justification for the use of the dramaturgical analogy is that the conventional distinction between words and actions, or appearance and substance, loses a lot of its usefulness in the context of international politics. Received opinion divides state behaviour into two realms. On one side is placed the passive world of diplomacy; its tools of the trade are words and its business is advocacy, not action. On the other side of the partition are the dynamic worlds of industry and defence. Its agents achieve tangible gain, changing reality 'on the ground'.

While containing a grain of truth, this oversimplified distinction misleads more than it informs. Of course solid economic achievement and a sound defence are vital; words cannot compensate for material weakness. What is overlooked is that in peacetime states do not impinge on each other in any direct, physical sense – like so many billiard balls – but can only modify each others' behaviour indirectly, by the exercise of influence, persuasion and negotiation. And this diplomatic dimension of power necessarily entails a process of communication or, to put it another way, the manipulation of symbols. Some of these symbols are familiarly verbal. Others are not.

Within this second, nonverbal category comes much of the conduct usually assumed to be unrelated to communication, because it involves doing rather than saying. It includes foreign visits, state occasions, diplomatic meetings, the whole calendar of leadership activities, sporting and cultural exchanges, trade and aid, military manoeuvres, decisions on arms expenditure and emplacement – indeed more actions and events than can be listed here. One can say that most intercourse between states has both an instrumental aspect (which may well be paramount) but also an *affective* or communicatory element. As we ruefully learned during the Falklands war, even apparently innocuous events, such as expeditions by 'scrap merchants', let alone the disposition of naval patrol vessels, can bear a vital message.

Finally, the theatrical metaphor does fit the reality of the age of television. Every evening the TV news reports on international affairs. Where people once received their information about the outside world via the printed or spoken word, it is the visual image that is now dominant. This involves a momentous change. For one thing television does not simply reproduce, like an unseen monitor, what is going on. Its very presence may alter the events which are being recorded. An occurrence which participants know is being filmed and will later be seen by millions on television necessarily becomes a performance, more or less contrived – a media event. Behaviour in the presence of the TV camera can hardly be spontaneous.

Now it is well known that television has greatly affected domestic politics, the conduct of elections and the public relations management of government. It has also influenced the presentation of foreign policy and in particular the business of inter-state communication. Symbols and images have always had a powerful effect on the imagination, arousing emotions that words might not reach. This is the very basis of modern advertising and propaganda. Since TV is of its essence a medium for transmitting images, it has provided governments (and, unfortunately, terror groups as well) with an unrivalled means of tacit signalling. A wealth of information can be transmitted visually to domestic and foreign audiences. The leadership appearances and public events which make up the lexicon of international nonverbal communication are grist to its mill. Moreover every broadcasting innovation has broadened the scope of television. One can only guess at the political consequences of direct broadcasting by satellite.

In a curious way, therefore, the separate requirements of public politics, peacetime diplomacy and media technology have converged to reinforce the role of nonverbal communication between states. There have been many occasions in recent years when governments have wished that television would go away – for instance during the Vietnam war, the Iran hostages crisis and the *Achille Lauro* affair (when President Mubarak of Egypt was embarrassingly caught out lying in front of the cameras). But for better or worse it is not about to oblige; it is here to stay. The least we can do is to look behind the scenes of the 'theatre of power', observing its working, in an attempt to understand both its logic and implications.

REFERENCES AND NOTES

1.   Haig A M 1984 *Caveat*. Weidenfeld and Nicolson, p 86

ACKNOWLEDGEMENTS

We are grateful to the following for permission to reproduce copyright material:

The New York Times Company for an extract from the article 'Iraqis, at Least Temporarily, Turn a Kind Eye to the West' by Drew Middleton in *The New York Times* (22/11/82); Penguin Books Ltd for the poem 'The Renegade' by David Diop trans by Gerald Moore and Ulli Beier from *Modern Poetry from Africa* ed Gerald Moore and Ulli Beier (Penguin African Library 1963) trans copyright (c) Gerald Moore and Ulli Beier 1963; Times Newspapers Ltd for extracts from articles in *The Times* (24/3/81, p 6; 13/11/81, p 1; 5/5/82, p 5).

Twice sing aloud my daughter
A mountain goat by dew-light

(the author)

Chapter one
DIPLOMACY AS THEATRE

From time immemorial diplomatic envoys have met to exchange views, negotiate agreements and iron out differences. An anarchic international system, in which sovereign states are paramount and any central authority absent, places the onus on diplomacy for the peaceful accommodation of usually selfish and frequently conflicting interests and aspirations. Since, simply put, diplomacy rests upon orderly dialogue, diplomats must endeavour to convey their intended message while excluding the unintended intrusion of irrelevant or confusing information. They may, of course, wish to be deliberately ambiguous, in which case they will avoid precision or clarity. But whatever the content of the diplomatic message the ideal is to achieve an identity of intended and perceived meanings.

It is generally assumed that the burden of diplomatic communication is carried by language. And indeed statesmen have evolved over the centuries a *language of diplomacy* making use of specialized terms and conventions so that messages can be conveyed, both orally and in writing, with a minimum of unnecessary misunderstanding. Specially trained officials, often with a legal background, ensure that statements of policy, official documents and the various kinds of treaty, are rigorously drafted so as to convey no more and no less than is intended.[1]

Now it is inconceivable that states could communicate with each other without the medium of language. But what is equally clear is that states have also become adept at using extra-linguistic forms of communication. These forms do not replace language, rather they complement, illustrate or supplement it. Sometimes they transmit messages which it is undesirable to convey linguistically, or which are less credible or even comprehensible if put into words.

The study of nonverbal communication at the diplomatic level is a natural extension and application of work under way for some years in the social sciences. While one should avoid overstating the comparative salience of this dimension of behaviour at the expense of language, a large and growing body of evidence does demonstrate the variety of extra-linguistic channels available to transmit information to our fellows. Posture, gesture, facial expression, body movement, dress and so on equally pass on important clues about such things as status, role, identity and feeling.[2]

Much of this theoretical material is certainly relevant to our concern. But while citing anecdotes from political life, most writers scarcely address themselves to the peculiar function of nonverbal communication in politics, apart from a brief bow in the direction of electoral campaigning. On the whole sociologists are concerned with the role of bodily gesture at the interpersonal level. Even the burgeoning body of research on intercultural communication is more interested in the problems posed when individuals from different ethnic backgrounds come into contact and not at all with the mechanisms developed by diplomacy precisely to overcome such obstacles.[3]

Within the fields of anthropology and political science Murray Edelman and Abner Cohen have pointed to the crucial function of symbol, sign and ritual in communicating and maintaining the great intangibles of social cohesion: authority, legitimacy, national purpose and identity. Highly suggestive in themselves, they again do not seek to tackle the question of nonverbal communication *between states*.[4]

The justification of this book must be to provide a systematic introduction to an area of nonverbal behaviour which not only falls outside the scope of previous work but is also subject to its own kind of semantic logic. As will be seen, the vocabulary of sign and gesture used by the diplomatic community overlaps in some respects with that found in everyday life: a handshake is a handshake. (In some cases diplomatic signals are striking and effective just because they exploit the language of personal relations as a metaphor for the quality of inter-state relations.) However, a number of distinctions must be drawn between interpersonal communication as such and diplomatic signalling.

First, diplomatic communication is bound, almost by definition, to seek cross-cultural comprehensibility. A nonverbal message is useless if it cannot be understood by one's audience. The diplomat must therefore try to reach beyond the cultural specificity of much bodily gesture. The problem is that some of the most resonant gestures shift their meaning across cultures. Conversely, different societies express the same message in quite different nonverbal ways.[5] Although local cues can be drawn upon by foreign envoys well versed in the customs of the host culture, they hardly provide the basis for international communication. Thus diplomats and statesmen are obliged to seek out appropriate signals which will be meaningful to observers irrespective of culture. They then have to combine these units into complex messages. This raises another cross-cultural problem. For even if there is agreement on the 'words', who is to say that the 'sentences' will be intelligible? It cannot be assumed that the perception of pattern is universal.

A second distinction to be drawn is between the degree of deliberation involved in interpersonal as opposed to international communication. To some extent private individuals as Jean-Paul Sartre and, more systematically, Erving Goffman point out,[6] do 'put on a show', at least in certain situations, for others. But this kind of self-conscious posing is possible for most of us for only limited periods. On the whole we pursue our private lives outside the gaze of strangers and without undue deliberation about the messages we are transmitting through our use of bodily gesture.

In the international community, however, all outward directed behaviour is the product of careful deliberation. When in public a governmental figure is always 'on show'. His behaviour will necessarily be scrutinized by observers and he must gauge his actions accordingly. Furthermore, if the gestures of private life are usually involuntary, conditioned by instinct and upbringing, signals transmitted at the level of the state are essentially political and therefore non-spontaneous acts. For the state is not a biological organism (though its agents arc) but an artificial construction controlled by processes of government. When an envoy makes a personal gesture in public he is, or should be, acting under instructions or at least in conformity with a predetermined policy.

Even when individuals do manipulate their appearance to make a conscious point (say, by dressing in a particular way for a certain meeting) it is hard to find examples from daily life of the conduct of an ongoing nonverbal dialogue, in which nonverbal messages are deliberately exchanged over an extended period. Yet this remarkable pattern of behaviour occurs all the time at the diplomatic level. Indeed it is fundamental to an understanding of inter-state communication to realize that nonverbal signalling is not a spasmodic, anomalous activity but a continuous, purposive instrument of foreign policy.

States are unlike individuals in another way. For the state there can be no escape from an insatiably inquisitive audience. Everything states do is under sustained and searching scrutiny. In an uncertain and dangerous world information about others' intentions and perceptions is a condition of sustenance and survival. Nor is self-isolation, even if feasible, any solution. The more a state does try to limit the contact of its citizens and representatives with the outside world, the more significance is imputed by spectators to those public enactments that are observable. In Communist regimes even sporting and cultural contacts are put at the disposal of foreign policy, not to mention more conventional areas of government activity such as trade.

On a shrinking globe both the opportunity and necessity for contact, moreover, are growing at an ever-increasing rate. Trade, security, environmental concerns and cultural solidarities inevitably thrust the nation on to the world stage. Before the invention of the railway, steamship and telegraph, many communities were free to conduct their affairs relatively undisturbed. Self-sufficiency was the rule rather than the exception. The concept of national identity, let alone regional identity, was unknown beyond the pale of European states. Cross-cultural intercourse was comparatively rare. Only 150 years ago an exchange of messages between London and Peking took up to nine months.

The communications revolution has changed all that. Inter-dependence is the modern watch-word; a state of affairs in which nations are unable to satisfy their own needs, both physical and spiritual, without recourse to others. Developments since the Second World War in such areas as the international division of labour, finance and commerce have bound states closer together. As a consequence many new problems have arisen for international law and order. And with the great increase in the scale and intensity of international relations has come a commensurate expansion in the scope for inter-state communication both linguistic and nonverbal.

One aspect of nonverbal communication between states to have drawn the attention of analysts is the demonstrative use of force. Tom Schelling and Coral Bell in particular have provided enlightening studies of military signalling during periods of crisis and confrontation, and James Cable has examined the role of 'gunboat diplomacy' in the modern world.[7] Very little needs to be added to these accounts and therefore diplomatic, rather than military, activity shall be the theme of the present book.

At an anecdotal level the theatrical side of international politics is frequently touched on in newspaper reports and diplomatic memoirs. But they hardly treat the subject either systematically or analytically. What I hope to add to these accounts – while drawing on the useful illustrative material they provide – is a demonstration of the simultaneous diversity and underlying consistency of the nonverbal medium.

There are many alternative instruments of nonverbal communication available to the diplomat – literally an entire lexicon of expressions and nuances. Some of these are self-evidently comparable, others appear quite unrelated. An overall survey of the field can show how different elements perform similar functions, follow common principles and fit together into coherent patterns of information.

To show how diverse modes of diplomatic conduct make up a recognizably distinct phenomenon one must first analyse the purposes to which nonverbal communication is put. The study of military signalling has emphasized the deterrent and persuasive roles performed by the demonstration of power. It should become evident that diplomatic signalling is capable of transmitting a somewhat more subtle and complex range of political messages. Such messages are neither trivial nor marginal but are central to the conduct of international relations.

Most important, a unified approach to the study of nonverbal communication in diplomacy reveals how the various kinds of signal mesh together – integrated by the underlying themes of policy as envisaged by the leadership. Like an artist painting from his palette of colours, the statesman draws upon a repertoire of diplomatically sanctioned gestures to create a harmonious pattern of impressions consonant with his overall political purpose. A Hitler seeks to awe opponents with an impression of overwhelming resolution and strength; a de Gaulle to dazzle the world with French *grandeur* and natural right to be included in the ranks of the great powers.

Alongside the metaphor of the statesman as artist (and 'statesman' is also being used here as shorthand for 'leadership group') a particularly fruitful way of approaching diplomatic signalling is suggested by the work of sociologist Erving Goffman. In his seminal work *The Presentation of Self in Everyday Life*, Goffman compares the individual to an actor on stage. Just as in the theatre, he argues, action takes place within a setting contrived or chosen for that purpose; there are props and items of costume made use of by the performer; there is the performance itself, in which the 'actor' manipulates gesture, movement and speech to conjure up a socially desirable impression for a watching audience. The only thing lacking for our purpose in this characterization is the role of producer or *metteur-en-scène* – the designing mind of the policy maker moulding the total performance.

There is a twofold advantage to the *dramaturgical* approach to diplomatic signalling. First, it draws attention to features of diplomatic behaviour one might otherwise overlook. Second, it emphasizes that element of integration and purposefulness which must be considered central to nonverbal communication between states. This book accordingly takes the theatrical metaphor as its organizing theme.

There is, however, one other crucial reason for adopting Goffman's approach. It is the old story of 'nature imitating art'; the diffusion of television has to some extent transformed metaphor into reality. Diplomacy today may not only be likened to theatre. In the presence of the television camera it has also willy-nilly acquired some of its characteristics. Since the Second World War developments in telecommunications have had a momentous impact on politics. Elections are now swayed by candidates' images rather than just policies. Diplomacy has not been immune from the effects of this revolution.

Let us consider, for instance, the Arab world. In the 1950s it suddenly became clear that the transistor radio had placed extraordinary power in the hands of a charismatic leader like Gamal Abdel Nasser. The lands of the Koran had always taken great pride in their rich linguistic heritage. They now provided a fertile soil for the pervasive rhetoric of the new nationalism broadcast over the Voice of the Arabs.

As the price of the transistor radio dropped to a few dollars, every household, from Marrakesh to San'a, could tune in to the potent message coming out of Cairo. The effect on national expectations, pan-Arabism and local struggles for independence was dramatic.

Since the 1950s a new landmark has appeared over every *casbah* and *suk* – the television aerial. What the Western world has long taken for granted has now arrived in the Third World. To the verbal resonance of the radio has been added the visual kaleidoscope of television. The consequences of this are far-reaching.

According to Marshall McLuhan, the revolution that started at Gutenberg, with the invention of the printing press, destroyed the traditional, face-to-face community. The printed word replaced the spoken word as the repository of tribal wisdom. Speech had engaged speaker and listener in an exchange bringing all the senses into play. Facial expression, gesture, intonation, atmosphere, 'presence', all combined to enrich and impart meaning to the oral tradition of the community. In contrast, McLuhan argues, the printed word, laid out in invariant uniformity, is an impoverished and desiccated source. Its effect has been to regiment man, sever him from the wisdom of the race and bankrupt his culture. But all is not lost. Television can rescue us from this debilitating predicament. By linking mankind in a vast network of telecommunications it can reconvene the tribal village on a global scale. The spoken word is restored to its former place of glory.[8]

Now, as a detailed argument, much of what McLuhan says is questionable. This is not the place to demolish him.[9] However, some of his general insights are deeply suggestive and relevant to what is now happening in international relations. Classic diplomacy, in the pre-electronic age, rested almost entirely on linguistic skills. The primary means of communication was the written word or a spoken message emptied of its emotive content. Obviously there was bound to be a certain element of theatricality in the conduct of diplomacy. Human beings were involved and not automata. But the ideal diplomat was supposed to repress emotion and individuality. His lodestar was Talleyrand's famous piece of advice: 'Above all avoid an excess of enthusiasm.' The remark characterized an entire diplomatic tradition. Any scope that might have remained for the leakage of nonverbal information was limited by protocol. Detailed manuals of rules and regulations were drawn up to govern conduct on every conceivable occasion. Spontaneity was anathema; deviation from the norm was 'bad form'.   The intrusion of television has altered the scope for 'theatricality'. Linguistic skills are no longer sufficient. The diplomat and the national leader are now required to be television performers. Those qualities of reticence formerly associated with the ideal diplomat are completely unsuited to the television screen. The image is the message. It is the visual impression even more than what is said that counts for the viewer. Whether he likes it or not the television performer is, by definition, on stage.

In the presentation of news, television, moreover, possesses characteristics quite different from those of the press or radio. It creates a sense of attending on events in a way that can only be compared to the immediacy of direct experience. The photograph, too, provides a visual image – and is sometimes a telling instrument of statecraft – but it is frozen and lifeless. Television depicts action, movement, 'reality'. It is excellent at depicting the sense of a human relationship, the intimate reaction of one individual to another. Thus television is the ideal medium for conveying nonverbal information.

Over the last decade technological advances have broadened the repertoire of television still further. Inventions such as the communications satellite and the shoulder-held camera have made it increasingly possible to cover foreign news as it occurs or for the next scheduled news broadcast. The inventory of international dialogue and interaction is now routinely screened for the general viewer: state visits, diplomatic shuttles, debates in the UN General Assembly, military manoeuvres, hijackings, terrorism and even full-scale warfare have become common fare. Events that previously occurred before restricted audiences or were never seen at all have been opened to the public gaze. We can now watch, in real time, an American president arriving on the soil of the People's Republic of China, an Egyptian leader making a momentous speech to the Israeli parliament, the holding by an insurgent group of a London embassy – and its liberation – and even the stately, if menacing, passage of a Soviet fleet through the Dardanelles. There is hardly anything, it sometimes seems, that an ingenious and courageous TV crew cannot film. Even closed societies, by accident or design, are falling under the purview of the ubiquitous camera. Riots in Warsaw, the attack by Afghani fighters on a Soviet supply column, the unsteady performance of a succession of decrepit Communist leaders, have all been screened in recent years.

All events, and certainly those that have been planned in advance, are potentially media events. Governments are now aware that any public action for which they are responsible may be transmitted worldwide. Should they so desire, even apparently 'private' or 'spontaneous' occurrences can be staged for their visual impact.

The first major diplomatic encounter to be structured around the requirements of prime-time television was the 1972 Nixon visit to China. Public-relations experts usurped the role formerly taken by protocol officials in its preparation. As a result, the significance of what occurred was unmistakably forced home to hundreds of millions of people. To the American public 'television established the reality of the People's Republic and the grandeur of China as no series of diplomatic notes could possibly have.' The banquets, televized live, 'performed a deadly serious purpose. They communicated rapidly and dramatically to the peoples of both countries that a new relationship was being forged.'[10] Such was the appraisal of Henry Kissinger. Outsiders were no less profoundly impressed. In Japan viewers watched the Nixon arrival and reception with trepidation. One official admitted its impact upon him: 'Watching television, I realize this is an historic turn-around after all. I am shocked.'[11] The Nixon trip made clear that communication between nations is no longer the preserve of a closed circle of leaders, their officials and officers. Everyone can look in.

Thus the neutral, flat formulations of diplomatic messages have been supplemented by pregnant and evocative – if equally painstakingly choreographed – visual images on the television screen. Nonverbal communication – gesture, symbol, ceremony, demonstration – may be beside the point when it comes to detailed negotiation. It has no place in the meticulous drafting of legal texts. No one should mistake the perennial importance of these instruments. But as international society takes on the intimate traits of McLuhan's electronic village, the burden of communication between states is becoming increasingly carried by a choreography of deeds and not just words.

The use of nonverbal communication in international relations did not, of course, suddenly materialize with the advent of television. There are many examples of the grandiloquent gesture in history. Indeed it is often the gesture rather than the word which is passed on by the national memory. (Who remembers what Magna Carta actually *says?*) In the twentieth century Hitler was the first master of the medium, exploiting to the full its remarkable potential for control and manipulation. His career and movement were founded on the mobilization of mass audiences. Even his speeches were sound performances rather than reasoned expositions. Powerful tribal symbols were evoked, woven into a tapestry of setting, light and pageantry.

Significantly, the Nazi regime broke new ground in exploiting the cinema for political purposes. Of the 1936 Nuremburg rally, immortalized in Leni Riefenstahl's satanic masterpiece, *Triumph of the Will*, it was perceptively said that the event was created for the film and not the film for the event. This was literally true in that the director herself was closely involved in the staging of the rally. Settings, props and the choreography of the Führer's movements in the stadium were carefully planned for their cinematic effect.

The same theatricality used to legitimize the regime internally, mobilize the German people and project the image of an infallible Hitler, was drawn upon for the achievement of foreign policy objectives. The 1936 Berlin Olympics were staged both to glorify the regime and to create an image of Nazi prestige, power, efficiency and purpose in the eyes of the world. They were a stunning success. Not for the last time the festival of international solidarity was exploited as a showcase of nationalist achievement.

Hitler's diplomatic encounters were also carefully orchestrated. One of the classic tricks used by Hitler when he received foreign dignitaries whom he wished to overawe was satirized by Charlie Chaplin in *The Great Dictator*. Film enthusiasts will recall how Hynkel plans his fellow dictator Napaloni's entry into the throne room in order to establish his own superiority: an endless trek from the main door; a lower chair for the guest. Extraordinarily enough, we now know that

Hitler did actually plan his new chancellery, together with Albert Speer, with attention to the need to impress foreign visitors. He told Speer: 'On the long walk from the entrance to the reception hall they'll get a taste of the power and grandeur of the German Reich!'[12]

Since the Second World War television and the cinema have been increasingly taken into account in the orchestration of diplomacy. Various factors have combined with the development and dissemination of the electronic media to bring this about: the growth in the number of independent states and the need of new leaders to mould a sense of nationhood; the extension of diplomacy beyond the old, largely European, 'magic circle'; the decline in the aristocratic bias in the manning of foreign services and governments; the emphasis on open diplomacy at the UN and international conferences; the new salience of regional diplomacy with its rhetoric of fraternity; in all, an immense increase in foreign contacts.

The fundamental point is that as communication proliferates across national boundaries both linguistic barriers and the inherent limitations of language project themselves with growing insistence. The spoken word, filtered through the medium of an interpreter, is just not a very good way of reaching out to a foreign audience. Particularly cultures with an oral rather than a written tradition of language, for which the sound and rhythm of speech are all-important, tend to be unresponsive to the language of outsiders. Ada Bozeman demonstrates this very clearly in her study of *Conflict in Africa*.[13] Such cultures have also always relied heavily on nonverbal means of communication. It is only natural that they should extend a rich, existing tradition to the international sphere.

Even the Arab states, with their long history of literacy – but with an equally developed sense of rhetoric and hyperbole – sometimes find it difficult to take seriously the understatement of the Western diplomatic tradition.[14] When one adds to the equation the emphasis placed by Arab culture on the personal dimension of political relationships, the result is a diplomacy for which nonverbal communication comes as second nature. Arabs are literally left cold by purely formal, impersonal contact and relish the warmth of personal intimacy. Similar considerations hold for many of those non-European societies falling into the category of what E. T. Hall calls *high context* cultures: cultures for which the burden of significance is carried by the extra-linguistic circumstances, accompanying cues and medium of a message, rather than by its explicit meaning alone.[15]

The ideas sketched out so far will be developed more systematically during the course of this book. However, much of what I have been arguing is well exemplified by the Sino-American dialogue at the beginning of the 1970s already referred to: two cultures, with a minimal common language, did succeed in conducting a productive dialogue under inauspicious conditions. How they did it can serve as a paradigm of international and also cross-cultural nonverbal communication.

A generation has grown up taking for granted the links between the People's Republic of China and the West. Yet until Henry Kissinger's secret trip to Peking in 1971, the idea of contact between the two rivals seemed impossibly remote. For years Communist China was painted in almost demonic colours, perceived as incorrigibly expansionist and bitterly hostile to all things American. One of the arguments for intervention in Vietnam was the need to contain the spreading flood of Chinese Communism.

As we now know, perceptions of Chinese intentions were inaccurate. Far from being an unstoppable juggernaut, mainland China was a weak, developing country, struggling with immense internal problems. From the death of Stalin onwards, relations between Peking and Moscow slid downhill at an increasing rate. By 1960 their quarrel was out in the open, though expert observers had been reading the signs for some time.

Since the early 1950s Peking had tried to get the message across to Washington that it wished the United States no ill and was interested in friendly relations. At the Geneva conference of 1954 Chou En-Lai offered his hand to John Foster Dulles but was cuttingly ignored. From 1954 onwards Chinese and American officials had regularly met to discuss issues arising out of the Korean war. Contacts continued in Warsaw even after outstanding issues were dealt with. Clearly the Chinese wished to leave the option of dialogue open. For years, though, established positions were simply reiterated. In the middle 1950s Chou had spoken out with surprising warmth of the United States, knowing the message would reach American ears. On a visit to Afghanistan he told local leaders that he had not forgotten the United States. American education, medical missionary work in China and wartime support against the Japanese invaders had put the Chinese people in America's debt. 'He was puzzled [an official at the United States embassy in Kabul reported home] why the Americans, by spurning China's desire for friendship, were allowing their great reservoir of good will in China to be replaced by the inbred hostility of a whole new generation.'[16] How can one account for this uncharacteristically churlish response on the part of the United

States? Partly it was the anti-Communist crusading fervour of the period, the strength of the China lobby, the fear of official Washington, after the McCarthy nightmare, of stepping out of line. But it was also because of the inherent limitations of conventional diplomacy. Who believes the protestations of friendship of a demon? How can mere words pierce the armour of prejudice and fear? In certain situations – crisis, embedded hostility, turning points in relationships – language simply lacks credibility, force, the capacity to deflect nations from their ponderous courses. The arid tedium of diplomatic language is excellent for the conduct of ongoing, routine relations. It rarely rises to more dramatic occasions. Words are too often worn out, flaccid, muted by surrounding voices and distractions or lost in the bureaucratic maze.

It was going to take more than a dry exchange of messages for the United States and the People's Republic of China to restore a working relationship. First, minimal confidence and credibility had to be painstakingly established after years of bitter hostility. Both sides were worried about being deceived and double-crossed. How could one be sure about the other side's sincerity? Might he wish, not to negotiate in good faith, but to compromise his interlocutor and then to let him humiliatingly down? The mere impression, in the eyes of the world, that one side was an impatient supplicant would have raised awkward questions. It would also have been embarrassing and counter-productive.

Second, any dialogue was bound to be protracted. Suspicions could not be removed overnight. Contentious issues lay around like a mine-field. Premature disclosure would enable domestic and foreign opponents of improved Sino-American relations to mobilize against the negotiating process in an attempt at sabotage. In some way, therefore, the dialogue had to establish confidence, construct an honourable symmetry of mutual commitment, and create an irreversible momentum. By the time news of the initiative was revealed to the world, it would have to have reached a point of no return.

Third, both China and the United States had to overcome the inertia and ingrained hostility of elements in government and public opinion. Years of propaganda had produced, on both sides, demonic images of the opponent. A sudden, unexpected and inexplicable shift might be unsustainable. If improved relations were to have any permanence, Chinese and American officials and citizens would have to be brought along.

The problem was especially acute for Chinese officials. In the past ideological upheavals had proved to be short-lived. Over-enthusiastic converts in the hundred flowers campaign and cultural revolution had later found their careers and reputations ruined when the wind had changed back. Why should they now go along with a policy which might be subsequently repudiated?

In the United States there was a wider problem of public opinion. 1972 was an election year. No president could risk, for political or substantive foreign policy reasons, a move that might be unpopular with the electorate. A way had to be found of accustoming people on both sides to the idea that improved relations were conceivable and tolerable. Education would have to be gradual, to avoid shocking domestic critics.

Finally, communication was complicated by the absence of formal diplomatic ties between the People's Republic of China and the United States. The irregular Warsaw talks could be (and, indeed, were) used to pass on messages. The disadvantage of this channel was that it had become institutionalized. A revolutionary breakthrough required, in the first instance, overcoming bureaucratic inertia and nit-picking, not adding to them. This was one further reason for seeking unconventional means of communication.

All in all messages were finally passed on along three primary channels. At the first level were carefully worded public statements intended to signal, to the initiated, the *possibility* of changes in policy in Peking and Washington. Such statements drew the attention of careful observers, at home and abroad, to an option not yet a reality. At the second level messages were passed on through the good offices of friendly third parties indicating a willingness for dialogue. No direct or formal contact was involved and so there was no commitment to be disavowed. Not a great deal could be said when the postman was reading the mail. What could be signalled was less substance so much as sincerity of purpose. By using a trusted intermediary the likelihood of a double-cross was reduced. However much the two sides might be tempted to let each other down, they would presumably recoil from embarrassing a mutual friend, valued by both of them, since this would damage their own interests. Thus, as is frequently the case in diplomacy, the medium of the communication was as expressive as the message.

At the core of the Sino-American dialogue, however, was a fascinating interplay of gesture, signal and symbol. Male cranes engage in a ritual 'dance' to determine the character of their relations. The United States and Communist China sought, by an analogous diplomatic minuet, to create the basis of a *modus vivendi*. Their manoeuvres, a subtle balance of conciliation with the merest hint of threat, were so much more suggestive than anything words could have expressed.

America's message was transmitted over a two-year period, from July 1969 to June 1971. It was largely contained in the gradual easing of a series of controls on trade and travel with mainland China first imposed at the time of the Korean War. At first derestriction covered only *Chinese-made* goods, purchased by tourists, up to the trifling value of $100. A few months later the $100 ceiling was lifted. Then it was announced that *US subsidiaries abroad* could trade with the people's republic. Soon *US-made components* were cleared for export as part of foreign orders. By July 1970, within a year of the first move, *US engines in Italian trucks* were given a green light. And so it went on, step by step, until, at the culmination of the process in June 1971, the administration announced that a broad range of non-strategic goods could be directly exported to Communist China.[17]

It was all deliberately low-key and technical. This had several advantages. Trade had always been a central feature of American ties with China. Given America's commercial reputation, and Communist stereotypes of capitalism, measures, however modest, aimed at restoring trade, could be expected to carry particular conviction. Further, nobody's prestige was at stake. As Dr Kissinger emphasizes, the moves did not require reciprocity or acknowledgement and so could not be rebuffed. Finally, coming in easy stages, no single step was controversial enough to arouse a domestic outcry but the cumulative effect would build up Chinese confidence in America's sincerity and consistency.

Underlying these gestures of goodwill there was also a less philanthropic theme. As unilateral acts of government, any concessions could always be withdrawn. Public opinion and Congress were not engaged. The form of the message contained a further hint. The United States was not giving anything away but simply removing restrictions on normal contact. So while China could look forward to an end to international leprosy, the United States was emphasizing its own power to grant or withhold the cure. As an index of status, the policy of decontrol implied just a touch of condescension. This is why, in the end, Kissinger and Nixon could afford to visit the Chinese leadership and not the reverse. Theirs was a concession of the powerful.

From the Chinese side came a number of signals that were as economical as they were subtle. If American images possessed the attention to detail of a Norman Rockwell portrait, those of the Chinese were as starkly symbolic as a study in oriental calligraphy. China's first move was brilliantly opportunist. On 16 July 1969 two American yachtsmen whose boat had capsized were taken into custody in Chinese waters. Instead of the anti-American hullabaloo that had marked such episodes in the past, Peking kept eloquently silent. In its own way this absence of a reaction might be as significant as the fact that the dog did not bark in the night in the Sherlock Holmes story. It might mean nothing or it might imply, as was indeed the case, a pointed abstention from an unfriendly act. On 21 July 1969 the State Department therefore announced, exploiting the timing, the first easing of restrictions on trade and travel to the People's Republic. Three days later the American yachtsmen were released.

On the surface, given the circumstances of the gesture (always significant in nonverbal communication) its meaning was obvious enough. It was a unilateral gesture of good will which committed the Chinese to nothing and could not be rebuffed. It also had some subtle touches. Apparently spontaneous, it was even more elliptical and disclaimable than the administrative exercises of the State Department. As a humanitarian gesture, it was good public relations, aimed perhaps to alter the sinister image of inhumanity attached to Peking in the media. By exploiting the human angle the Chinese indicated a grasp of American psychology and the mechanics of public opinion. Since the signal was aimed at both government and public opinion Peking was intimating that it could always go over the head of the administration and appeal directly to the people. Hanoi had used this very stratagem in its anti-American propaganda with devastating success.

On two further occasions China released American detainees. In December 1969 two other yachtsmen were set free. Nothing new was being signalled, but the very fact of reiteration suggested that Peking retained its interest. By July 1970, with the dialogue well under way, the Chinese ratcheted up their interest another notch. This time they released an American bishop, James Walsh, who was serving a twenty-year prison sentence for spying. The innovation was not only in the rank of the citizen set free, but his status: Walsh's release was an official act of clemency.

China's big gesture came on 1 October 1970. Ironically, it was overlooked by the administration at the time! It involved the use of a classic device of Communist choreography. Mao Tse-tung was photographed together with the American writer Edgar Snow, who had written the sympathetic account *Red Star Over China*, reviewing the annual anniversary parade. Now it is a central convention in the Communist world that a meeting between the party leader and a foreign visitor is a privileged mark of friendship. The ultimate accolade for a guest is to be invited to the reviewing stand alongside the party leader at one of the two great Communist holiday parades. It is doubtful whether the parading masses have any idea of the identity of the visitor. The point is the symbolism of the display. The gesture is an act of political theatre, intended to broadcast a political message. As an individual the guest is of no inherent interest to Peking. His significance only derives from the country or movement he is thought – or picked out – to represent. Nor, in the Communist system, do things take place by accident.

Here, then, was Edgar Snow, an American citizen, a distinguished writer and known friend of the Chinese Communist movement since the 1930s, being held up to the regard of the Chinese people. The intention could only be to honour the United States. It was, therefore, the most unmistakable signal to date of Chinese willingness at the highest level and in full public view to cultivate friendly relations with the United States.

As usual, appearances were not the whole story. Edgar Snow was also a journalist and in fact was given an interview by Mao a few weeks later. Again the option of an appeal to US public opinion was being suggested. Finally, the very public nature of the gesture emphasized a theme that the Chinese were to reiterate. This was to be no hole and corner affair. Only an open relationship would serve Chinese purposes: to gain full membership of the international community and to obtain a visible counterweight to the USSR. Having said all this, the fact is that the gesture was completely missed in Washington. So nonverbal signals are not infallible. Nevertheless the lesson of the episode must be to underline the need for greater sensitivity to this form of communication on the part of the sometimes too literal-minded West.

The culmination of China's campaign came in the spring of 1971 with the invitation of the American ping-pong team to the People's Republic. It was a bravura performance. At one level it repeated and amplified previous themes: the wish for friendship, the insistence on an open relationship, the people-to-people motif. But now the Chinese government had gone dramatically and irrevocably public. It was no longer a question of releasing unwilling detainees or receiving proven friends. The invitation was extended to a group of ordinary Americans representing their country at sport. Pictures published at the time show Chou En-lai laughing together with the president of the US table tennis association and Chinese passers-by greeting Americans with warm smiles. For Dr Kissinger such graphic evidence provided him with the assurance that an official American emissary 'would step on friendly soil'.[18]

As before, the aesthetics of the gesture excite admiration. If the United States had eased trade restrictions – emphasizing what it did best – the People's Republic had invited a table tennis team – emphasizing what it did best. No admission of supplicant status here. At the same time as the American visit, six other teams (who had also been playing in the world championships in Japan) were invited to China. It all symbolized, for the benefit of party cadres and outside observers, a great turning outward. The United States would have to note that the dyke against Communist China would be breached whether Washington liked it or not. Not all the cards were in the American hand.

One final image, among many, is worth recalling. Alongside the carefully staged photos of happy Americans and smiling Chinese we find Chou En-lai chatting with a young, long-haired American sportsman. 'I understand you,' Chou is reported as saying. An entire sub-culture and period of history were encompassed by Chou's image: the Vietnam war, the protest movement, the erosion of American authority. All this Chou understood; it was dire necessity, not philanthropy that drew the two sides together. . . .

Within a short time the intricate courtship display by which China and America sought to attract each other resulted in an invitation for an American envoy to come to Peking. In July 1971 Dr Kissinger made his astonishing first trip. The barriers had finally come down.

REFERENCES AND NOTES

1. Cohen R 1981 *International Politics: the rules of the game*. Longman, ch. 5
2. Good introductions are: Knapp M L 1980 *Essentials of Nonverbal Communication*. Holt, Rinehart and Winston: New York;   Burgoon J K, Saine S 1978 *The Unspoken Dialogue: an introduction to nonverbal communication*. Houghton Mifflin: Boston; The *Journal of Nonverbal Behavior* covers current research in the field
3. The best introduction is Gudykunst W B, Kim Y Y 1984 *Communicating with Strangers: an approach to intercultural communication*. Addison-Wesley: New York
4. Edelman M 1964 *The Symbolic Uses of Politics*. University of Illinois Press: Urbana;   Cohen A 1974 *Two-Dimensional Man*. University of California Press: Berkeley
5. For example, see Wylie L W 1977 *Beaux Gestes: a guide to French body talk*. Undergraduate Press: New York
6. Sartre J-P 1956 *Being and Nothingness*. Philosophical Library,

New York; Goffman E 1969 *The Presentation of Self in Everyday Life*. Penguin

7. Schelling T C 1960 *The Strategy of Conflict*. Oxford University Press; Schelling T C 1967 *Arms and Influence*. Yale University Press, New Haven; Bell C 1971 *The Conventions of Crisis*. Oxford University Press; Cable J 1971 *Gunboat Diplomacy*. Praeger: New York

8. McLuhan H M 1962 *The Gutenberg Galaxy*. University of Toronto Press: Toronto

9. For an effective critique see Miller J 1971 *Marshall McLuhan*. The Viking Press: New York

10. Kissinger H 1969 *The White House Years*. Little, Brown: Boston, pp 1067, 1069

11. Meyer A H 1974 *Assignment Tokyo*. Bobbs-Merrill: New York, p 164

12. Speer A 1970 *Inside the Third Reich*. Macmillan: New York, p 103

13. Bozeman A 1977 *Conflict in Africa*. Princeton University Press: Princeton

14. See Prothro E T 1955 Arab-American differences in the judgement of written messages, *The Journal of Social Psychology* 42: 3–13

15. Hall E T 1976 *Beyond Culture*. Anchor Press: New York

16. Meyer A H 1974 *op cit*. p 149

17. Kissinger H 1979 *op cit*. chs 8, 18

18. *Ibid*. p 710

Chapter two

WHY NONVERBAL COMMUNICATION?

Most of the time, words suffice. Routine diplomacy, which carries the overwhelming burden of inter-state contacts, is basically a highly sophisticated verbal exercise. Nonverbal communication, then, performs a special function. What is it and why is it needed?

To begin with, a working definition. By nonverbal communication at the international level I mean both the deliberate transfer of information by nonverbal means from one state to another and also from the leadership of a state to its own population on an international issue.

An act of communication must, first and foremost, be deliberate – there must be a conscious intention to convey a message. After all, if speech is meaningful by definition, actions are assumed to have a practical purpose. An aircraft carrier may make a subtle political point, but it is still a fearsome weapon of war. The agencies of symbolic action are instruments in their own right.

Having said this, a genuine paradox presents itself. For an act to constitute a signal, it must clearly be intended as such. But if it is explicitly acknowledged by its initiator to be a signal, it may lose its point. The advantage of a nonverbal signal may lie precisely in its being ambiguous and disclaimable.

After the event one can look at the records to discover just what was or was not intended. Many of my examples were obtained in this way. For instance, Henry Kissinger has subsequently made it quite plain that a political intention lay behind the administration's modification of its trade embargo with the People's Republic of China in the years 1969–71. The actual change, he writes, 'was unimportant but the symbolism was vast'. And again: 'The fundamental purpose was a political gesture that Peking could hardly misunderstand.'[1] This was not, however, actually said. Some plausible technical explanation was given which avoided controversy.

At the time, therefore, an observer is obliged to infer the significance of an action on the basis of internal evidence such as timing, context and convention.

Does this not leave a large area of behaviour, the reader may wonder, of indeterminate status? May we not, in some cases, be reading too much into acts which have no ulterior motive? Or is there not a danger that other genuinely meaningful acts be overlooked or misinterpreted? The answer to these questions is fundamental to inter-state communication. It can be called the *assumption of intentionality*. Contemporary observers can never be absolutely certain of others' real intentions. Hence they have to assume that actors do indeed intend the ostensible meaning of their acts. Since all actors know (or quickly learn) that all public acts, except those self-evidently accidental or inadvertent, may be considered significant, the assumption tends to become a self-fulfilling prophecy.

Obviously it is not an iron-clad law of nature. All human behaviour is probabilistic rather than determined. But the assumption of intentionality is observed to be a working convention among diplomats and national security officials.

Reinforcing the assumption is the awareness that in an uncertain and interdependent world no action of foreign relevance can avoid scrutiny. With self-consciousness inevitably comes responsibility. And the more controlled a society is thought to be, the greater the control it is obliged to exert over its observable actions.

Even if a diplomat does have a cold, he may find it difficult to cancel his engagements without this being understood as a deliberate gesture. Like any actor on stage, the public figure knows that he must not allow the mask to slip for an instant; the show will go on, whether he likes it or not.

A macabre example of the working of this convention can be found in the strange appearance of Soviet Prime Minister Alexei Kosygin at the 1967 May Day parade. He was observed, with curiosity, by a foreign diplomat:

> He had stood there, motionless and ashen-faced. Only the next day did
> it become known that, the night before, his wife and life-long
> companion had succumbed to a long and incurable disease. The Soviet
> order of things made it impossible for him to absent himself from the
> festivities. The true reason would not be believed, but speculation that
> his non-appearance meant political disappearance would find
> widespread credence. For the presentation of his public life he had to
> forgo the privacy of mourning his wife's death.[2]

The assumption of intentionality can be a real headache for protocol officers responsible for steering non-diplomats through the maze of a foreign visit. They know – usually from rueful past experience – that quite inadvertent slips may be blown up into embarrassing diplomatic incidents.

Former Canadian Prime Minister Pierre Trudeau made more than his fair share of diplomatic gaffes. His relaxed, informal style was acceptable and attractive in North American terms. It was less successful on foreign tours. On a round the world trip to dramatize the North–South dialogue, Trudeau stumbled from pot-hole to pot-hole. In Austria, where he was booked to discuss problems such as that of world hunger with Chancellor Kreisky, a snow-storm trapped him and his party on a mountain-top retreat for the rich. Forced humour, at the end of the ordeal, about a shortage of avocados, was not well-received. Algeria, to be the next stop on the tour, was not amused to hear that the Canadian party would arrive a day late. It cancelled the invitation. Arriving in South America, Trudeau's Brazilian hosts were taken aback to find their distinguished guest reviewing an honour-guard in trainers. It was taken as an inexcusable slight. And of course it was. No leader can expect to put his comfort and life-style before the courtesies of diplomatic life without being accused of arrogant disrespect.

The international system is like a great stage on which the states are, at one and the same time, both actors and audience. Any public act of government may be taken as a meaningful gesture to be carefully interpreted. The claim that 'I did not mean it' is not an admissible excuse. On the contrary, it simply compounds incompetence with ignorance.

The substance of nonverbal communication is self-evident enough. Whereas conventional diplomacy is largely thought of as involving the exchange of written or spoken messages, nonverbal communication concerns, in principle, all other means of transferring information.

In practice it is not always possible to maintain a rigid distinction. Some forms of behaviour, known as 'illustrators', are closely tied to speech; they do not stand by themselves, but illustrate or amplify what is being said. Conversely, words themselves, especially in the mouth of a skilled orator, may evoke resonant associations. A rhetorical appeal may be as steeped in symbolism as a physical act. Finally, the contents of a message are sometimes less significant than the fact of its delivery. A telegram of condolences may convey a message of recognition or support 'written between the lines'.

Bearing these reservations in mind, it is nevertheless possible to identify a characteristic lexicon of gestures, symbols and actions used for signalling purposes in international politics. This lexicon can be ordered along three dimensions: leadership, diplomacy and violence. In this book we shall be concentrating on the first two.

Leaders make use of a varied repertoire of signalling devices including exemplary action, the manipulation of symbols, the projection of a particular style of government and all the traditional aids of theatrical performance – props, costume, gesture, setting and script.

Diplomacy draws upon a store of conventions, stylized gestures and nuances of protocol, as well as such indices of cooperation as aid and cultural and sporting ties.

Violence subsumes the demonstrative use of violence and terror by both regular and irregular forces and the display of military power in its various forms.

The common denominator unifying these three dimensions is that each one is an instrument of national purpose. The leader, at the focus of decision-making power, is an arbiter of his country's fate. In the eyes of observers at home and abroad he becomes identified with the nation he leads. The foreign service also performs a dual representative and executive function. It is both a vehicle and an expression of a state's membership of the international community. Lastly the armed forces of a state are the ultimate symbol of sovereignty and instrument of the national will.

As symbols of the nation, crucially associated with the disposal and exercise of power on its behalf, all three instruments draw the attention and respect due to the state itself. What more appropriate and effective heralds could a state possess in order to communicate about the great issues of international life – war and peace; nationhood; power and status; alliance and conflict; independence and tutelage?

Beyond the aesthetic appropriateness of nonverbal communication there is an even more fundamental set of reasons which accounts for its use. The heart of the matter is that nations, and the bureaucracies that manage their foreign policies, are collective entities. Symbolic action provides the answer to problems of communication that arise which are insoluble by more conventional methods.

A collective body – a state or a bureaucracy – is not an individual. Legal fictions, that consider such bodies as persons, should not obscure the sociological reality. Collectivities are made up of a large number of individuals each one of whom possesses a separate will and personal perspective. Presumably they have an at least minimal shared interest in the survival and prosperity of the community. But beyond that basic involvement, the main concern of private citizens is the conduct of their own business. Even officials, employed in the administration of the nation's affairs, can only be concerned with a very small part of the total picture. There may have been a time when government could be carried round in the head of the king or his chief clerk. That time has long since passed.

The 'collectivization' of foreign policy can be demonstrated by some representative statistics. In 1830 the British Foreign Office employed thirty officials in London to run the affairs of the world's greatest power. One hundred and fifty years later about 4,000 home officials are engaged in the management of the foreign affairs of what is, today, an important but not dominant power. To this number can be added the several thousand personnel working abroad in British missions, not to mention the large number of officials from home departments – such as trade and defence – involved, one way or the other, in foreign relations. Even a relatively small power, the Netherlands, employs 1,600 officials in its foreign ministry.

Such a huge increase in staff is a direct result of the explosion in the sheer quantity of international relations. From 1820 to the present day the number of states in the international community has increased from 23 to more than 160. At any one moment a contemporary medium-sized country finds itself immersed in a great flood of foreign business – multilateral conferences, bilateral negotiations, membership in regional and international organizations, alongside the routine but still onerous management of ongoing relations with the other 160-odd states in the world. The organizational diagrams which map out the structure of modern foreign ministries have begun to resemble the family tree of some particularly prolific royal dynasty. Not surprising, therefore, that the sheer volume of information handled has escalated almost out of control. The number of telegrams received at France's Quai d'Orsay has multiplied by fourteen since 1948 alone.[3]

All this means that no single minister or senior official can any longer effectively grasp the full sweep of foreign affairs. At best he can focus on a handful of major issues. Lord Palmerston, British foreign secretary in the 1830s, wrote most of his own despatches. Today's statesmen do not even write their own speeches.

Administration and the coordination of policy have become a nightmare. The right hand hardly knows what the left hand is doing. The increasing involvement of other government agencies complicates matters still further, raising problems of 'bureaucratic politics', that is, inter-departmental rivalry.

The consequence of this complexity are far-reaching from the point of view of communication. To get through to a single listener, an all-powerful prince, is one thing. To make an impression on a diffuse collectivity like a foreign ministry (and immeasurably more so on the nation as a whole) is quite another. The fate of nations is no longer determined by face-to-face encounters between heads of state. They simply set the seal on the labours of the bureaucracies.

It is against this background that the increasing salience of nonverbal communication is to be understood. For certain crucial purposes it turns out to be the most suitable medium for inter-state and inter-bureaucratic relations.

THE ATTENTION FACTOR

The first quality possessed by the medium of nonverbal communication is its ability to capture the attention and interest of large numbers of separate individuals. If I am correct in claiming that the modern state is not at all like a 'unitary actor' under a single ruler – as it may have been at the time of Machiavelli – then this quality of attractiveness must be of the utmost importance.

Symbolic action possesses this quality because it is inherently dramatic. Just as theatre is fascinating, political set-pieces are of absorbing interest. There is no coincidence in this; it is because audiences switch on drama that governments and political parties turn public encounters into drama. If nonverbal communication did not exist, it would have been invented by public relations officers.

Why drama grips is a problem of aesthetics or psychology and need not detain us. What is suggestive about political theatre, at both the domestic and international levels, is that, when totally successful, it reminds one more of sacred ritual than of secular entertainment. A treaty signing, a state visit, indeed any kind of ceremony at the national level, have a strangely moving quality.

Roland Barthes, in his study of myth, argues that performances of this kind work by supplying a 'sensory reality', in opposition to the mental associations of language. Furthermore, they lend their theme 'a natural and eternal justification ... a clarity which is not that of an explanation but that of a statement of fact'. Finally, by acting parsimoniously, they abolish 'the complexity of human acts', give them 'the simplicity of essences', organize 'a world which is without contradictions'.[4] In short, they mythify.

Political ritual surely does just this. It transforms mundane reality into historical myth. The great gestures of international history have transcended their periods and become as timeless as myths. How natural it is for British and French statesmen, during periods of cooperation between their two countries, to evoke the spirit of the *Entente Cordiale*, which entered their national memories not the least as a result of President Loubet's magnificent and historic visit to London in July 1903?

The great state visit is one of the devices used by governments to supply an historic dimension to a diplomatic turning point. Although we as yet lack an historical perspective, there is a strong presumption that events such as the de Gaulle trip to the USSR, the Nixon-Mao meeting and Sadat's mission to Jerusalem, have indeed 'entered history'.

Over and above the mythification of events, symbolic action, as Barthes hints, also has the major task of giving concrete form to the otherwise elusive concepts at stake in international relations.

The basic unit of international relations, the state, is a collective noun – what philosophers call a *category word* – applied to a set of institutions, procedures and events. Though frequently personified for legal and rhetorical purposes, it is not a tangible object as such. The nation itself is indeed made up of flesh and blood individuals. But the ties that bind those individuals into a nation – shared loyalties, beliefs and memories – are abstractions (though no less powerful motive forces for that). This is not meant to imply that the state is not a 'reality'. Whether or not a mental construct, the state, via the agencies of which it consists, clearly effects the lives of its own and other citizens.

If the state itself is an abstraction then relations between states must be equally abstract. Any physical transactions that occur, such as warfare, trade and personal contacts, are conducted, again, by agencies of the state and not the state itself – there is no 'itself'. The labels by which we choose to characterize those relations – friendship, respect, disapproval and so on – are convenient metaphors borrowed from everyday life. States are no more 'friends', in the sense that people are friends, than parrots can actually talk. States can enter into an alliance and may cooperate to pursue shared interests but that is something else.

Instead of using metaphors drawn from personal relations to describe international relations we could just as well make use of a quite different vocabulary altogether, for instance that of mathematics. 'Power' is already understood by some specialists not as a tangible commodity but as a vector – the mathematical expression relating two points in space. One of the aspects of international politics repellent to outsiders is that the calculations of professional strategists and diplomats are so cold-blooded. The personifications and sentimental judgements beloved of popular discourse have no part in the objective analysis of interests and capabilities.

When it comes to the implementation of policy, however, popular attitudes become highly relevant. The language of geopolitics makes little sense to the general public. Abstractions have to be given concrete form so that they can be grasped and related to. Thus the state is objectified by symbols and ceremonies such as the flag, the Crown and armistice day. Relations between states are objectified by the symbolic actions of leaders, diplomats and soldiers, in themselves personifications of the nation. Alliance is made comprehensible by the vocabulary and external forms of friendship and hospitality – the embrace, the cordial gesture, the banquet. A conflict of interests becomes tangible in stylized rituals of anathematization.

Professional soldiers may cheerfully go to war against an 'enemy' whom they have never met in their lives. Diplomats may recommend courses of action that will bring suffering to thousands of unknown and innocent civilians. For the professional there is 'nothing personal' in it all. They are simply acting, as duty obliges them to, as fiduciary agents of the state, just as a lawyer acts dispassionately in the best interests of his client. But for the public there has to be something personal in the carnage and the suffering. Only by personalizing it all, therefore, can the community affect the perceptions and actions of its members in the directions its interests require. Conscripts have to hate in order to fight; taxpayers have to feel some kind of sympathy if they are to go along with grants of foreign aid. However fictitious the description, by the mere fact of attributing friendship or enmity to another group, the community is creating a reality with real consequences.

Without symbolic action dramatizing and objectifying their policies, governments would have difficulty in implementing any initiatives going beyond the routine programmes of the bureaucracies or the fixed attitudes of public opinion. Both kinds of collectivity are impervious to verbal persuasion.

Bureaucratic obtuseness is a result of classic organizational necessity – the principle of the division of labour. For the efficient conduct of business foreign ministries are bound to communicate via regular channels that link together responsible officials and exclude others. The greater the quantity of information, the greater the need for its selective dissemination. Considerations of security and status reinforce practical requirements.

The upshot of all this is that, inevitably, information-flow in a bureaucracy is designed for sound management and not collective education. Information which, as a matter of standard operating procedure, has universal circulation, is likely to be low-grade and unnoteworthy.

Where foreign affairs is concerned, the general public has less access to information than the most over-burdened and specialized official. Research has consistently demonstrated popular uninterest in the subject most of the time. Mass-circulation newspapers ignore it. Nothing could be less calculated to impress the public than an address on foreign policy. A foreign leader receives even shorter shrift.

Only dramatic public events, whether spontaneous or stage-managed, have the resonance and diffusion to seize the attention of foreign or domestic mass audiences and bureaucracies. Where words would be overlooked, acts have a direct and unavoidable impact.[5]

Public opinion polls, so far as they go, do provide some evidence for the dramatizing effect of symbolic action. Between February 1946 and October 1949, during the opening stages of the Cold War, a series of surveys were conducted in the United States on the saliency of foreign policy issues.

In the face of a perceived Soviet threat it was vital for the Truman administration to educate the American public away from traditional isolationist attitudes towards an awareness of the need for American involvement in world affairs. Dramatic presidential actions such as endorsement of Churchill's 'iron curtain' speech (symbolically delivered in Truman's presence, in his home state of Missouri), enunciation of the ringing Truman doctrine, the Marshall plan for European recovery and the conclusion of the North Atlantic treaty, were all stages in the education of the American people as well as important policy statements and measures.

They proved to be remarkably effective on both counts. From a low point of 11 per cent of respondents holding foreign policy issues to be paramount in June 1946, numbers rose to 73 per cent in April 1948 during the key debate in Congress over the Marshall plan.[6]

Murray Edelman, the pioneer of the study of symbolic politics, has described the mechanism at work: government acts, he argues, are one of the few forms of activity perceived to concern the interests and needs of the whole society. At the beginning of the Cold War the administration made use of this capability to dramatize the emergence of an external threat. He concludes:

> The political acts to which the mass public responded may have been
> rational and effective or they may not. That question remains
> controversial and also irrelevant to this inquiry. That the response of

spectators was to these acts, however, and not directly to exhaustive and dispassionate analysis of the military situation, is central. The public is not in touch with the situation, and it 'knows' the situation only through the symbols that engage it.[7]

THE CREDIBILITY FACTOR

The second problem raised by communication with a collectivity is that of achieving credibility. It is one thing to attract your audience's attention; quite another to actually convince it. Bureaucracies are notoriously conservative beasts. General publics are highly resistant to changes in images of the outside world. To compound this difficulty it has been shown that relatively anonymous, mass information sources – the press and the radio (but not television) – carry far less conviction than local opinion leaders such as clergymen, physicians, respected businessmen and so on, actually known to people personally.[8] (These communal figures are equivalent to the face-to-face sources described by McLuhan.)

In other words, the most credible sources for influencing public opinion, respected members of the local community, are those least likely to be active on foreign policy issues.

(In parenthesis, it should be remarked that the strength of Jewish support for Israel in the United States is sustained precisely by the local affiliation of Jews to organizations associated with Israel in all kinds of ways – religious, charitable, social, etc. It is at this grass roots level that Israel pitches much of its information effort and it is at this level that counter-information, carried by the national media, is least likely to convince. Hence the immunity of Jewish opinion to the unfavourable image of Israel projected at various times by administrations to neutralize the Jewish lobby.)

It is, therefore, very difficult for governments to shift public attitudes to the outside world, since these tend to be both stable and relatively impregnable.

Faced by this challenge, governments hold two basic weapons in their information armoury: in the long term, to maintain a consistent trend of explanation on an issue, in the hope that this will have a cumulative effect; in the short term, to engineer some really spectacular happening.

In the whole post-war period perhaps the most striking and influential international development was the launching of *Sputnik I* followed by the consistent success of the Soviet space programme. Its worldwide impact on perceptions of Soviet prestige was truly far-reaching. Opinion polls taken in Western Europe in November 1957, just after the space shot, revealed that 21 per cent more people believed the USSR to be ahead of the USA in scientific development than the reverse. Later surveys showed that though numbers might fluctuate, especially in the light of America's subsequent achievements, Soviet leaders had permanently disposed of an historical image of technological backwardness.

The Soviet space programme has had a great bearing, as it was intended to, upon perceptions of Soviet power, particularly long-term military capabilities. In West Germany, for instance, the number of people who believed that the United States was stronger than the Soviet Union dropped between 1957 and 1961 from 38 to 26 per cent.[9]

From the perspective of today, thirty years after the launching of *Sputnik*, there is no doubt that this spectacular event was a turning point in perceptions of the balance of power between the superpowers. We now know that in quantifiable terms – the ability of the USSR actually to fight a war with the USA – little had changed between September and November 1957. Despite contemporary panic-mongering about a 'missile gap' it was years before Russia disposed of a serious ballistic missile force.

No, the true effect of *Sputnik* was psychological. Nevertheless the consequences of Western dejection and the Soviet Union's reciprocal elation were no less real for that. In Western Europe the campaign for nuclear disarmament became an important factor. The Berlin crisis of 1958–61 and the 1962 Cuba crisis, the first attempts to change the post-war *status quo* for over a decade, were uncomfortable evidence that the Soviet Union was beginning to feel a new confidence and to assert itself globally.

Quite deliberately, the Soviet leadership, obsessed by an historical sense of technological inferiority to the West, had set out to create an image of scientific achievement, the key in the twentieth century to prestige and influence. In *Sputnik* it had hit upon the quintessential symbol – condensed, simple, dramatic.

Before *Sputnik* the Kremlin had self-consciously brandished its achievements in aircraft development as proof of Soviet sophistication. In his memoirs the then first secretary, Nikita Khrushchev, returns again and again to this theme: at the 1955 Geneva conference of the big four, he writes, it was 'embarrassing' to compare his own twin-engined Ilyushin-14 with the 'more impressive' four-engined planes at the disposal of Western delegations.

When the massive Tu-104 came on the scene in 1956, Khrushchev did not lose an opportunity to show it off. He flew in it to Britain in

1956. 'This was one of the first jet passenger planes in the world, and we wanted our hosts to know it.' An important Yugoslav delegation to Moscow was offered the plane for the flight home only very shortly after arriving in its own Dakota. The Yugoslav ambassador understood that the Soviets 'would like to appear in Belgrade with this plane as soon as possible'.

By September 1957 the Tu-104 had landed at Delhi, Rangoon and Jakarta, as well as in Western capitals such as London and Paris. Later the Soviet government was to adopt the practice of placing the monster jet at the disposal of visiting third-world statesmen – such as President Nasser – whom they wish to overawe.[10]

With the launching of *Sputnik I* Moscow geared its entire communications apparatus to publicizing this most powerful of all images of Communist achievement. Even stamps, paintings, models, public displays and children's toys took up the same theme. No opportunity for publicity was passed up. Distinguished visitors to the Kremlin would be subtly reminded of Soviet space prowess by a display of models of rockets, space craft and aeroplanes positioned on a side table in the conference room. When Khruschev visited the United States in September 1959 (travelling non-stop in the stretched Tu-114, in itself a sinister signal of the new Soviet capability to deliver nuclear bombs as far as the American continent) he presented President Eisenhower with a duplicate of the Soviet pennant which had been landed on the moon. De Gaulle, the following year, received a model of the original *Sputnik*.[11]

The remarkable success of the Soviet space programme in political terms can be accounted for by the combination of a spectacular initial event followed up by a sustained series of further achievements over a long period. This is the classic strategy, though rarely with such impressive results, invariably adopted by governments to alter collective stereotypes on foreign issues.

At the first stage an impressive public display is put on encapsulating the desired message which is reinforced over time by the repetition in various ways of the theme in question. A familiar gambit of this kind, at a turning-point in inter-state relations from hostility or indifference to friendship, is the careful staging of a great show of esteem and affection by one leader for another. It is amusing to read in newspapers at the time assiduously briefed stories to the effect that 'the leaders really hit it off together; they really like each other'. Instant friendship. Obviously this is part of the effort of enacting a national, political convergence in comprehensible human terms.

(Anthropologists would also point out the resemblance of such national ceremonies to the 'rites of passage' within communities to symbolize the transition from one period of life to another – baptism, confirmation, marriage, death.)

Demonstrations of this kind can only be the starting point for a careful cultivation of attitudes and relations. They are intended to provide the initial jolt needed to overcome inertia.

The Sadat visit to Jerusalem, in November 1977, had a two-tier impact on Israeli opinion. At the societal level the sight of an Egyptian leader on Israeli soil had an electrifying effect. It convinced the average Israeli of Sadat's sincerity. Opinion polls measured an increase from 50 to 90 per cent of respondents who believed that Egypt was seriously interested in peace.[12] After all, by coming to Israel, accepting full honours from her representatives and even entering the very citadel of her sovereignty – the *Knesset* – Sadat was unequivocally recognizing Israel's nationhood.

In political terms the overall image of credibility acquired by Sadat stood him in good stead on the weary road of negotiations ahead. As he often remarked, Sadat had won for himself powerful allies *within Israeli society* – the mothers and wives he had specifically addressed in his *Knesset* speech. He had thus skilfully reduced the room for manoeuvre available to the Israeli government. He himself, the *Rais* of an authoritarian regime, had greater breathing space. In the final analysis the imbalance of pressure on the negotiators (and let us not forget Sadat's equally adroit manipulation of American opinion) was fully reflected in the terms of the final settlement. In exchange for the Sinai peninsula, Israel received a set of promissory notes.

At the level of Israel's political elite the Sadat visit earned credibility in an even more direct manner. The Egyptian president was able to work his charm in person – not from the television screen or from a speeding motorcade. During the three days of his trip Sadat was introduced to hundreds of key figures in Israeli public life. The eagerness of the Israeli government to display its genuine desire for peace, to amplify the occasion as much as possible and to forestall potential domestic critics, all determined this high exposure policy.

As a result, Sadat was able to win over, in the traditional politician's manner of pressing flesh, sceptical members of the elite. His technique of face-to-face persuasion was irresistible. During his very first moments in Israel, at the foot of his aircraft's steps, he was presented to some of the most hard-bitten of the Israeli leaders, especially present or former military men. Sadat, who was well aware of the power of Israel's defence establishment, made full use of his considerable charm. He specially stopped on the reception line to exchange a few words with Generals Sharon, Dayan and Gur. Gur, the chief of staff, had told the press that he considered the proposed visit as a 'bluff', a deception stratagem in the prelude to a new war. Sadat murmured: 'I wasn't bluffing.' No, indeed. In the event, the military establishment, represented by Defence Minister Weizman, former Defence Minister Dayan and head of the general staff's planning department (and a key figure) General Avraham Tamir, was to play a decisively moderating role in the negotiations.[13]

THE MOBILIZATION FACTOR

The third problem of communication at the collective level is that of inducing action: how does one move a nation? Individuals can be persuaded to act in their own personal interest; groups are moulded by socialization to conform to general norms of behaviour. But to bestir collectivities to action going beyond the basic requirements of social order and sustenance poses a different kind of problem – that of *political mobilization*.

The classic answer to this problem was perceived by the French writer Gustave Le Bon nearly a hundred years ago in his famous study of collective behaviour, *The Crowd*. According to Le Bon, crowds (by which he means all collective groups) are not impressed by reason, but only by 'a startling and very clear image, freed from all accessory explanation'. 'It is only images that terrify or attract [crowds] and become motives of action.

For this reason theatrical representations, in which the image is shown in its most clearly visible shape, always have an enormous influence on crowds ... *The entire audience experiences at the same time the same emotions*.'[14]

Le Bon describes here both the mechanism of collective motivation and its working. Groups act in unison because the individuals who make them up are separately moved to action. It is the simultaneous performance of many separate, but coordinated, actions that creates the overall impression of a collective personality endowed with traits above and beyond those of its constituent members.

Looked at from this perspective it is clear why nonverbal communication – Le Bon's 'images' – rather than reasoned argument moves groups. Only the most basic public, and therefore shared, symbols, whose meaning is grounded in the common culture of the collectivity, have the capacity to induce a unified response among separate individuals. Nonverbal communication, drawing on such a collective heritage, can mobilize groups for precisely this reason.

Political rhetoric can also do this to the extent that it conjures up Le Bon's 'striking and very clear images' in the imagination of spectators. Neither private symbols nor reasoned argument, however, can move groups, because they cannot evoke shared assumptions and sentiments; they mean different things to different people. To arouse a public response requires a public stimulus.

Given that it is the convergence of individual reactions that produces the appearance of a collective response, we have still to account for the animating effect of 'images' or symbols in the first place. Why do they move us?

Murray Edelman explains that symbols have the unique ability to store up a great charge of association and emotion. 'They condense into one symbolic event, sign or act, patriotic pride, anxieties, remembrances of past glories or humiliations, promises of future greatness: some one of these or all of them.' When brought, in the appropriate circumstances, into political discourse, symbols can galvanize groups into action in a powerful discharge of emotion. They provide, in brief, 'rallying points for group action'.[15]

Drawing on the condensed and suggestive vocabulary of symbol and gesture, nonverbal communication is able to tap the deepest well-springs of national sentiment. It expresses and evokes the very feelings and instincts which bind together and move nations: pride, loyalty and identity – the substance of nationhood; sympathy and affection – the motives of kinship and friendship; anger, hatred and fear – the motives of enmity; resolution and confidence – the sinews of independence; submission and demoralization – the ingredients of defeat and subjugation; respect and admiration – the qualities of prestige.

Nations are not impelled to action by mathematical calculations. To move a nation, indeed merely to retain a sense of collective purpose, requires a medium of communication that taps the sources of human feeling. Thus it is that gesture and symbolism address themselves to the fundamental bed-rock questions which are not amenable to cost-benefit analysis or operational research: Why obey authority? Why belong to one nation rather than another? Why die for your country? Why die for your country's ally?

Such irreducible questions can only be answered at the deepest, non-rational, emotional, level. Means can be chosen by calculation. Values cannot – they are existential properties of the community. To evoke loyalty to a cause, it is futile to appeal to the report of a scientific inquiry. No nation went along the path of painful alliance or bloody conflict as the result of forensic analysis. Experts, it is true, may determine the optimal course of action with a slide-rule. Governments will only mobilize support and sustain relationships by eliciting a normative response grounded in national sentiment.

Symbolic action, then, is intended to appeal to the community at a level that precludes debate – where debate would only engender inaction. Symbols provide answers to questions without answers.

Argentine behaviour in the Falklands war provides a recent example of political mobilization in the field of foreign policy. At the outset it was easy for the government to generate popular support to 'liberate' the British-held islands. The Malvinas, as they are possessively called by the Argentines, have long been a potent symbol of patriotic aspiration. 'The Malvinas are ours,' one Argentine explained, 'and we feel we have a strong moral justification for what we are doing. Equally importantly, we have a passionate attachment to the islands which has been imbued throughout our schooldays.'

The problem for the Argentine government, in fact, was not to justify the initial invasion, which was virtually seen as an act of simple repossession. As the conflict escalated out of hand, and it was disquietingly realized that the war was not to be a push-over but would involve full-scale military action against Britain, it became imperative to sustain initial enthusiasm.

Classic symbols of patriotism were accordingly resorted to. The pale blue and white flag was displayed everywhere: on public buildings, in mass demonstrations and in the mass media. The film clip of the flag fluttering over the Falklands became a standard feature. President Galtieri assured his compatriots: 'The blue and white flag of Argentina will never come down from the Malvinas.'

Television played a central role in the war. Great prominence was given to carefully chosen shots of the armed services, both 'in action' on the islands and in training. Planes streaked into the sunset and battleships ploughed through the waves to the sound of the national anthem. The high-point of the television campaign was a 24-hour non-stop patriotic broadcast linked to a funds drive. Above all television was the medium by which all other forms of symbolic action were presented to the Argentine people.

Religious motifs were extensively drawn upon: in photographs and on television the leadership could be seen, now on their knees at a mass for victims of the war, now in the company of important church figures. Even popular sports stars were lined up by the regime to endorse the struggle. One photo showed the Argentine national soccer team holding up the sign: 'Las Malvinas son Argentinas'. In a country in which soccer is a great focus of national pride and passionate interest, this was more than a trivial gimmick. Mass demonstrations and commemorative occasions were exploited by the regime both to express and evoke popular support: May 17, Navy Day; May 25, Independence Day; and May 29, Army Day, were all opportunities for banging the drum and handing out medals, as well as recalling the glories of the past. Finally, the country's leadership was frequently pictured in various symbolic postures intended to symbolize such themes as sacrifice, resolution, national unity, historical legitimacy and so on.[16]

Altogether it was a most impressive exercise in political mobilization. Unfortunately the patriotic fervour generated by the campaign proved ultimately counter-productive. So much stress was placed on the glorious symbolism of the Argentine forces and the historical justice of their cause that more down to earth considerations about the real likelihood of success were swept aside. When the dreadful consequences of the invasion became clear, there could be no backing down. The Argentine junta found itself hoisted with its own petard.

THE DISSONANCE FACTOR

The final aspect of nonverbal communication to be considered is the exploitation of its ambiguity. We have already seen that ambiguity can be of benefit in permitting a message to be signalled whilst avoiding the sort of commitment – or provocation – involved in an explicit verbal statement. In essence, what happens in a situation of this kind is that at the nonverbal level one signals one thing while saying something quite different.

One example of this occurs when an ambassador is brought home to indicate disapproval. Now the recall of an ambassador, or, worse still, the breaking off of ties, is a very extreme step for a country to take, an official mark of a severe deterioration in relations. Unless unavoidable, states dislike such irrevocable measures because they are very hard to reverse and weaken contacts when communication is most needed. Sometimes states have severed relations and then been unable to find a suitable occasion to restore them for years, at great diplomatic cost.

To avoid this undesirable complication, to burn no bridges, and yet to leave no doubt about their attitude, states often resort to the device of ordering their ambassador home and announcing that he is being brought back for 'routine consultations'. When the atmosphere improves he can therefore return to his post without any loss of face or too much being read into the gesture.

Beyond this useful tactical advantage, symbolic action possesses a unique quality: the ability to incorporate contradictory messages *at one and the same time*. Put another way, the rules of logic prohibit the simultaneous appearance of opposites, p and -p, in a single proposition. They do not apply to nonverbal symbols.

Take the proposition 'Jesus is alive and Jesus is dead'. From a logical point of view it is not well-formed, it does not make sense. Either Jesus lives or Jesus does not live – but not both at the same time. What symbolism can do is to permit the coexistence of contradictory assertions in a single form, not at the logical level but at the emotional, affective level.

Hence the symbol of the cross, in all its suggestiveness, succeeds in reconciling opposite assertions about the nature of Jesus: that he was crucified and that he is risen; that he was man and that he is God; that in the abyss of despair he was at the pinnacle of hope. It is precisely because key symbols incorporate in an intelligible unity disparate and even contradictory meanings and relationships that they possess the fascination and potency they do. Since when were the great emotional, motive forces of human life based upon consistency?

Nonverbal communication, then, has the remarkable property simultaneously to assert and deny a given proposition. As a consequence the medium is uniquely qualified to perform the task of manipulating dissonance in and between collective bodies. Three separate functions are referred to here: (a) The arousal of contradictory feelings in one or more international actors, for instance fear together with hope, friendship together with enmity; (b) the creation of different expectations in different actors, for instance, optimism in one and pessimism in the other; (c) the avoidance of disunity within a single body by affirming a new policy or doctrine while apparently confirming an old one.

(a) The arousal of mutually contradictory feelings

At the death of President Brezhnev in November 1982 the People's Republic of China sent its foreign minister, Huang Hua, to the great state funeral in Moscow. While there Huang made a speech calling for better Sino-Soviet relations and praising Mr Brezhnev. Even more remarkably, at a Kremlin reception he stood before a large black-bordered portrait of the late Soviet leader and bowed his head in respect.

Following on months of hints and signals of various kinds it was obvious enough to most observers that this was intended as a demonstration of good will, of a willingness to improve ties with the

Soviet Union on the part of China. Huang was the most senior Chinese representative to visit Moscow since 1964, when Chou En-lai had failed to patch up relations in the wake of Khrushchev's fall from power.

There was, however, more to it than that. The Chinese had something else to say. One day after his return to Peking, Huang Hua resigned on the grounds of ill health. On the face of it, this did not make sense. Were the Chinese repudiating the gesture of their own foreign minister? Hardly likely, given the strict principles of collective responsibility extant in China at that time. Moreover both Deng Xiaoping and Hu Yaobang, the top leaders of the Chinese Communist party, had publicly associated themselves with the principle of improving relations with the USSR at the very moment Huang Hua was in Moscow. But if Huang was not being fired for his views, why then risk giving that impression? Indeed, why send a 'lame duck' foreign minister on such a clearly important mission?

The answer to the puzzle is surely that it was precisely these kinds of doubts and uncertainties that China was interested in fostering, even while saluting the departed Soviet leader! Huang Hua's choice for the Moscow mission 'was not a coincidence'. First, Huang was closely involved in the break-through in relations with the United States at the beginning of the 1970s. In the Kissinger memoirs he is actually referred to as 'my new friend'. He was also one of the strongest critics of Soviet policy. Second, Huang's resignation had been gazetted for some time before the Moscow trip, so it was not in itself a surprise. Rather, the significance lay in the timing.

Accordingly, the following interpretation suggests itself. A pro-Soviet gesture would come with added emphasis from America's 'friend', Huang Hua. (Its significance would also be painfully clear in Washington.) However, the foreign minister's immediate departure from the scene – understood to have been *planned in advance* – balanced the promise with a warning: the conciliatory signal was far from irrevocable; no reputations were tied up with the policy; its herald had been used and discarded. Moreover, as a diplomat and not a Communist party official, his gesture implicated the state, but not the party – always a significant reservation in a Communist regime, where the party is paramount.

Huang Hua's successor, Wu Xiuquan, was associated with neither Russia nor America. But it was known that he was fluent in English . . . thus the constructive ambiguity of Chinese foreign policy was reinforced, opening options and improving China's negotiating position towards both superpowers.[17]

(b) *The creation of divergent expectations*

As the previous study hints, nonverbal communication can also permit one of the parties in a triangular relationship to play the other two sides off against each other. By exploiting China and the Soviet Union's reciprocal fears, the Nixon administration was able to extract concessions from both of them. Under the Reagan administration China was enabled to play off the USSR against the USA.

This kind of triangle is particularly amenable to manipulation by nonverbal means because symbolic action is at the same time public, economical and subtle. It avoids the dangers of a brazen policy of blackmail that might easily boomerang, yet gives sufficient food for thought to worried imaginations.

There is surprisingly wide scope for this particular strategem – especially for third parties in a bipolar world of Soviet–American competition. A nice demonstration of this kind was put on by the Iraqi government which, though tangled in a war with Iran, successfully managed to manoeuvre between the superpowers.

The situation in Baghdad at the end of 1982 was that Iraq was massively dependent on Soviet arms and advisers, but somewhat disenchanted by Moscow's (albeit temporary) discontinuation of military assistance early in the war. An unsuccessful Soviet attempt to mend bridges with the Khomeini regime was yet more ominous. The United States, the third side of the triangle, had not had full relations with Iraq since the 1967 Arab–Israel war. It was, however, fully represented by a team of senior diplomats lodged in an interests section in the Belgian embassy.

The gesture itself was a minor gem of diplomatic indirection. The story is told by Drew Middleton of the *New York Times*: 'An American diplomat on a routine visit to the Iraqi foreign ministry found the Hungarian ambassador waiting in the outer office of the Iraqi official the American wished to see. To his surprise, the American envoy was ushered into the official's room immediately. When he emerged after a half-hour discussion, the Hungarian was still there.'[18]

This little scene was clearly intended to signal that the United States was being given priority over an ally of the Soviet Union. (Note: not the Soviet Union itself; that would have been dangerously blatant.) From our theoretical perspective the episode is interesting because the Iraqis succeeded in encapsulating encouragement to the United States and a snub to the Soviet bloc in a single elegant act. The Hungarian ambassador was kept waiting, poor man, not only as a stooge – but also as a witness!

(c) The avoidance of disunity

Nowhere is the ambiguity of symbolic action more useful than in the avoidance of doctrinal conflict within a collectivity. The sort of divisive ideological contradictions that could not possibly coexist in open debate can be reconciled at the nonverbal level. All regimes face the need for symbolic reassurance during periods of change when tradition or dogma is obliged to bow before innovation. It may be difficult indeed to mollify outraged conservative forces. The Soviet Union after the twentieth party congress at which Stalin was denounced, China after the death of Mao or the Roman Catholic Church following the second Vatican council, drew widely on symbolic expedients to soothe change.

The most dramatic example of this strategy, though, involves the Palestine Liberation Organization. Now the PLO is not a homogeneous body. It is, rather, an umbrella organization which takes in a range of constituent groups of sometimes widely differing social and political orientations. These have included the mainstream *Fatah*, the pro-Syrian *Saiqa*, the Marxist PFLP and PDFLP and so on. Not the least of chairman Yassir Arafat's achievements was to maintain overall unity for as long as he did.

It was the invitation to address the UN General Assembly in November 1974 which called forth the full measure of Arafat's leadership skills. At the heart of his appearance lay a paradox. On the one hand it was the climax of the PLO's diplomatic drive to achieve legitimacy and respectability in the international community. On the other hand it could not fail to suggest the abandonment of the strategy of the armed struggle. Enshrined in the Palestinian covenant – the foundation charter of the PLO – the doctrine was perceived to be essential in maintaining the unity and morale of the organization, and coercive pressure on Israel.

While it was quite feasible, from a tactical point of view, to run diplomacy and violence in tandem, it created serious strains. Internally, the moderate style and rhetoric inherent in the diplomatic option infuriated ideologues within the movement, such as George Habash, who were not even prepared to countenance concessions for tactical purposes. (Habash, in fact, withdrew his PFLP from the PLO in October 1974.) More flexible proponents of the diplomatic track were anathematized and sometimes actually assassinated.

Externally, the combination was equally precarious. Friends of the PLO, who insisted on the real moderation of the movement and its ultimate willingness to compromise, were continually embarrassed by the juxtaposition of moderate words and extreme acts.

For appearances' sake the contradiction could be mitigated by the PLO establishing clandestine groups – such as Black September – which would perform acts of sabotage and murder that the parent body could disclaim. Still, this device hardly withstood objective investigation.

It was on the podium of the UN General Assembly that this dilemma presented itself with full force. In the body of his speech it was relatively easy for Arafat to obfuscate the substantive issues. Emphasis was placed at the philosophical level of justice and rights. Jewish nationalism was equated with colonialism, imperialism, neo-colonialism, racism, anti-semitism and collaboration with Nazism. Palestinian nationalism was equated with peace, freedom, justice, equality, development and self-determination.

So far so good. But to sidestep any reference to the future role of violence would leave the impression that the PLO had bought international respectability at the price of self-immolation.

Arafat resolved this dilemma by the use of symbolism. At a rhetorical level he concluded his words with the following dramatic image, gripping because of the tension between two diametrically opposing symbols: 'I have come bearing an olive branch and a freedom fighter's gun. Do not let the olive branch fall from my hand.'

But it was at a theatrical level that his belief in the armed struggle was most effectively conveyed. The device used was that of Arafat's own personal appearance. There he stood, in the temple of international diplomacy, dressed in desert attire – *kaffiyah*, three-day beard, tinted glasses, white windbreaker and open shirt. No concession to convention here. An armchair, normally reserved for heads of state, had been thoughtfully provided for the PLO leader. Arafat declined to take a seat. As delegates applauded his speech he remained standing, one hand on the chair.

Then, in acknowledgement of the ovation, he raised his hand in salute. Under his windbreaker could quite clearly be seen a revolver holster. It was shockingly expressive: the 'freedom fighter's gun'.

Afterwards there was some disagreement about whether it did or did not contain a weapon. An official aide to the PLO leader claimed that the holster was empty. Two UN security guards – eye witnesses – stated that they had seen a gun. It was beside the point who was correct. Arafat always appears with a posse of armed bodyguards. And a shoulder holster is not much use against a sudden assassination attempt. No, the holster was a prop meant for the audience. Its message: here stood, when all was said and done, a guerrilla fighter. .... [19]

REFERENCES AND NOTES

1. Kissinger H 1979 *The White House Years*. Little, Brown: Boston
2. Rafael G 1981 *Destination Peace*. Weidenfeld and Nicolson, p 173
3. All statistics from Steiner Z 1982 *The Times Survey of Foreign Ministries of the World*. Times Books
4. Barthes R 1972 *Mythologies*. Wang and Hill: New York, pp 117, 143
5. See Deutsch K W, Merritt R L 1965 Effects of events on national and international images, in Kelman H C (ed), *International Behavior*. Holt, Rinehart and Winston: New York
6. Almond G A 1960 *The American People and Foreign Policy*. Preager: New York, pp 76–7
7. Edelman M 1971 *Politics as Symbolic Action*. Markham Publishing Company: Chicago, pp 7–9; Edelman M 1964 *The Symbolic Uses of Politics*. University of Illinois Press: Urbana, p 173
8. Lazarsfeld P F, Berelson B R, Gaudet H 1948 *The People's Choice*. Columbia University Press: New York, pp 150–8
9. Deutsch K W, Merritt R L 1965 *op cit.*, pp 149–51, 163, 175–6
10. Talbott S (ed) 1970 *Khrushchev Remembers*. Little, Brown: Boston, pp 395, 406; Micunovic V 1980 *Moscow Diary*. Chatto and Windus, p 247; Barghoorn F C 1960 *The Soviet Cultural Offensive*. Princeton University Press; Princeton, p 208; Heikal M 1978 *The Sphinx and the Commissar*. Harper and Row: New York, p 95
11. Heikal M 1978 *The Sphinx and the Commissar op cit.* p 11; Menon K P S 1963 *The Flying Troika*. Oxford University Press, p 247; De Gaulle C 1971 *Memoirs of Hope*. Weidenfeld and Nicolson, p 234
12. Lewis A 1979 The peace ritual and Israeli images of social order, *Journal of Conflict Resolution* 23: 697
13. Haber E, Schiff Z, Yaari E 1979 *The Year of the Dove*. Bantam Books: New York, pp 61–3
14. Le Bon G 1896 *The Crowd*. T Fisher Unwin, pp 78, 76 My emphasis
15. Edelman M 1964 *The Symbolic Uses of Politics*. University of Illinois Press: Urbana, p 6; Firth R 1973 *Symbols: public and private*. Cornell University Press: New York, p 77
16. *The Times* 23 Apr. 1982, 5 May 1982, 10 May 1982, 18 May 1982; *New York Times* 26 May 1982, 30 May 1982
17. *The Times* 16 Nov. 1982, 17 Nov. 1982, 20 Nov. 1982
18. *Ibid.* 23 Nov. 1982

19. *New York Times* 14 Nov. 1974; Yodfat A Y, Arnon-Ohanna Y 1981 *PLO: Strategy and tactics*. Croom Helm

Chapter three

THE LEADER AS PERFORMER

At the centre of power's stage stands the national leader. He (or she) is uniquely qualified to take the key part in the drama of politics. In the nature of things the leader, whether in free or totalitarian societies, is an object of unmatched media attention. As a nineteenth century bishop wrote of the pope: he had the diplomatic corps by his side; unlimited means of communication; moral power; the eyes of the world always upon him; ears always stretched to hear his words; in short, 'illimitable, invincible publicity' accompanying his every action.[1]

True, not every leader has the magnetism or newsworthiness of a pope, but he does have at least his own national media more or less at his disposal. Given such benefits, he has the opportunity to communicate both to his own community and to the wider world. Indeed, in Western societies he may find it more difficult to evade, rather than attract, the surveillance of the press and television.

Public interest in leadership is not hard to account for – a product of a fascination for power and its trappings, the need to personalize momentous forces affecting the welfare of all, and a tendency for the public to focus even individual resentments and hopes on the most prominent authority figure. But from the point of view of symbolic politics and the communicatory role of leadership, the main point is that the leader is identified with the state that he heads. Both for his own people and foreign audiences the leader represents, symbolizes, his country. For countless millions, Mrs Gandhi was India, a mother-goddess of the nation. A conference of world leaders is not simply a convention of officials; it is perceived as an assembly, in microcosm, of the races of the earth. A summit of the nonaligned movement, for all its ringing rhetoric – and insubstantial practical results – is a moving occasion for this very reason: the deprived of mankind meeting in brotherhood and, for a few days, shared, symbolic endeavour.

The tendency to personify the nation in the shape of its leader can be carried to extremes. The supposed qualities of the leader may even be taken to reflect traits of 'national character' or the state of national morale. Neville Chamberlain, for instance, who was actually a very tough prime minister, assiduous, domineering and intransigent, was quite mistakenly believed to embody the softness and decadence of a declining empire. Mussolini, the Italian dictator, actually described Chamberlain and other British officials (on a visit to Italy in January 1939) as 'the tired sons of a long line of rich men, and they will lose their empire'.[2] Well, the Duce lost his first. That the Chamberlain government chose, in the absence of alternatives, a foreign policy of conciliation, and needed Italy as an ally in the Mediterranean, had nothing at all to do with the 'moral fibre of the British nation' – whatever that might mean.

As a national symbol, however far-fetched the conclusion sometimes drawn from this, the leader is placed in an unrivalled position to perform the role of dramatic communicator, enacting in his own person the aspirations, intentions and attitudes of his people in the international arena. In this chapter I shall consider four dimensions of this performance: the leader as a paragon of appropriate behaviour, signalman of national attitudes, staker-out of political commitments and finally as a priest, providing legitimacy and inspiration.

THE LEADER AS PARAGON

First, the leader is seen as an exemplar of fitting conduct in ideological, social or political terms. Should a government wish to inculcate some mode of behaviour the most visible, striking and unmistakable method of education is that of personal example.

David Ben Gurion, Israel's first prime minister, set great store by this teaching role, seeking in his own public life to establish certain standards of simplicity and the pioneering spirit. He dressed in plain khaki, was known to have few possessions apart from his books, lived in a spartan apartment. In retirement he moved to a hut on kibbutz Sdeh Boker in the Negev desert, wishing to encourage the settlement of that arid region. In the tense period preceding the 1956 Sinai campaign, seeking to rally the people round the government, and strengthen home defences, Ben Gurion launched a movement of volunteers to fortify border villages. The newspapers showed him stringing barbed wire and digging trenches.[3]

The same kind of public education by leadership example is an established feature of political life in the People's Republic of China. It is common for photographs to be displayed in the press of China's leaders performing everyday tasks, such as helping with work on a dam or mingling with labourers on a commune. A portrait of party chairman Hu Yaobang released in February 1982 showed him sweeping leaves with other workers. As well as setting a personal example of manual labour the picture may have been aimed at disposing of speculation about the absence of party leaders from public view over several weeks. It is also tempting to wonder whether the photo was not intended, more elliptically, to emphasize the determination of the top leadership to persist in a current campaign to prune the government bureaucracy and 'sweep away' unsuitable party cadres.[4]

It is but a short step from the leader's exhortatory role in domestic affairs to his exemplary role in the arena of foreign relations. The people look to him for guidance in their attitudes and reactions to the outside world. Leadership in this sense consists in demonstrating what is right and fitting.

In a crisis – a test of national resolution – the leader's behaviour acts as a paradigm. He is both mentor and champion. Hesitation, defeatism or simply lack of energy remorselessly communicate themselves to the general public at home and to watching foes and supporters abroad. In this way the conduct of leadership, by acting as a focus of expectations – right or wrong – can affect actions and hence outcomes.

To strike the right balance between the needs of domestic guidance and those of external policy poses a real difficulty for a leader. A display of internal modesty may create a mistaken impression abroad of plain weakness. Domestic flamboyance may be understood as the precursor of an aggressive foreign policy. (Though the experience of regimes such as those of Sukarno of Indonesia and Qaddafi of Libya suggests that pomp and bombast may indeed be translated into self-assertion abroad.)

A classic example of the rare golden mean is found in the courageous behaviour of Finnish President Paasikivi in the face of Soviet pressure. In February 1948 the government of Finland were the recipients of a letter from Stalin that could only have aroused extreme concern: was Finland prepared to sign a treaty of mutual assistance with the USSR similar to Soviet treaties already concluded with Hungary and Romania? Given Finland's defeat at Soviet hands in 1944 some sort of pact could hardly be avoided. Paasikivi, however, had no wish for Finland to be reduced to satellite status.

Finnish intentions were signalled by a series of steps taken by the president, of dignity and studied deliberation, in which the factor of time was exploited with skill and originality. Not for Paasikivi the hurried and unseemly 'journey to Canossa' at Hitler's command of a Schuschnigg or Hacha. Paasikivi took his time. He waited five days to inform his government, then acknowledged Stalin's letter with a brief note, pointing out his constitutional requirement of consulting the representatives of the people. By the time parliamentary groups had reported, a delegation been appointed, instructions drawn up and approved, and the delegation finally seen off, more than a month had passed.

Max Jakobson, former Finnish ambassador to the United Nations, summarizes Paasikivi's tactics thus: 'The timetable of the Finnish preparations was eloquent in itself. It was an assertion of Finnish independence and a demonstration of the democratic process. The Finnish people were being reassured: their interests and rights were not going to be signed away by frightened men in hasty and secret deals.'[5] The Soviet Union, moreover, was being put on notice, Jakobson might have added, that Finland was not intimidated and would bend the knee to no one. And indeed the subsequent Soviet-Finnish friendship treaty was successfully to preserve the form as well as the substance of Finnish independence.

Sensitivity to Soviet concerns without subservience has been the mark of Finnish policy toward her great neighbour. The self-discipline of the Finnish people as a whole, in avoiding providing the USSR with any pretext to disturb this delicate and ambiguous balance, is not the least due to the cool-headed and restrained example set by Paasikivi and his successor Kekkonen.

THE LEADER AS SIGNALMAN

Alongside his role as bell-wether, setting an example for his flock, the national leader is looked to by foreign observers for an authoritative indication of his government's intentions and orientations. He, it is assumed, provides – in both word and gesture – a true guide to his country's positions on foreign affairs. Such personalization of government, while obscuring its more complex nature, is a succinct and most expressive means of dramatizing – and hence better communicating – policy.

On the home front the first opportunity a newly installed leader has of indicating his political preferences and setting the tone of his administration comes at his inauguration.

Jimmy Carter, seeking to remove the presidency from its pedestal, to restore trust and to bring government to the people, chose to walk hand-in-hand with his wife Rosalynn along Pennsylvania avenue. On journeys he carried his own briefcase and appeared on television in an informal sweater. His close advisers were permitted to wear jeans and open-necked shirts to the office. Ironically, it soon became clear that the American public was not at all interested in downgrading the dignity of the presidency.

François Mitterrand, in reaction to the aloof, 'monarchical' incumbency of his predecessor, Giscard d'Estaing, dedicated his own presidency at the Panthéon, the shrine of the revolution. There he placed red roses (the French socialist symbol) on the tombs of Jean Moulin, a hero of the Resistance, and Jean Jaurès, the father of French socialism. Even the *Marseillaise* was played, at Mitterrand's instructions, at a brisker, more exuberant tempo than previously.[6]

President Mubarak of Egypt, for his part, deliberately avoided the pomp and splendour of an American or French-style inauguration. Turning his back on the highly personalized, pharaonic – but also corrupt and inefficient – regime of the assassinated Anwar Sadat, Mubarak projected a low profile, technocratic image. Any hint of a new personality cult was eschewed. Billboards ceased to carry huge posters singing the president's praises. Political opponents of the late president were ostentatiously released from prison. A group of distinguished former internees including Mohamed Heikal, Nasser's confidant, were received at the presidential palace in front of television and press cameramen. Domestic reconciliation and rejection of at least some of Sadat's policies were clearly to be a leading theme. A striking symbol of the downfall of the old order came in the shape of the much-photographed demolition of one of Sadat's holiday homes next to the pyramids on 'environmental grounds'. A number of other rest houses popular with the Sadat entourage were 'handed back to the nation'.[7]

Most new governments have no set-piece diplomatic occasions, equivalent to an inauguration, at which foreign policy changes can be hinted at. The common custom of giving a reception for the diplomatic corps is invariably tightly hemmed-in by protocol and not a time for giving favour or offence.

Where the former incumbent has died in office his state funeral may, however, provide an opportunity for the new leadership to signal its reaffirmation or reappraisal of previous positions. The presence of Israeli Prime Minister Begin at the Sadat funeral and his embrace of the new president seemed to signal that the Mubarak regime planned to continue the peace process with Israel.

The Brezhnev funeral was an especially fascinating occasion. The exceptional attention paid by new party leader Yuri Andropov to Chinese Foreign Minister Huang Hua has already been noted. It was not the only significant innovation. Observers remarked that Heng Samrin and other officials of the Vietnamese-supported Cambodian regime were separated from the 'fraternal' delegates from Laos and Vietnam. In the list of delegations printed in *Pravda*, the ruling Cambodians appeared among those Communist parties *not in power*. Similarly, the Afghan delegation led by President Babrak Karmal was listed, insultingly, after the minor Communist parties of Guyana and the Dominican Republic. Both gestures could be read as hints of possible Soviet flexibility on two of the outstanding issues between Moscow and Peking – Vietnamese influence in Cambodia and the continuing Soviet occupation of Afghanistan.[8]

Quite different was the treatment accorded to the PLO delegation. Yassir Arafat, though neither a head of state or government nor a Communist, was to be found away from the Third World grouping at the side of important Communist bloc leaders such as General Jaruzelski of Poland, Fidel Castro of Cuba and Janos Kadar of Hungary.[9] Clearly the Soviet commitment to the PLO and its aspiration to statehood was being doubly emphasized. The juxtaposition was also eloquent about Soviet plans for a future Palestinian state and its role in the Soviet scheme of things.

Apart from exceptional occasions like a state funeral, a new leadership is bound to make use of early diplomatic contacts to redefine (or reaffirm) its foreign policy orientations.

By convention, it is thought to be an unusual mark of favour for a foreign diplomat to be the first envoy to be received by a newly-installed foreign minister or head of government. In 1954 Soviet Foreign Minister Malenkov, wishing to signal the onset of a thaw in the Cold War, invited British ambassador Sir William Hayter for the 'inaugural' visit of a foreign diplomat. John Kennedy, on his arrival in office in January 1961, picked out French ambassador Hervé Alphand for that signal honour. Kennedy, the envoy wrote, 'insisted on receiving first of all the ambassador of France, because he wished to have the best relations possible with that country and deeply admired General de Gaulle, whose advice he sought'. (The recalcitrant but influential French president was also the first foreign leader received by President Johnson after the Kennedy funeral, despite the tension in Franco–American relations following the French veto on British entry into the EEC of some months previously.[10])

Ronald Reagan, on his accession to the presidency in January 1981, had a very clear and different set of priorities in foreign policy from that of Jimmy Carter: a de-emphasis of human rights, a tougher approach to the Soviet Union, more consistent and open support for anti-Communist regimes and especial emphasis on the affairs of the Western hemisphere. Accordingly, the first foreign head of government to visit the White House was Jamaica's prime minister, Edward Seaga. The latter was a free market, pro-American conservative, who had recently defeated the pro-Castro regime of socialist Michael Manley. Generous economic assistance promised to Jamaica indicated that here was one administration that knew how to look after its friends.

Another early visitor to Washington was the new leader of South Korea, Chun Doo Hwan. His imprisonment of former rival Kim Dae Jong and a human rights record which had distressed the Carter administration were overlooked. A senior official explained: 'It is not the purpose of this Administration to look into the internal affairs of Korea.'

But the most momentous departure came in relations with the USSR. Newly-appointed Secretary of State Alexander Haig was eager to broadcast the change of course as quickly as possible. He comments in his memoirs: 'In the morning of an Administration, the air is fresh and still relatively quiet, and friends and adversaries are alert and watchful. It is the best time to send signals. Our signal to the Soviets had to be a plain warning that their time of unresisted adventuring in the Third World was over . . . .' Haig's first move, taken together with outgoing Secretary of State Edmund Muskie, was a demonstration of naval power in support of Morocco. The Moroccan seizure of Soviet fishing trawlers had resulted in the Soviet stationing of several warships in the Atlantic, off the Moroccan coast. Against the background of Soviet support for the Polisario front, fighting for independence of Morocco in the Western Sahara, it was perceived by the Moroccans as 'a serious threat'. Haig himself viewed the incident in a larger perspective. It was 'an opportunity to show support for Morocco, to demonstrate opposition to a leftist insurgency, and to warn the Soviets early on'. A US navy guided missile cruiser and its support vessels were accordingly diverted to the Moroccan coast, and the Soviet ships withdrew.

Haig's next signal was conventionally diplomatic, but its timing and tone were significant. In his first letter to Soviet Foreign Minister Gromyko, Haig pointedly avoided the sort of platitudes usually expressed. Instead he stated American concern over the Polish situation and Soviet suppression of human rights in Eastern Europe. Nor did he conceal 'our displeasure over cynical and unhelpful Soviet propaganda in connection with the hostage situation in Iran'.

Ironically, the gesture that received most publicity had not been planned by Haig at all, at least in the first instance. Since the time of Kennedy, Soviet ambassador Anatoly Dobrynin had been granted the courtesy of entering the State Department through a basement garage, thus avoiding reporters at the building's main entrance, and then ascending a private elevator to the secretary of state's inner office on the seventh floor. In Haig's words: 'This trivial but highly symbolic perquisite acknowledged the special nature of the relationship between the United States and the other superpower.' However, when Dobrynin arrived for his first meeting with Haig he found his usual entrance barred by a security officer, who ordered the embarrassed ambassador to proceed to the main entrance, in full, humiliating view of the media.

Haig wishes in his memoirs that he 'could claim credit for this inspired gesture'. In point of fact the decision had been made at a bureaucratic, not political level. The assistant secretary of state for European affairs had ordered the move at the instigation of the chief of the Soviet desk in the State Department in order to indicate disapproval at the lack of Soviet reciprocity in their treatment of US ambassadors in Moscow. (As Soviet defector Arkady Shevchenko points out, Dobrynin's privileged access in Washington actually worked to the detriment of the United States, since it lessened the need for the Soviet government to make use of American diplomats in Moscow, leaving them even more isolated than necessary. So presumably part of the rationale for the recommendation of the Soviet desk was, sensibly, to restore the balance of access.)

Whoever made the decision, the snub turned out to be most effective. A self-important individual had been taken down a peg or two. It was just the kind of thing to catch the attention of both the American public and the prestige-conscious Soviet leadership. The USSR had been given notice that the cosy compliance of the Carter years in Soviet expansionism – as the Reagan Administration saw it – was to be replaced by a new, hard-nosed realism.

But if the gesture was not deliberate, the reader may wonder, how could it possess political significance? The answer is that it was Haig's retrospective approval that confirmed that the whole affair 'was not an accident'. The Soviet Union would anyway assume American intentionality, as Haig well knew. In the absence of an apology or of a restoration of the privilege, this initial assumption became, willy-nilly, a political fact.[11]

The vocabulary of personal gesture as used by statesmen and diplomats does have its own conventions and special features (as we shall see in Ch. 5). But it also draws on the mannerisms of everyday life, albeit writ large. Very subtle signals – a cocked eyebrow or a nuanced smile – are sometimes found (more likely in the performance of oriental than Western figures). On the whole, though, the body language of the leader tends to resemble that of a ham actor rather than a character from a Henry James novel. Since he is very much 'on stage' he has to choose gestures unlikely to be overlooked by his audience. It is, therefore, the bear-hug, the long, slow handshake and the big smile that have become the clichés of televised or photographed diplomacy. Nikita Khrushchev got it just right when he cheekily remarked to Vice-President Nixon on the latter's 1959 Moscow visit as they came out from dinner to meet the photographers: 'Keep smiling; otherwise they'll say we just had a quarrel!'[12]

More seriously, the personal gesture can communicate to a watching audience, as nothing else can, the tangible reality of a complex political development. An outstanding description of one such display has been given by one perceptive witness to the January 1963 signing of the Franco-German friendship treaty by General de Gaulle and Chancellor Adenauer:

> as the two men stood facing each other, de Gaulle was seen to step forward, extend his huge arms, pull in his sizeable stomach, and stoop to press the dry little old man against himself and then to bestow two sonorous kisses on the wrinkled cheeks of the strange Mongol face. The spectators were stunned; everyone held his breath as he witnessed this unique scene. Tears, real ones, clouded the eyes of the German Chancellor. His hand sought that of his French friend. The picture that one hundred million European viewers saw on television ... had a much greater impact, a much clearer meaning, than any speeches about reconciliation or treaties of cooperation. In politics, appearances count for more than reality; on that day appearances were everything, the reality almost nothing. The kiss of peace confirmed a sentiment, abolished an entire past, offered a promise. It is plain that the most spontaneous gesture, the most gratuitous act is, for de Gaulle, the result of political calculation.[13]

THE LEADER AS STAKER-OUT OF COMMITMENTS

The repertoire of leadership is clearly based on certain simple, almost self-evident principles. First and foremost is the idea that the meaning of a gesture at the personal level – pleasure, intimacy, dislike, etc. – directly translates into a political statement at the national level. Thus de Gaulle embracing Adenauer, a sign of deep personal affection, commonly used in French society between relatives or close friends, becomes an expression of 'fraternity' or 'reconciliation' between the French and German nations. This equation is possible because the leader is seen in some sense as embodying or at least representing his own people. The gesture is consequently seen as a metaphor for state policy.

A second principle governing the symbolic dimensions of leadership behaviour is the convention, apparently universal, that the presence of the leader constitutes approval or support of the individual, institution or state being visited. Physical proximity is thought to imply political endorsement. Psychologically, as advertising firms have long known, the principle is well grounded. A media personality who is pictured together with a product sets on it his seal of approval. The difference between the world of politics and that of advertising is that political endorsement carries along with it a degree of responsibility not assumed by manufacturers of sports shoes. When a leader endorses an idea he is making a political commitment to its fulfilment or protection.

As a way of signalling the establishment or maintenance of a political commitment the leadership visit is one of the mainstays of diplomacy. It has a large number of variations, but at this point it is sufficient to describe a single example – the ritual enactment of a security commitment.

Since a visit as such does indeed carry a range of possible connotations, the expression of a defence commitment has to take a very pointed form. One variant involves the visiting leader actually travelling to the border between his ally and the opponent in question and being photographed in some posture of determination or vigilance. At the Berlin wall, a frequent place of pilgrimage for NATO leaders, a permanent vantage point has been set up from where allied visitors can peer through binoculars into East Berlin. Every American president and secretary of state since the time of John Kennedy has visited the spot to symbolize the continuing US commitment to the defence of West Berlin. Similar observation posts exist at Panmunjom, on the armistice lines between North and South Korea, and at Shibetsu in Northern Japan overlooking the Kuril Islands, occupied by the USSR since 1945.

A slightly different version of this gesture replaces or supplements binoculars with a hand gun (and is therefore not recommended in the presence of nervous frontier guards). On a visit to the border between Pakistan and Afghanistan in 1981 Mrs Margaret Thatcher, the British prime minister, was pictured 'examining a captured Soviet rifle', thus graphically associating her government with the guerrilla struggle against Soviet occupation. More crudely, Zbigniew Brzezinski, President Carter's national security adviser, made a similar point by posing on the great wall of China and lunging with a borrowed Chinese rifle in the general direction of the barbarians to the north. ... [14]

Clearly this kind of gesture does have its melodramatic side. It can, nevertheless, provide a very informative guide for observers to the priorities and commitments of the signaller. Some months before the Israeli attack on the PLO in the Lebanon in the summer of 1982 Israeli Defence Minister Ariel Sharon, the 'architect' of the Lebanese war, paid a much-publicized visit to the friendly 'Free Lebanese' force of Major Said Hadad. It was made known that Sharon was looking into the problem of guerrilla incursions into Southern Lebanon 'in order to decide on what steps to take'. Such visits, moreover, had rarely been publicized in the past. Observers were in no doubt that the trip was intended as a clear warning that Israel would act against continued infringements of the ceasefire.[15]

THE LEADER AS PRIEST

Finally, we come to the leader as priest. In solemn ceremonies and on days of commemoration or dedication the leader can manipulate sacred symbols of the nation in order to legitimize his government and sanctify otherwise pragmatic and self-interested acts of national policy.[16]

In the past kings were seen as possessing priestly attributes and their authority was buttressed by the concept of divine right. Relics of that tradition are retained in the coronation service, certain ceremonial practices and customs, and the aura of reverence surrounding the monarch. Some of these features have reappeared in modern leadership. Popular myths of supernatural power have enveloped even blatantly secular figures such as Eva Peron and Kwame Nkrumah.

Still, in an era when power is acquired by the ballot or the bullet, and not by inheritance, it might be thought unusual to stress the sacred side of leadership. It is simply that religious or pseudo-religious themes and rituals continue to play an important role. One is led to conclude that the spread of materialist doctrines and the decline of traditional cultures have not removed the continuing need for a transcendent dimension to human affairs.

The inspirational potential in leadership can remain dormant for long periods and then re-emerge to surprise us. In recent years the relationship of a Polish pope or an Iranian ayatollah to his people provides a reminder of the potent results produced when raw faith is infused into political life. In both cases sacred symbols, myths and rituals were powerfully harnessed in the cause of national mobilization. On his catalytic 1979 visit to Poland John Paul II made full use of the panoply of Polish Catholic symbolism. The Black Madonna icon of Czestochowa, for instance, which synthesizes, in one evocative symbol, the triumphs and tragedies of Polish national and religious history, was frequently placed next to, if only in reproduction, the person or image of the pontiff. Indeed it was clear that in a very real sense he was considered her priest and the latest instrument of her purpose for the Polish nation.

In a different religious context the image of the ayatollah Khomeini and symbols of Shi'ite martyrdom were without doubt of great inspiration to Iranian armies in their war effort against Iraq.

In the final analysis one may wonder whether it is at all useful to classify phenomena of this kind as narrowly political. Were these not authentic religious occurrences in their own right, albeit with momentous socio-political consequences? They seem more on a par with messianic phenonema such as the Crusades and the Sabbatian movement of the seventeenth century, than with the modern Soviet exploitation of pseudo-religious ritual in the service of the state. Wojtyla and Khomeini were not acting as priests; they were priests. The movements they helped to precipitate were largely spontaneous upheavals of collective aspiration and not cynically engineered political contrivances.

What these examples do indicate is the extraordinary potential for popular galvanization packed into symbols of religious belief. It is not surprising, then, that such motifs are deliberately drawn upon by national leaders to serve political ends. Two separate uses of religious symbolism can be distinguished in the area of foreign policy: the evocation of the authority of religion to legitimize a controversial political initiative; and the appeal by national leaders engaged in a process of reconciliation or alliance to shared symbols of fraternity.

For President Sadat of Egypt the journey to Jerusalem and the subsequent negotiations with Israel were fraught with danger. Acceptance of the existence of Israel flew in the face of a long-established Arab taboo; for years the cause of Palestine had been a touchstone of loyalty to the wider Arab nation – as much an abstract credo as a real issue to be concretely pursued. For his good intentions Sadat risked being isolated in the Arab world and anathematized as an apostate and traitor. Even in Egypt, where war-weariness and local nationalism had eroded sympathy for the Palestinians, the predictable opposition of pan-Arabists, Nasserists and the Left could not be overlooked. The Islamic fundamentalists, who were later behind Sadat's assassination, combined a burning faith in Islamic unity with a profound antipathy for that race – the Jews – which had not accepted the election of the Prophet.

Thus both at home and abroad Sadat sought to legitimize his policy of peace with Israel by the use of Moslem symbols and ideas. His speech to Israel's parliament, the *Knesset*, was redolent with religious themes: war was an offence against God's creation, man, and opposed to his teachings of love, sincerity, purity and peace. Stressing the benevolent, rather than militant, dimension of Islam, Sadat appealed to the tradition of Umar ibn al-Khattab, the second successor to Muhammad, who developed the idea of tolerance and respect for non-Moslems.[17]

Sadat also drew upon religious symbolism for the timing and programme of his Jerusalem mission. For the first day he deliberately chose the Feast of the Sacrifice (*Id al-Adha*), which commemorates Abraham's willingness to sacrifice his son – thereby recalling the common ancestor of both Arabs and Jews. From an Islamic perspective the evocation of Abraham also carried with it the pious suggestion that Sadat, like the founder of the Arab race, was submitting to the will of God, not out of weakness but out of deep belief.

The very first call made by the Egyptian president in Jerusalem was at the El Aksa mosque, the third holiest shrine in Islam. The elegant image of the adjacent El Sakhra mosque, the more familiar structure on the Haram es-Sherif, had appeared on several Egyptian postage stamps dedicated to the Palestinian question issued during Sadat's period of office. It also featured, side by side with a portrait of the president, on the commemorative issue released following the Jerusalem visit.[18] The choice of a peaceful religious symbol as a synonym for Palestine anticipated the peace intiative. Sadat's visit to the site itself, with its religious and Palestinian national associations, became the fulfilment of a symbolic prophecy. It was also, of course, a dramatic and effective demonstration of his continuing commitment to the Palestinian cause.

By choosing a festival for the occasion of his journey, Sadat ensured that millions of Arabs throughout the Middle East would be at home to view him on their television screens. Their initial, crucial, impression of his mission would be of the president as true believer and pilgrim, kneeling at prayer with his Palestinian brothers in the Holy City. It was a compelling image of piety and devotion – certainly not of surrender to Israel. In this holy place, Sadat was saying, in effect, I dedicate my mission to the cause of peace and Palestine.

The use of Moslem symbolism to legitimize the peace initiative went hand-in-hand with a search for religious motifs shared by both the Jewish and Islamic traditions. One of these, as we have seen, was the recollection of Abraham, the common ancestor. Another, at a later stage in the negotiations, was the idea of building a mosque, synagogue and church on Jabal Musa, Mount Sinai to Jews and Christians, where Moses was said to have received the tablets of the law. It would have been a dramatic way of reviving the talks, then going through a difficult period. Israeli Defence Minister Ezer Weizman correctly perceived the political idea behind the gesture: 'The peace process had forced Sadat to comb through his people's traditions for some way of presenting Israeli society in a favorable light. This was particularly difficult in view of the anti-Zionist ideology prevailing in Egypt for decades. His solution was to focus on the age-old link between the religions – a link symbolized by Mount Sinai.'[19]

Such shared symbolism is a way of bridging the psychological gap between separate nations involved in a quest for reconciliation or friendship. It carries the message to both peoples that their differences are subsumed within a deeper communion.

Between co-religionists – Christians or Moslems – a resort to joint prayer and common motifs is natural and can, indeed, be frequently observed in practice. More unusual is the use made of this device by Communist regimes in relations with non-Communists. Perhaps it is a deliberate ploy to correct the impression of Communists as anti-religious iconoclasts.

Whatever the motive, it has taken some curious forms. One unusual example of this can be seen in an episode from Sino-Indian relations. It took place during a visit by Mrs Pandit (sister of Indian Prime Minister Nehru) to Peking in 1952, at a time of great optimism in relations between the two ancient, yet emergent, Asian giants. To welcome the Indian delegation a troupe from the Chinese academy of dance had prepared a special ballet for the occasion based on an idea – as the guests were pointedly informed – of Chinese Prime Minister Chou En-lai himself. At the climax of the performance the stage filled with immense lotus flowers. From each one emerged a girl, while the prima ballerina came out of the central flower.

What are we to make of this remarkable scene? It is not hard to see that it was intended as a symbolic act. In fact, Chou En-lai had envisaged it as a great compliment to India and her ancient civilization – an acknowledgement of the debt owed by China to the influence of

Buddhism. Chou was not only evoking a religious and cultural heritage received by China from India, but also, by doing this, flatteringly hinting at Indian seniority. (That he could afford such a generous gesture was actually an index of China's enormous cultural self-confidence.) He was also, with rare economy, paying a direct compliment to the person of Mrs Vijaya Lakshmi Pandit.[20]

The dance was derived from a classical theme of Indian mythology, the birth of Lakshmi – after whom Mrs Pandit was named – wife of the great god Vishnu. This mother-goddess of fortune and beauty, according to the epic poetry of the *Mahabharata*, emerged from a lotus which sprang from the forehead of Vishnu. To Indian taste the lotus has always been considered the most beautiful of all flowers and is associated with ideas of purity, perfection and immortality. Prominent in Indian art and literature, its ornamental use and symbolic meaning were brought to China and the countries of the Far East by the spread of Buddhism. No more apt or tasteful symbol of Sino-Indian ties could have been conceived.

Few statesmen are capable of that combination of artistic sensibility and political subtlety at which Chou was matchless. Only perhaps Charles de Gaulle (helped by André Malraux) and Anwar Sadat could make a claim to that supreme skill which can harness aesthetic appreciation to the expediencies of *realpolitik*. At its most successful, art or drama in the service of politics enables the statesman to appeal to both heart and mind. Playing the sacred chord is calculated to touch the deepest emotions of an audience, overcoming all scepticism and apathy.

Perhaps it is not so unusual for a Communist ideologue to resort to a classic Buddhist myth to convey a political message. Timeless, universalist themes are, after all, best suited to suggest international fraternity. For all the effort that they have expended on the project, Marxist regimes have not succeeded in displacing traditional symbols. The Lenin cult arouses minimal enthusiasm beyond Soviet borders. Pagan symbols, also cultivated by the Nazis, in folk culture and sport, deserve mention, but are vehicles for chauvinist pride as often as altruistic brotherhood. How ironic to find the Soviet postal service resorting to the biblical image of the sword beaten into a plowshare as a symbol of universal peace!

When Social Democrat and Communist meet they must seek their shared heritage, therefore, in Christianity. It was to Guestrow cathedral that Erich Honecker, general secretary of the East German Communist party, took his guest Helmut Schmidt to celebrate the ceremonial climax to their 1981 talks. The bishop officiating pointed out that the cathedral and the brick Gothic churches of the Baltic region were symbols of the two Germanies 'common past and memories'.

Reporting to the *Bundestag* on his return, the West German chancellor described his emotion at the experience. But, as he well understood, he was not the only one to be moved. The television scene of the leaders 'sitting next to each other in the choir stalls' gave citizens of both countries 'a more important indication of the common ground between us than any after-dinner speeches and communiqués or resolutions can do'.[21] In an electronic and secular age the ancient themes can still be the most effective instruments of leadership.

In the following chapters we shall examine in detail the props used by the leader in his role as performer.

REFERENCES AND NOTES

1. Quoted in Seton-Watson C W 1967 *Italy from Liberalism to Fascism*. Methuen, p 219
2. Muggeridge M (ed) 1947 *Ciano's Diary 1939–1943*. Odhams Books, pp 9–10
3. *Yediot Ahronot* (Hebrew) 9 Oct. 1981; Rafael G 1981 *Destination Peace*. Weidenfeld and Nicolson, p 53
4. *The Times* 13 Feb. 1982, 19 Feb. 1982
5. Jakobson M 1969 *Finnish Neutrality*. Praeger: New York, pp 38–9
6. *Time* 1 June 1981; *Le Nouvel Observateur* 25–31 May 1981
7. *The Times* 26 Nov. 1981, 5 Feb. 1982; *Yediot Ahronot* (Hebrew) 16 Dec. 1981
8. *The Times* 17 Nov. 1982
9. *Ma'ariv* (Hebrew) 8 Dec. 1982
10. Parrott C 1977 *The Serpent and the Nightingale*. Faber and Faber, p 62; Alphand H 1977, *L'étonnement d'être*. Gaillard: Paris, pp 349, 416
11. Haig A M 1984 *Caveat*. Weidenfeld and Nicolson, pp 96–102; Shevchenko A N 1985 *Breaking With Moscow*. Knopf: New York, p 195
12. Kornitzer B 1960 *The Real Nixon*. Rand McNally: New York, p 315
13. Viannson-Ponté P 1964 *The King and his Court*. Houghton Mifflin: Boston, p 74
14. *The Times* 9 Oct. 1981, 31 Mar. 1982
15. *Yediot Ahronot* (Hebrew) 3 Nov. 1981; *Ma'ariv* (Hebrew) 4 Nov. 1981

16. See Apter D E 1963 Political religion in the new nations, in Geertz C (ed) *Old Societies and New States*. The Free Press: New York
17. Salem-Babikian N 1980 The sacred and the profane: Sadat's speech to the Knesset, *Middle East Journal*, 34: 13–24
18. *Stanley Gibbons Stamp Catalogue* Part 19 Middle East 1980. Nos. 1184, 1206, 1333–4. Also see nos. 1069–70, 1366
19. Weizman E 1981 *The Battle for Peace*. Bantam Books: New York, p 317
20. Panikkar K M 1955 *In Two Chinas*. Allen and Unwin, p 172
21. German embassy press release 18 Dec. 1981

Chapter four

COSTUME AND COMMUNICATION

In the presentation of self – Erving Goffman's phrase – dress is an extension of the personality of the wearer and, with bodily gesture, the most conspicuous and yet intimate vehicle of self-expression. The immediate impression we receive of an individual is largely the effect of his external appearance.

As a social instrument dress defines role and bestows rank. Pascal noted long ago the judge's need of robe and wig. Without them he would be stripped of half his authority.[1] In politics dress performs no less a purpose. Revolutions have used it as one means in their consolidation of power. Napoleon reintroduced the style of dress of the *ancien régime* in order to buttress the legitimacy of the new ruling class. In contrast, the bolsheviks rejected the clothing conventions of the pre-revolutionary period and adopted a drab working uniform, precisely to signify the overthrow of the old order.[2]

In foreign policy the scope for diverging from the norm and therefore of making a political point is limited by two factors. First, if a message is to be comprehensible, it must draw upon a recognized convention. It is clearly insufficient for the article of clothing to have some private significance. Second, the community of officials and ministers involved in the conduct of foreign policy is, on the whole, conformist from the point of view of dress. Diplomats do not usually wish to draw attention to their appearance. Furthermore protocol lays down detailed guidelines for the form of dress appropriate for various occasions – say for a daytime ceremony or an evening function. Improvization is at a minimum.[3]

What room, then, remains for political communication? There are two levels at which choice of dress may be significant. At a collective level the national group can choose to conform to or diverge from the clothing conventions generally accepted by the international community. At an individual level a statesman can give greater scope to his personal preferences than can his subordinates. First let us turn to the clothing convention chosen by the national group, in an attempt to determine its underlying logic.

Under the 'old diplomacy' of the pre-First World War period clothing conventions were rigid and uniform. Guides to diplomatic protocol could lay down, with marginal national variations, the costume demanded of a particular occasion – whether in London, Buenos Aires or St Petersburg. Such sartorial conformity reflected, in the first instance, a social and cultural consensus. Diplomats, of whatever nationality, were members of a select club with its own jargon and 'club rules'. Members shared a common educational and cultural background, and usually came from the same social strata – the ranks of the nobility or the wealthy upper bourgeoisie. Selective admission procedures based upon personal connexions, the need for a private income and the assumption of certain customs and manners, ensured that the diplomatic community remained restricted to a social elite. Forms of attire current in government and diplomacy in the nineteenth century were simply based upon those found in the upper echelons of society at the same time.

However, uniformity of dress signified more than just social homogeneity and the defence by a class of its own privileges and position. Agreement on manners went hand-in-hand with – indeed was a metaphor for – agreement on ideology. Membership of the diplomatic club entailed commitment to the preservation of the existing structure of international society and the assumptions upon which it rested: in economic terms, capitalism and the sanctity of private property within and beyond national boundaries; in cultural terms, the hegemony of European, Christian civilization; in legal terms, the primacy of a system of international law grounded in Western experience and values.

In circumstances such as these, to don the frock-coat and top hat of the European diplomat was to adopt the attitudes of a class and the premises of a civilization. If one wanted to join the club, one agreed to maintain the rules. External conformity in clothing signified compliance with contemporary norms of international society. To flaunt convention would signify symbolic rejection of society itself as presently constituted.

The first newcomer to question the forms of classic diplomacy was the United States. As its envoy in Paris, Benjamin Franklin found the methods and ethics of European politics totally repugnant. Like other American diplomats after him he had no wish to entangle the infant republic in the snares of old world cynicism. But reality proved more powerful than predilection. Were the American revolution to survive it had no choice but to seek the recognition and support of monarchist France.

The compromise on principle that this entailed was outwardly demonstrated by a compromise on form. On first arriving in Paris in 1776, Franklin, as befitted a no-nonsense egalitarian, appeared at court in a plain suit, no wig and brandishing a knotty crab-apple cane. But within a short time he realized that to succeed in his mission he would have to adapt himself to the elaborate customs and costumes of the court.[4]

Nowadays no American diplomat would dream of offending against local habits, sartorial or otherwise. Yet the egalitarian tradition and its distaste for *realpolitik* and the protocol that seem to symbolize it, run deep in American culture. 'Protocol and striped pants', President Truman once wrote, 'give me a pain in the neck.' Most Americans would heartily agree and probably sympathize with the attitude of Thomas Jefferson, who once received the British minister while sitting in an old chair in his bathrobe and tossing a slipper about on the end of his toe.[5] Much later, Lyndon Johnson was to behave in much the same way.

A later newcomer to the diplomatic arena was Japan. Unlike the United States, which was, after all, an offshoot of European civilization, Japan was a great civilization in its own right and naturally possessed its own traditions and forms of dress. For it to adopt Western diplomatic garb would require more than conforming to accepted convention; it would entail the adoption of unfamiliar foreign costume. Would this not convey an admission of cultural subordinacy? To catch up with the West, Japan was prepared to make the sacrifice. The spirit of Japanese diplomacy was summed up in the expression *Datsu-A nyu-O* – meaning a willingness to reject things Asian and welcome things European.[6]

In 1872 a Japanese mission, led by the royal official Iwakura Tomomi, visited Europe and the United States. It was to act as a diplomatic embassy and a commission of inquiry into Western life. The Tomomi mission is considered the starting-point for Japan's foreign policy in the modern era. It proved a useful opportunity to learn the rudiments of Western diplomacy. In the United States members of the mission initially appeared in customary Japanese court attire: silk kimono. However, they quickly grasped that traditional costume made an unfortunate impression of 'backwardness'. In the words of a contemporary observer: 'This was their last appearance, in what to our eyes appeared a grotesque costume, and no doubt did so to the shrewd observation of the Ambassador Iwakura, for not one member of the Embassy ... ever appeared afterwards in public, with what we would call feminine garments made of silks and satins.' Henceforth the delegates wore Western-style suits.[7]

Whatever psychological difficulties novice American and Japanese diplomats might have had in adopting formal diplomatic attire, they had no objections on the grounds of ideology. Both sought admission to the international community and were prepared to abide by the rules. Not so the first representatives of Soviet Russia. Leon Trotsky, first people's commissar for foreign affairs after the bolshevik revolution, believed he could simply 'issue some revolutionary proclamations to the peoples and then close up the shop'.[8] Old-style diplomacy was to be as redundant as the nation state and other irrelevant – and doomed – institutions of the capitalist system.

But it was the Communist regime, and not the outside world, that was to teeter on the brink of collapse. The Soviet leadership had no choice but to accommodate itself to the facts. The new economic policy, restoring the mechanism of the market on the home front, entailed, as a natural corollary, a foreign policy of conciliation abroad. Not for the last time a Communist regime looked to the West for succour. Chicherin, Trotsky's successor at the foreign ministry, admitted in 1920 that a *modus vivendi* had to be found with the capitalist system.[9]

In April 1922 with famine at home a Soviet delegation, headed by Chicherin, made its diplomatic debut at the Genoa economic conference. 'Old-time diplomats noticed with pleasure that the Soviet representatives, in frock coats and striped trousers, behaved exactly as diplomats were expected to behave. Chicherin even went to a royal reception and exchanged toast with an archbishop. Henceforth, Soviet diplomats became known as sticklers for diplomatic etiquette.'[10]

With the dissolution of the colonial empires since the Second World War, new issues have arisen. Given that there is now a large Third World majority at the United Nations, it is far from self-evident that membership of the international community should entail the adoption of Western dress. Yet a study of photographs of the UN General Assembly, the assembly of the Organization of African Unity or summits of the nonaligned movement indicates that the Western lounge suit overwhelmingly predominates.

Now this is surely a most curious finding. No one today would dare to look askance at the wearing of national dress. Indeed the diplomats of Saudi Arabia, Nigeria, India and various other states commonly do dress traditionally. One would think it natural for the delegate of a non-Western state, where Western clothing is not customary, to wear some variant of his native costume. That this is not so, on the whole, requires explanation and not the reverse.

One explanation for the phenomenon is that new states simply and unquestioningly conform to existing convention in dress as in other aspects of protocol. The fact that it happens to derive from Western practice is no more than a historical accident. It is more convenient to follow existing precedent and no deeper significance should be read into it. Most new members of a club prefer conformity to obtrusiveness. When membership of that club is considered an important attribute of national independence, there will be a natural desire to follow the rules.

An alternative explanation is that the adoption of Western dress derives from a deliberate wish to emulate Western prestige and technological achievement. According to this hypothesis, the willingness to exchange traditional attire for a lounge suit reflects a deeper cultural ambition.

Western clothes undoubtedly do arouse powerful associations in former colonial territories. In Africa, dress was one of the instruments of political and cultural subjugation employed by the colonial powers. Entry into a European institution, such as a school, church, hotel or restaurant – assuming they allowed admission to Africans at all – was strictly in Western clothes. Employment might carry with it a similar requirement. For instance, male servants, of all ages, were obliged to wear a uniform of shirt, shorts and – humiliatingly – an apron. Conversely, whites were equally unprepared to concede to blacks the 'privilege' of full Western dress, seeing this as a dangerous pretension to equality.[11]

Against this kind of background it is hardly surprising that European clothes came to symbolize the achievement of autonomy and equality for some but, equally, a reminder of past discrimination and oppression for others.

For Presidents Senghor and Houphouet-Boigny of the former French colonies of Senegal and the Ivory Coast, men deeply imbued with French language and culture, the choice of anything other than Western clothes would have been unthinkable. Such leaders looked towards European civilization and were proud of the fact.

In socialist Tanzania Western dress was also adopted as an instrument of policy, though on different grounds. In 1968 the government deemed the traditional minimal body covering of the Masai to be an undesirable symptom of backwardness. The Arusha area was placed out of bounds to those clad in this way: At the same time the wearing of the *hangd*, the red-ochre-dyed toga of the Barabaig, was banned, to be replaced by shirt and shorts.[12] In both instances the Tanzanian authorities were seeking a tangible symbol of 'progress' (defined as the adoption of European culture) and also a means of de-emphasizing tribal differences. Where ethnic identity is strongly associated with bodily decoration and tribal rivalry is a real threat to nationhood, the attack on ethnic costume doubtless has a compelling logic.

A similar logic can also be seen to be at work at the pan-African level. In Africa national boundaries are simply relics of colonial rule reflecting past administrative convenience. Tribal loyalties cut across these borders. Between countries with overlapping tribal populations, the adoption of ethnic costume by one could easily be seen as an appeal to tribal kinsmen in the other – in effect a challenge to national integrity. Seen in this light, it may be, paradoxically, more desirable to introduce a non-African style of national dress than a potentially provocative and divisive traditional costume more appropriate on cultural and aesthetic grounds.

This is surely why African statesmen and diplomats meeting at *African* forums, such as the Organization of African Unity or the Economic Community of West African States – and not just wider international organizations – invariably wear the ubiquitous lounge suit. The desire to conform and to emulate Western 'achievement' is reinforced by the logic of good neighbourliness.

It might be wondered why African states have not evolved a peculiarly African variant of the diplomatic uniform as a symbol of their wider community. In fact there has been, in a modest way, a spontaneous development of this kind. At the beginning of the 1960s the safari suit began to make an appearance among African leaders. Initially it seems to have been copied from the uniform worn by Chinese officials in the aftermath of Chou En-lai's tour of Africa at the turn of 1963/64. Certainly the earliest pictorial evidence I have for this fashion is from March 1964 and shows Kwame Nkrumah, the first president of Ghana, playing table tennis in Peking with Chou En-lai. Both leaders are dressed in the characteristic high-necked, plain tunic.[13] At about this time the style was also adopted by Presidents Kaunda of Zambia and Nyerere of Tanzania.

Alongside its Chinese (and therefore, presumably, Third World and 'progressive') associations the safari suit has much to commend it in an African context. It is modest and modernistic; moreover it is highly functional – cool, loose-fitting and comfortable. Finally, it is neither Western nor regional. Among those who have taken up the fashion can be counted Sékou Touré of Guinea, Mobutu of Zaire, Numeiry of Sudan and others. However, in most of these cases the safari suit has become one style among other more common alternatives, especially the lounge suit and, increasingly, military dress uniform or populist combat fatigues. It has not developed into an emblem of African identity.

As I have already remarked, the very connotations which impel one national movement to assume Western attire might equally militate in the opposite direction: the proud assertion of national identity by an emphasis on traditional local symbols. A Senegalese poet has powerfully expressed his revulsion at the aping of Western culture:

> My brother you flash your teeth in response
> to every hypocrisy
> My brother with gold-rimmed glasses
> You give your master a blue-eyed faithful look
> My poor brother in immaculate evening dress
> Screaming and whispering and pleading in the
> parlours of condescension.[14]

Mahatma Gandhi was one of the first leaders to exploit national attire as a weapon in the struggle against colonialism. He was unquestionably a master of symbolic politics. His march in protest at the salt tax was a skilful expedient for mobilizing the people of India against the British Raj. The choice of a spinning-wheel as a symbol of self-sufficiency in the face of British textile imports was equally inspired. But, whether by design or accident, it was by virtue of his remarkable personality that Gandhi became a legend in his own lifetime and successfully guided his people to independence. He came to represent the soul of India – part holy man, part simple peasant.

No small contribution to this image was made by Gandhi's personal appearance. His figure was slight and emaciated, utterly devoid of all affectation; naked from the waist upwards, he was clad only in the white *dhoti* – loin cloth – of the male Hindu and *khaddar*, cloak of homespun cloth. He called to mind, to an European eye, nothing so much as Christ on the cross. 'A very powerful personality', Lord Irwin, the viceroy of India, summed up, 'very poorly endowed with this world's trimmings.'[15] Quite.

For Indian nationalists such gestures provided potent encouragement. For opponents they were infuriating. Churchill described it as

> alarming and also nauseating to see Mr Gandhi, a seditious Middle
> Temple lawyer, now posing as a fakir of a type well-known in the East,

striding half-naked up the steps of the Viceregal Palace, whilst he is still
organizing and conducting a defiant campaign of civil disobedience,
there to negotiate and to parley on equal terms with the representative
of the King-Emperor.[16]

Against the might of an empire, Gandhi was pitting, with stark
simplicity, the power of an idea. It was truly unnerving.

After Indian independence in 1947 there was a period of some years,
as India sought her vocation in the international arena, during which
her representatives abroad conformed to prevailing Western fashion.
Photographs of Jawaharlal Nehru, first prime minister of India, in
London, Paris, Washington, New York (at the UN) and Ottawa from
October 1948 to June 1953, show him in an elegantly-tailored lounge
suit and tie. At home, in contrast, he is never seen in anything other
than jodhpurs, long linen coat buttoned to the neck and, in public,
white Congress cap.

As yet, it should be remembered, the movement to decolonization
had not gained full momentum. At the 1953 coronation Elizabeth was
crowned queen of a still considerable portion of the globe. The concept
of a nonaligned grouping, distinct from the great industrialized blocs
of the capitalist and Communist, worlds, remained inchoate.
Sartorially, this state of transition was reflected in Nehru's willingness
to assume Western clothes when in Western settings. A sign of things
to come, though, was Nehru's retention of his national costume on
visits to Indonesia in June 1950 and Egypt in June 1953.

The sea-change in Indian policy on this issue came in 1954 with the
breakthrough in relations with China, the agreement on Tibet and the
panch shila – the five Buddhist principles of coexistence. Suddenly
India had found her vocation as an Asian power. Together with China
she would step forward as a leader of the developing world,
unbeholden to either bloc. The immediate fruit of this revelation was
the holding of the seminal Bandung conference of African and Asian
peoples in April 1955.

No longer had India any need to apologize for being different. How
natural for the new sense of pride and self-confidence in India's
mission to find outward, symbolic expression in a style of dress that
was characteristically Indian and owed nothing to foreign culture. At
the June 1954 reception in New Delhi for Chou En-lai Indians were
required to wear national costume. Foreign diplomats, on their part,
would continue to wear formal dress.[17] In protocol terms the one was
to be considered on a par with the other.

From this point on Nehru is never, ever, seen in Western dress.
Whether in Peking, Moscow, Prague, Saudi Arabia, Washington,

New York, Ottawa, Colombo or Oslo, the Indian prime minister retained the clothes of his native country when abroad.[18] Subsequent Indian leaders – Shastri, Moraji Desai, Mrs Gandhi and her son Rajiv – have all, in their own way, continued the Nehru tradition.

National costume, then, being a sign of distinctiveness, is an expression of pride in one's identity. But this cannot be all that there is to it. Other states, no less proud of their culture and history, demonstrably prefer to conform to the prevailing, more anonymous mode. In the case of India there is surely an added hint of that nation's sense of mission to lead and set a moral example.

A similar sense of mission can also be discerned in the aims and style of the foreign policy of Nkrumah's Ghana, the first black African state to gain independence (in 1957), and Nigeria, the most powerful black African state, with its wealth of natural resources. Nkrumah was personally convinced that he had been chosen as *osagyefo* or redeemer of Africa. This was reflected in the resplendent multicoloured toga, or *kente*, with which he is associated. The beautiful gowns worn by Nigerian civilian leaders are equally impressive symbols of eminence, proclaiming the statesmanlike stature of their wearers.

From what has been said so far it can be seen that the wearing of national dress on the international stage is not at all a simple, unselfconscious act. On the contrary, by eschewing the norm it necessarily involves a deliberate demonstration; it is a request for attention. Nor can it be taken for granted that the cultural affiliation portrayed by the costume is a settled matter. It may be for some leaders. But even Nehru, it has been suggested, emphasized the external signs of distinctiveness precisely because of the extent of his intellectual and cultural debt to the West. In many cases the display may reflect an aspiration rather than a settled reality. Identity – such an ambiguous and difficult word – is often *what one wishes to be thought to be* and is not at all a straightforward existential self-definition.

The abandonment by Kemal Atatürk, the founder of modern Turkey, of clothing associated with the Moslem religion was a central, symbolic part of his drive to secularize and modernize Turkish society. Thus the relevant decree ordered all civil servants to wear the costume 'common to the civilized nations of the world' – suggesting that until then Turkey had not fallen into that category. Presumably by donning a suit and tie officials would join the ranks of the 'civilized'.[19]

More recently the pendulum has swung the other way in the Moslem world. In Iran the Khomeini revolution has countermanded the Westernizing reforms introduced by the deposed shah's father, Reza Shah, in the 1930s in emulation of Kemal Atatürk's reforms. The removal of the veil, according to Khomeini, was 'spiritually damaging to the country and ... forbidden according to the law of God and the Prophet'. The Western hat was a 'disgrace of the Islamic nation' and a stain on Iranian independence.[20]

Pakistan has taken the same route. For years Pakistani representatives conformed to Western dress in their international relations without feeling that this in any way detracted from the Islamic vocation which underlay the creation of the state in 1947. The formation of the nonaligned movement had no effect on this; Pakistan remained steadfast in its Western orientation. The turnabout occurred as a result of the loss of East Pakistan – Bangladesh – in 1971. For one thing, the geographic focus of Pakistani policy altered. Pakistan was now determined to develop closer relations with the Moslem states of the Middle East. Prime Minister Bhutto, and the man who executed him, General Zia ul-Haq, made great efforts to develop an 'Islamic' foreign policy, hosting a series of Islamic summit conferences and drawing especially close to the oil-rich states of Saudi Arabia and Libya. Internally, the 1971 trauma resulted in a renewed emphasis on Islam as a way of life and ordering of society. A state pulled together in 1947, with no historical antecedents and marked by ethnic, linguistic and cultural diversity, Pakistan was obliged to fall back on its only unifying force – religion.

This intertwining of external and domestic imperatives is naturally reflected, as Edward Mortimer perceives, in the cultivation of an 'Islamic' style in public life.

> Zia himself makes a point of setting an example of piety and austerity, for instance by using wooden chairs rather than sofas at public functions, wearing 'national' dress (the *kurta* tunic and baggy *shalwar* trousers, a style in fact imported from central India) when not in uniform and urging others to do likewise; insisting that men and women be segregated at official dinners; and so on. He aspires, apparently, to be a kind of Atatürk in reverse.[21]

When Princess Anne visited Pakistan in 1983 she was greeted by local officials, all dressed traditionally, it was reported, at the orders of the president; the women's heads were covered with cowl-like *dopattas*; a girl guide guard of honour appeared in white *shalwar* and long *kameez* shirt. Nor is the past left alone. Muhammad Ali Jinnah, the founder of Pakistan, is now portrayed, in his official portrait – which is hung everywhere – in traditional costume. In fact in real life he usually wore a lounge suit and tie.[22]

No discussion of the role of national dress in politics would be complete without a look at the People's Republic of China. As in the case of Pakistan, domestic and foreign motives are inextricably bound together. Both states, in their own way, see clothing as an instrument of social change. But whereas Pakistan uses Moslem motifs as an act of wider affiliation, China adopted its own style as an affirmation of self-sufficiency.

The high-collared, severely plain tunic and working trousers (*chungshan*) which, under Mao, was the uniform of Communist China, were actually not the inspiration of the 'great helmsman' at all; it was Sun Yat-sen, the founder of the Chinese nationalist party, the *Kuomintang*, who adopted them early this century. At one and the same time the uniform suggested equality, modernity and labour. By taking it over for themselves the Communists acknowledged their debt to Sun Yat-sen and his movement, and reaffirmed their ideological commitment to those same goals.

As worn by Chinese diplomats the *chungshan* also became, in the view of R. P. Dore, a defiant statement of self-reliance at a time of international ostracism: 'In breaking the convention of dress one declares symbolically one's non-concern with any of the conventions of the international culture in which one may yet have a low ranking.'[23] One may also add the very tangible impression of austerity and discipline other diplomats would receive at the sight of a Chinese delegation, identically clad in dark grey uniformity. Since these delegations also tend to be extremely large, the effect must have been highly disconcerting – like facing a remorseless force against which all argument is futile.

With the departure from the scene of Mao Tse-tung, the defeat of the 'gang of four' and the rise to ascendancy of Deng Xiaoping in 1977–78, Chinese policy has undergone dramatic changes across the board. A programme of modernization (the 'four modernizations') based upon radical reform has been introduced; ideological restrictions have been relaxed; and in its foreign policy China has abandoned much of the baggage of the Mao era. Though relations with the USSR have steadily improved, good relations with the United States and Western Europe have a high priority. This seems to be dictated by both economic and strategic logic. On the one hand it greatly increases China's freedom for manoeuvre. On the other hand Western markets, credits and modern technology are essential if China is to modernize. The most remarkable sign of this orientation was the September 1984 Sino-British agreement on Hong Kong by which China committed herself to preserve capitalism in the territory for fifty years from 1997.

Support of 'national liberation' movements, a central tenet of the

Maoist credo, has greatly declined and aid to southeast Asian guerrillas has been all but discontinued. At a bilateral level Peking continues to cultivate relations with Third World countries, but the ideological commitment to the nonaligned movement as part of Mao's global struggle of the 'city' against the 'countryside' is absent.

These departures under Deng from previous dogma have been amply reflected in the style of dress. At a diplomatic level Zbigniew Brzezinski noted this 'symptom of changing times' in his diary for 11 December 1978. He wrote: 'When Ambassador Chai came to see me today accompanied by his two colleagues in Mao-type suits, he startled me by appearing in a brown suit with fashionably wide lapels, a blue shirt with a long collar, and a very multicoloured tie. A total sartorial transformation, symptomatic of the ideological transformation of contemporary China.'[24]

Brzezinski might have added that Chai's appearance was not only a symptom, it was also a statement of intent. Brzezinski was supposed to observe and deliberate on the significance of the change. One may see it as a declaration of pragmatism in foreign policy.

In general, visitors to China, of whom there are ever-increasing numbers, are struck by the return of colour and variety to city streets – a development eloquent of the post-Mao flexibility in economic and social policy. Not even the People's Liberation Army has remained immune from Deng's innovations. On Army Day, 1 August 1983, the armed policemen on guard outside foreign embassies and important monuments in Peking appeared in a new style of uniform. Instead of the familiar, baggy army fatigues, smart dress uniforms were now on issue. Meanwhile, in the army itself, smart dress and good drill were the order of the day.

Presumably the new uniform was intended to convey a message to the army commanders themselves. Deng was attempting to shift the PLA away from political involvement to exclusive emphasis on national defence and from reliance on outdated guerrilla strategy to competence in modern warfare. Top army commanders, however, had proved recalcitrant. Indeed television news on Army Day showed senior generals attending a reception in the old, ill-cut uniforms, with no marks of rank, of the Mao period. (Since 1983, incidentally, senior officers have been replaced on a large scale.) One may also conjecture that foreign embassies were being informed that the PLA, after its disappointing performance against Vietnam in February–March 1979 – with all this implied for China's strategic value and deterrent capacity – was not to be left behind in the campaign for modernization.[25]

It is against the background of international convention and national style that the individual leader projects his own particular image. Occasion and expediency will be factors in his design. Nor can domestic politics and protocol be ignored. Politicians who, as in the Western world, are hedged around in the performance of their duties by the requirements of law and tradition, are not free agents; they are simply not at liberty to dress, with some exceptions to be discussed below, as they might otherwise see fit. The obverse is equally true: the more untramelled the political power of the leader, the greater his scope to use dress for dramatic purposes.

A glance through one of the albums depicting the career of Winston Churchill illustrates this hypothesis. Before becoming prime minister in May 1940 Churchill was as conformist in his public appearances as any minister in British public life. After assuming his pre-eminent position – which he combined with the post of minister of defence – Churchill's public wardrobe became increasingly individual. We see Churchill, with a fine eye for the occasion, in an assortment of uniforms – now Royal Air Force, now Royal Navy, now Army; other photos catch him, at the Kremlin or in Cairo, in his famous siren suit; in the desert he wears safari costume; he even permits himself to be photographed in a dressing gown! Altogether his wartime portrait gallery accurately reflects the unique ascendancy of a man wielding greater power than any British prime minister this century. But his power was not arbitrary. For his monarch or Parliament Churchill meticulously reverted to protocol. Even then his individualism peeped through in a personal touch: his ubiquitous bow-tie.[26]

At the other end of the constitutional spectrum it is easy to observe the freedom from convention of such absolute leaders as Tito, Sukarno, Idi Amin, Qaddafi, Bokassa, Stalin and so on. Men in their position do not follow protocol; they make it to suit themselves.

Assuming, then, that there is some scope for self-expression, we can distinguish four separate political functions of clothing: (a) role definition; (b) indication of status; (c) identification with an ideology or culture; (d) reflection of mood.

(a) ROLE DEFINITION

From the policeman's uniform to the chef's apron and hat we are all familiar with the use of costume to indicate role. At the level of political leadership – as opposed to purely ceremonial pageantry – clothing has hardly been retained in the Western world as an emblem of authority. The practice of displaying authority by the wearing of some special garment or adornment of office tends to continue only in more traditional societies such as Saudi Arabia, Swaziland or Bhutan.

In foreign policy dress can be most useful in differentiating between two basic dimensions of role performance: the leader as warlord and as peacemaker. The precise political purpose of this display varies according to circumstances; the general aim of wearing military uniform is to trigger off patriotic associations of past glory and present duty.

At the beginning of her first term of office and following the Mountbatten assassination Mrs Thatcher appeared in Belfast in an army jacket. It was a simple but graphic way of boosting army morale and signalling that the commitment of her government to Northern Ireland had not wavered. Delivering an ultimatum to the Western allies on Berlin in 1961, Khruschchev assumed full military uniform. Here it was employed as an emphatic device accompanying a belligerent verbal message. In both cases uniform was an *illustrator*, a visual prop, to a political message being conveyed in other ways.[27]

The wearing of military dress by Polish Prime Minister Jaruzelski had a more complex significance. Domestically the device clearly implied that the General remained a military man, obliged by the force of events to enter government until power could be restored to the rightful hands of the party. Since the army was the only institution untainted by corruption and popular contempt, stress by Jaruzelski on his military rank was also politically advantageous.

More puzzling was his habit of wearing uniform for visits to the USSR. Reminders that Communism in Poland rested, not on popular consent, but the power of the army, could hardly be welcome. Jaruzelski did, frequently, appear in civilian clothes, so retention of uniform was not just a point of general principle with him. One answer may be that by showing off his military rank he was, in fact, emphasizing to his Soviet allies that Poland had proved quite capable, through its own efforts, of 'guarding Socialism' – without Red Army intervention. Another possibility is that the display, for the benefit of Polish and Soviet observers alike, was a way of hinting that General Jaruzelski's authority and legitimacy derived from his national background as a distinguished officer of the Polish Army and that he was far from being a Soviet puppet.[28]

The modern masters of political role display were Presidents Sadat and de Gaulle. In the 1973 Egypt–Israel War it was natural for Egyptian President Sadat, himself a former career officer, to present himself in the uniform of supreme commander of his country's armed forces, symbolizing a supreme national effort and his personal attention to the conduct of hostilities. After the cease-fire, though, Sadat shrewdly retained his uniform. His intention was to signal to the United States and Israel that he preserved the military option until a separation of forces agreement had been reached. During the wearisome 'shuttle diplomacy' of Secretary of State Henry Kissinger of January 1974 it was useful to Sadat to conduct negotiations under the shadow of the sword. That way he could hope to extract a better agreement.

The point was not lost on Dr Kissinger, acting as mediator between the two sides. Eventually an accord was reached to the Egyptian president's satisfaction. In an unprecedented gesture he then drafted a personal message to be conveyed by the secretary of state to Israeli Prime Minister Golda Meir, assuring her that the disengagement was the prelude to negotiations for peace: 'When I talk of peace now, I mean it.' In Israel there was scepticism tinged by hope. Mrs Meir returned an equally forthcoming reply, handed to Sadat by Secretary Kissinger. The scene is sketched in the Kissinger memoirs:

> There followed a scene out of a sentimental motion picture. Sadat had finished reading the letter, folded it, and taken off his glasses when his assistant Ashraf Marwan came into the room and whispered something in his ear. Sadat rose and walked over to me and kissed me on both cheeks: 'They have just signed the agreement at Kilometer 101,' he said. And then he added: 'I am today taking off my military uniform – I never expect to wear it again except for ceremonial occasions. Tell her [Golda] that is the answer to her letter.'[29]

Thus, in the most vivid way possible, the warlord donned his new role of peacemaker. In the Middle East symbolism is the very stuff of politics; often not a means, but an end in itself. Four years later, following Sadat's Jerusalem mission, an Israeli negotiating team arrived in Cairo to begin detailed talks on the conclusion of a treaty of peace. As if in acknowledgement of Sadat's original gesture the Israelis ruled that even their military personnel would appear in civilian clothes. 'We thought it would help improve the atmosphere,' writes Israel's then defence minister, 'if we tried to avoid anything that could evoke bitter memories.' Remarkably, the Egyptian team, presumably by an identical process of reasoning, had arrived at precisely the same conclusion. They too appeared in mufti.[30]

For General Charles de Gaulle, president of France from 1958–69, the wartime uniform of brigadier-general was an essential element of the historical role he had created for himself. As de Gaulle, with remarkable self-insight was fully aware, there were in a sense two de Gaulles. The one – the real man of flesh and blood, with his weaknesses like any other. But this private person was unknown to the world. It was the other de Gaulle, the public persona, who acted out a series of roles on the stage of history and, in the Gaullist version, had saved the honour of France in 1940. Thus for de Gaulle to 'dress up' in his old uniform was to assume the character of this national hero, the wartime saviour. In protocol terms he had, as civilian president of France, absolutely no obligation to wear military uniform.

Fully to grasp the associations evoked by the image of de Gaulle, the leader of the Free French, one must appreciate the trauma of the war years. Out of the shame of surrender he had, believing himself called on by fate, thrust himself forward and fought on to liberation. His career was calculated to blot out of mind the ugly events of those years – the collapse, the collaboration and the division of France. In their place de Gaulle put a necessary legend of unity and struggle.

It was on this inestimable fund of credit and prestige that de Gaulle drew in 1958 when he presented himself yet again in the role of national saviour, this time from the civil strife that threatened to engulf a France painfully divided over the fate of Algeria. The uniform was one, not unimportant means by which de Gaulle conjured up the image of his wartime mission and sought, as on 18 June 1940, to rally Frenchmen and women around his standard.

Once again, on 18 June 1958, the eighteenth anniversary of the London broadcast which launched his movement, de Gaulle visited the Tomb of France's Unknown Soldier dressed in his famous uniform. Travelling to Algiers to face the restive French Army he again put on his general's *képi*. What better way to arouse the forces' loyalty and obedience?

De Gaulle himself was quite aware of the artifice of his own performance. For instance in 1960 General Massu, the recalcitrant French commander in Algeria, was recalled to Paris in the midst of a rapidly deteriorating situation and with a question mark over the obedience of some sections of the army. De Gaulle determined to act decisively and presented himself on television and radio to demand discipline from the army and support from the people. He laconically notes in his memoirs. 'I had donned my uniform.'

David Schoenbrun, a career-long observer of the general, perceived a double symbolism in the pose: 'it was the uniform of a national hero and served also as a reminder to the army that the President of the Republic, Commander-in-Chief of all the armed forces, was a military man, a general talking to generals, not just a civilian politician of Paris'. Lest the symbolism be misunderstood, de Gaulle made it explicit in his opening words: 'If I have again put on my uniform to speak to you today on television, it is to stress the fact that I do so as General de Gaulle, as well as in my capacity of chief of state.'[31]

When de Gaulle wore his uniform for trips abroad he was also evoking, with equal calculation but obviously with different intent, the wartime legend. On his historic visit to the USSR in June 1966 he did this to evoke the spirit of wartime comradeship-in-arms and the 1944 pact of friendship. More subtly he was hinting at a present shared concern – the future of Germany – and France's interest in its continued division.

Should de Gaulle have no interest in recalling the war years, he refrained from wearing military uniform. This was the case on his great state visit to West Germany of 1962 when his main political aim was to heal old wounds, not to reopen them. On Adenauer's return visit to France, a few months later, de Gaulle appeared in uniform only once, at a joint parade of French and German troops. He changed back into civilian clothes immediately afterwards.

French relations with Britain and the United States under de Gaulle were complex and often strained. On visits to those countries in 1960 de Gaulle was well satisfied to be received, as he saw it, in splendid acknowledgement of his own prestige and France's present national recovery. But he most assuredly had no intention of reminding his audiences of those painful years when France, in truth, had been no more than a nominal combatant and some of his bitterest battles had been waged against his own allies in order to preserve an independent voice for France. It was easy to forgive Germany; she had been laid low. What de Gaulle could never acknowledge was the debt owed to the two powers who had liberated France. And so, neither in Washington nor in London, was the leader of the Free French allowed to regain the stage. De Gaulle left his uniform at home.

On two occasions only in North America did the wartime figure reappear. Once was at the Eisenhower funeral in 1969, when the gesture was a personal one. The other set off momentous reverberations. It was on the dramatic visit of July 1967 to Quebec. Determined from the outset to galvanize French Canadians into an awareness of their peculiar identity – and the political possibilities that might flow from this – de Gaulle and the Quebec authorities set out to recreate, on Canadian soil, the atmosphere of a French provincial visit and, most importantly, the spirit of the 1944 liberation of France.

Travelling along the ancient *Chemin du Roi* from Quebec to Montreal *General* de Gaulle – in military uniform since his arrival the previous day – passed under symbolic *arcs de triomphe* and was greeted on all sides by enthusiastic crowds waving the French tricolour and the

Quebec fleur-de-lis inherited from the Bourbon kings. From the balcony of the Montreal city hall de Gaulle told his hosts: 'Here tonight, and all along the route, I found an atmosphere resembling the liberation of France in World War II.' And then the words that were to rock the Canadian federal government: 'Vive le Québec libre!' – the slogan of the separatist movement. Some said he did not understand its significance; others that he blurted it out on the spur of the moment. But the fact is that it was as inevitable a culmination of his tour as the final chords of a symphony. His message had been clear and consistent throughout. Just as he had liberated France, so had he come to liberate Quebec. . . .

(b) INDICATION OF STATUS

Sartorial splendour is a classic device for projecting status. Here goes, a fine costume proclaims, a person of substance. But, as Molière and other observers of the human condition have noted, ostentatiousness can just as easily reveal the shrill insecurity of the *nouveau-riche*. To over-dress is to protest too much about one's worth.

So it is perhaps unsurprising that sartorial extravagance has become, on the contemporary international scene, often a mark of national pretentiousness rather than of true status. The leaders of the superpowers have other ways of asserting their pre-eminence and usually appear in lounge suits of the utmost sobriety.

Among the more outrageous of modern world leaders is Colonel Muammar Qaddafi of Libya. Drawing on his country's immense oil-wealth to buy influence, assist insurgent movements and interfere in the affairs of his neighbours, Qaddafi has seen himself as a figure of pan-Arab and even international status. On foreign visits he has presented himself in accordance with this ambitious self-image. In Peking he arrived resplendent in a white and gold uniform, dark glasses and stylish hair-do, flanked by women guards in drab green battle fatigues.[32] In terms of conventional diplomacy it was ludicrous. Looked at from a show-business perspective it made sense, gaining international press coverage. Who could imagine that Qaddafi was the ruler of a nation of scarcely two million people, visiting the capital of a nation of one thousand million people?

One of Colonel Qaddafi's erstwhile allies was the Ugandan tyrant Idi Amin. Dismissed as a figure of fun, Amin's lust for international attention produced acts of mischief that were far from amusing in their consequences. Like his Libyan mentor, Idi Amin's megalomania found symbolic form in a predilection for pantomime costume. At the

Organization of African Unity meeting in Gabon in July 1977, where he proclaimed himself Conqueror of the British Empire, he appeared in a brilliant blue field marshal's uniform weighed down with numerous campaign medals and other decorations.[33]

What the Amins and Qaddafis of this world have grasped is that the media's attraction for the picturesque and bizarre has presented otherwise minor figures with an unrivalled opportunity to strut the world's stage. Lacking more conventional achievements such leaders have succeeded in acquiring notoriety by counterfeiting the visual accoutrements of fame. This must be counted one of the more outlandish by-products of the modern power of the image.

All this would be of no more than curiosity value if such sartorial flamboyance was restricted to eccentric individuals of secondary significance. Its scientific interest lies in its being part of a more general phenomenon – what Ali Mazrui has called the 'monarchical tendency' in political culture.[34]

Writing about Africa, Mazrui sees the 'monarchical tendency' as combining four elements of political style: the personalization of authority around the figure of the leader; the sacralization of authority, that is, the glorification of the leader in religious terms; the quest for a royal historical identity to supplement national dignity; and, finally, the quest for aristocratic effect. It is the latter that concerns us here, consisting as it does of personal ostentation in the form of a taste for palatial accommodation, expensive cars and other forms of conspicuous consumption, as well as a partiality for splendid attire.

Mazrui accounts for the phenomenon in various ways, seeing it as a way of reinforcing political legitimacy, enhancing personal prestige and an expression of the search for historical identity. In the international arena he argues that flamboyant self-assertion can be explained as a reaction to historical humiliation at the hands of the colonial powers. For those who have been treated as inferiors by an alien occupier, status in the eyes of the world becomes a psychological requirement of the very first order.

Thus on the one hand there is a tendency for post-colonial leaders to be excessively flattered by external marks of favour bestowed by other states, while on the other hand displaying great sensitivity to real or imagined slights. When Mazrui wrote he had in mind such colourful figures as Kwame Nkrumah of Ghana. However, his analysis also fits well Jean-Bedel Bokassa (who, following his hero Napoleon, crowned himself emperor of the Central African Republic/Empire) and Idi Amin, both of whom arrived later on the scene.

Outside of Africa the idea of a 'monarchical tendency' is relevant to understanding leaders like Marcos of the Philippines, Sukarno of Indonesia and, most curiously, Tito, for many years ruler of Communist Yugoslavia.

Josip Broz Tito was, by any standard, a remarkable character: wartime hero, symbol of national unity and international statesman. Under his leadership Yugoslavia succeeded in freeing itself from the Soviet grip and becoming one of the founders and leading lights of the nonaligned movement. Tito's foreign policy was valued in its own right as a prop to an otherwise fragile independence. But it also contributed to strengthening the national identity and unity of the motley collection of republics which make up the Yugoslav federation.

For the audacious programme of national construction and international assertion he envisaged for Yugoslavia, Tito staged a powerful show of self-confidence and pride. To withstand Stalin's pressure (after the Yugoslav Communist party's expulsion from the Cominform in 1948), subsequent economic deprivation and internal strains, strong, charismatic leadership was essential. Although the head of a European state, Tito's problems were more akin to those faced by post-colonial leaders. Colourless, technocratic leadership would have been quite insufficient. It is surely no coincidence that Tito was later to find a common language with the rulers of newly independent states in Africa and Asia. They, like him, sought to mould a national identity out of disparate elements and to emerge from behind the umbra of an imperial power. Circumstances, therefore, reinforced no doubt by personal inclination, imposed upon Tito a role of stunning incongruity: that of Communist monarch.

A fascinating portrait of the Tito court has been painted by Milovan Djilas, the man who was Tito's wartime comrade-in-arms and a leading official of the Yugoslav regime until, disenchanted, he broke with it in 1954. According to Djilas, Tito conducted himself as the virtual successor of the exiled Karadjordjevic dynasty. Royal property was expropriated and the palaces restored and put at the personal disposal of Tito. Only the finest works of art and furnishings, taken from national museums, were fit for these residences. Extravagant building projects were put in hand; parks were landscaped; zoos installed. Tito's predilection for luxury became a byword. He travelled in a Rolls-Royce, hunted enthusiastically, reintroduced horse-racing and built up a considerable stable. Monarchical traditions were continued – even the blatantly religious custom of the ruler acting as godfather of the ninth boy in any family; no matter that there might be no priest and no baptism. On his trips around the country Tito bestowed charitable patronage like any feudal seigneur. His expenses for the maintenance of such a life-style were reckoned to surpass those of the former king. 'Tito's court', Djilas concluded, 'was in no way inferior to the royal court that had preceded it; in ostentation it surpassed its predecessor.'

At the centre of this glittering setting was the larger-than-life figure of this Marxist Louis XIV:

> His uniforms were edged with gold. Everything that he used had to be just right and very special. His belt buckle was made of pure gold, and was so heavy that it kept slipping down. He wrote with a heavy gold pen. His chair was impressive and always placed at the centre of the room. He changed his clothes as often as four times a day, according to the occasion and the impressions he wished to create. In the presence of the army leaders he wore the uniform of a marshal. When he turned up in military uniform among civilians, or with Central Committee members, that might mean he wished to convey the idea that, whatever the issue at hand, he had the army behind him. He used a sun lamp regularly to maintain a tan. His hair was dyed, his teeth were false and gleaming white. Though he was naturally vigorous, in public appearances he often made a special effort to be animated and high-spirited.[35]

Tito worked hard to develop this style. The 'monarchical tendency' was carefully contrived, Djilas argues, as a demonstration of power. For the common people (and, indeed, other world leaders) pomp and circumstance were accepted as the outer form of authority. Sensing this, Tito adopted the regal pose and traditional props of the Yugoslav monarchs. Since he was not, in fact, the king, the show also, paradoxically, possessed revolutionary implications: Tito was appropriating the trappings of others.

In the conduct of foreign relations the grand style provided the backdrop to a policy of great panache. Visitors would be received at one or other of Tito's palaces or at his famous villa on the island of Brioni. On his own travels Tito made use of a yacht with a destroyer escort. If others were to take the man at his own estimation, he was a leader of world stature.

On the whole, they did so. Maurice Couve de Murville, de Gaulle's foreign minister and no stranger to the 'monarchical tendency', felt that Tito might have exaggerated his role as the leader of the nonaligned states, but makes clear that France had to take Yugoslavia seriously. Tito's view of the international situation carried the serene mark of the 'total and uncontested authority' he exercised at home.[36] Eden, Nasser, Nehru and Kissinger among many others were fascinated by him. And indeed his was truly an extraordinary achievement. Thanks to the skill and bravura of his performance, Tito succeeded in acquiring prestige and influence far beyond the material assets of what was otherwise a poor and vulnerable country.

His finest hour on the diplomatic front was in May 1955 when the post-Stalin Soviet leadership, eating humble pie, came to Belgrade. Tito laid down his own terms for the reconciliation: Yugoslavia was to retain full independence in internal and external affairs and was to be treated on a footing of full equality. The message was hammered home in negotiations and in the press. Nonverbally it was adroitly conveyed at Belgrade airport even before the visit started. Tito, with characteristic art, had prepared a little tableau for his guests and other observers. Waiting for the Soviet Ilyushin jet to land, Tito lolled back in his new Rolls-Royce, nonchalantly puffing on a cigarette holder. He was splendidly attired in a braided cap, sky blue military jacket and red-striped trousers. He radiated a palpable air of unrepentance and defiance. Marshal and monarch, Tito was unquestionably master in his own domain.[37]

(c) IDENTIFICATION WITH AN IDEOLOGY OR CULTURE

Imitation may or may not be the sincerest form of flattery. However, the adoption by a visitor of local dress is certainly a readily comprehensible and prominent way of indicating good will. 'I am', the gesture signals, 'one of you.'

The precise nuance intended will depend upon local and historical circumstances. It was, for example, right and fitting for the foreign minister of the German Federal Republic to don a skullcap on his visit to the Jerusalem shrine of remembrance to the Holocaust (*Yad Vashem*). Not only was it called for by custom but also conveyed something of the contrition and indemnification that have characterized West German policy towards the Jewish state since the time of Konrad Adenauer.

For Anwar Sadat, though, on his controversial peace mission of November 1977 to Jerusalem, the skullcap possessed unacceptable connotations. For political purposes the visit to *Yad Vashem* was a shrewd mark of respect. A more blatant gesture would have been counter-productive. Sadat heard out his host's account of the Jewish practice of covering one's head during prayer or in a sacred place. But the hat given to him remained in his hand. 'There is no doubt,' one spectator noted, 'that Sadat was afraid of a photograph of him wearing a skullcap. Such a picture would have served the propaganda against him better than any other publication.'[38] Wisely, the Israelis overlooked the apparent solecism. Sadat's was clearly a very special case.

Subject to the exact shading lent by time and place, several distinct tones are suggested by assuming local costume. First and foremost it conveys an intimate sense of association. In ordinary life only very close friends indeed wear each others' clothes. In consequence it is an effective way of signifying both existing friendship and reconciliation, the transition from hostile to amicable relations.

For visitors to the United States, with its populist traditions, insularity and mistrust of 'stuffed shirt' diplomats, the gambit is one good way of breaking the ice. Unfortunately the range of local dress to choose from is limited! A visit to Texas, however, always provides the opportunity to put on a cowboy hat. A photograph of German Chancellor Ludwig Erhard in a ten-gallon hat at a barbecue on the Lyndon Johnson ranch was a successful ploy from the point of view of US–West German Relations. It infuriated General de Gaulle, however, who, a master of visual imagery himself, saw it as symbolizing the change for the worse in Franco–German relations after the departure of his friend Adenauer from the scene. 'Voilà', de Gaulle is supposed to have exclaimed. 'He now takes himself for a cowboy.'[39] In geopolitical terms it hinted that West Germany had preferred loyalty to the United States over its former special relationship with France.

It must have been no less galling for the Soviet leadership poring over reports and pictures of Deng Xiaoping's trip to the United States at the beginning of 1979. Films of his stop-off in Texas would have shown the unique spectacle of the diminutive Chinese leader in a cowboy hat almost too big for him, riding around a rodeo arena in a stagecoach. The American media loved it. Gestures like this, at which Deng was adroit, were helpful in clearing away residual suspicions left over from the years of conflict.

Some items of clothing can come to represent an ideology or a cause; they become a sort of trade mark – a readily identifiable badge of affiliation.

The Bedouin *kaffiyah*, actually worn by millions of Arabs, is internationally associated with the PLO and the Palestinian cause. (It was the 'familiar checkered scarf of the *Fedayeen*' that revealed to US ambassador Sullivan that those responsible for the first attack on the American embassy in Teheran in 1978 had been trained in PLO camps.[40]) When Britain's Lord Home, after his Harrogate speech of October 1970 recognizing the 'legitimate aspirations' of the Palestinians, was pictured in full desert attire, stroking a camel in front of the pyramids, it strongly conveyed, as it was intended to, the pro-Arab orientation of British policy. The artifice of Home's costume becomes clearer when one realizes that neither the Egyptian villager nor townsman wears this kind of dress, which is restricted to the few desert Bedouin in the country. Had he wished to wear Egyptian dress Home would have had to put on the nightshirt-like *jalabiyya*. But this would not only have made him look ridiculous; it would also have been incomprehensible to the world at large.

King Hussein of Jordan assumed the Palestinian *kaffiyah* (which is slightly different, in fact, from that of his own Bedouin people) for the benefit of TV cameras during talks with PLO chairman Yassir Arafat in November 1982. Years of bad blood had separated them after the clashes of 'Black September' 1970 in which thousands of Palestinians were killed. Now they were trying to make up so that they might join forces to wrest the West Bank from Israel. But the gesture carried a hint of ambiguity. Hussein was pressing for 'power of attorney' to negotiate on the PLO's behalf. Whatever happened, Hussein was signalling, he would be the Palestinian's king in all respects and would continue his policy of integrating them fully into the life of the kingdom. He was not prepared to accept a separate Palestinian state, only autonomy under the Hashemite flag and with Amman as the federal capital.

The beret, worn by Fidel Castro and Ché Guevara, is an earlier symbol of revolution and national liberation. The Zanzibari rebels of January 1964 adopted Cuban guerrilla attire as their uniform. 'Revolutionary emulation', in Ali Mazrui's phrase, may also have underlain African borrowing, at the same period, of the 'Mao' suit. It was not by coincidence that Ch'en Yi, foreign minister of the People's Republic of China, wore it with a somewhat French air, on Chou En-lai's 1964 African tour.[41]

One further use of sartorial imitation is as a device for a visiting leader to display his respect and admiration for the host culture. Newly independent states, as we have seen, invariably emphasize indigenous customs and traditions in their 'search for identity'. They are also sensitive to any hint of a patronizing attitude on the part of westerners. The wearing of local costume is a conspicuous way a visitor can turn such sensitiveness to his advantage.

Khrushchev was especially adept at this ploy. Indeed, one of the reasons for the success of the Soviet diplomatic offensive in Asia and Africa after the death of Stalin lay precisely in a skilful manipulation of local symbols. On their epoch-making tour of India in 1955 – one of the key moves in wooing that country into the Soviet camp –

Khrushchev and his colleague Bulganin 'went native' with great enthusiasm. In the words of one Indian official, 'they took to native food, native customs and native costumes with gusto'.

> In Bombay they wore Gandhi caps, regardless of the fact that the Gandhi cap is the emblem of the Congress Party, which has given no quarter to communists in India. In Bangalore they wore gold-embroidered cloth over their coats; in Jaipur they put on fine, flowing Rajput turbans. In Madras, young damsels put *kumkum* on their foreheads; and wherever they went they were covered with garlands of flowers. When they greeted Indians, they invariably folded their hands in the Indian fashion and said, 'Namaste'. They concluded a number of speeches with the Hindi slogan 'Hindi-Russi bhai bhai'. All these gestures coming naturally from them endeared them to the people.[42]

Such an objective observer as the Canadian ambassador to India concluded that the Soviet leaders had 'gone a long way towards destroying in the minds of a large number of the Indian people the old picture of Russia as a barbarous, dangerous northern bear, and by their joviality and friendship and offers of aid they had substituted a picture of a great, friendly, progressive, peace-loving country which had no quarrel with either the internal or external policy of India.'[43]

It would clearly by simplistic to explain the success of Soviet policy in the Third World solely in terms of diplomatic choreography. Without an underlying convergence of interests it would not have helped. On the other hand it is to Soviet credit that they grasped the psychological element in the preoccupations of countries like India, Egypt and Indonesia. The need for recognition and approval was and remains considerable. Attention to local detail was one way of signalling both the importance attached to good relations and also Soviet willingness to conduct them on a basis, if only symbolic, of cultural equality.

(d) REFLECTION OF MOOD

Khrushchev may have been a skilful performer at 'playing to the gallery'. In one respect, though, he – involuntarily – let down his country's diplomacy. He lacked presence. Now no one could blame him for his squat shape or his over-exuberance. But he should have found himself a better tailor. Dressed in ill-fitting jackets and baggy trousers he did not look like the leader of a superpower to whom all respect was due.

Whether this mattered or not is hard to say. On the Belgrade visit of 1955, already mentioned, he cut a shambling, unkempt figure next to the crisp, self-confident Tito. On his trips to Western capitals he could not help looking like a peasant on an outing to the big city. For the leader of a country painfully concerned with status and overcoming a deep-rooted sense of inferiority, this did not, surely, convey the desired impression. There seems little doubt that the Khrushchev style discomfited the Soviet elite, though he was popular with the Russian man in the street. Together with more substantive errors of foreign and domestic policy it probably contributed to his fall.

Be that as it may, long gone are the days when a Soviet leader, in a suit that looks slept-in, bangs his shoe at the United Nations or scratches pigs on foreign visits. Today's men in the Kremlin dress smartly and conduct themselves with dignity. They are serious-minded and pedantic about protocol. If Khrushchev allowed style to go by default, Brezhnev for one most certainly did not. His photographs show him to be immaculately tailored to meet any occasion. The point is that elegance, cut and colour, convey an impression and create a mood no less than a demonstration of deliberate symbolism. Statesmanship is associated with an appearance of substance and dignity. Untidiness spoils that impression.

Others learned this lesson long before the Russians. Anthony Eden, a fumbling and indecisive British foreign secretary in the 1930s, established his widespread popularity and reputation on a debonair, youthful image. 'Very disarming, very endearing, and his sartorial splendour makes every one else look shoddy', wrote Sir Henry 'Chips' Channon, who was not otherwise impressed.[44] He looked like one expected the foreign minister of a great power to look.

Chou En-lai, seeking to project a sense of the wisdom, moderation and elegance of a great civilization (despite the revolution), succeeded in appearing smartly turned out even in the proletarian 'Mao' suit. This was carefully contrived. His suit was impeccably cut. Where surrounding officials wore dark clothes, his were light blue-grey. On the breast-pocket was embroidered the slogan, ingeniously distinguished: 'In the service of the people.' His proud, elegant bearing never failed to impress.[45]

Margaret Thatcher, dedicated to a revival of British power and prestige after years of painful decline, has proved herself highly conscious of the importance of personal style. Always cool and well-groomed, her wardrobe, though simple, is elegant. Her personal advisers are known to pay close attention to her image and to match her dress to the occasion.[46] As a woman relatively unencumbered by the requirements of protocol Mrs Thatcher knows that she is subject to close and critical scrutiny.

In her international appearances, subtle use of colour is made to create mood. At the EEC summit of March 1982 to mark the twenty-fifth anniversary of the organization, for example, Mrs Thatcher forcefully presented her government's dissatisfaction with the state of the Community and particularly its budgetary provisions. She was dressed in funereal black. There was, she implied, no cause for celebration. During the Falklands war, in the aftermath of British losses, she was similarly sombrely dressed.

In contrast, when a more cheerful, gregarious touch is called for – at a meeting with a friendly foreign leader such as President Reagan – Mrs Thatcher often chooses something light or patterned.

She seems especially skilful at regulating the mood of negotiations. At the Stuttgart European summit of June 1983 the subject was the size of the rebate to be paid to Britain from the Community budget. It was an issue on which the prime minister had staked considerable personal prestige. On the first day of the conference the lady wore dark blue – a sober, business-like colour, calculated perhaps to convince her negotiating partners of the seriousness of her position. On the second day Mrs Thatcher pitched into battle in cyclamen pink – an expression of assertive feminity. Was she trying to exploit the gallantry of her colleagues? For dinner that evening, and more hard bargaining, she changed tack, into the reddest dress anyone could remember. Red is the colour associated with war, bloodshed and victory.[47] Is it totally far-fetched to argue that an element of 'theatrical' calculation entered into Mrs Thatcher's wardrobe?

Informality is one of the hardest moods to get right. If the leader misjudges his audience he runs the risk of being thought to have diminished from the dignity of his office or of giving offence to his hosts. Pierre Trudeau's trainers were quite out of place in Brazil. But this is not to say that a leadership style of some irreverence and zest does not make sense for a young nation like Canada. Bound by geopolitics to NATO and economics to the United States, the Canadian government has sought to project a distinctive identity and as independent a foreign policy as possible, especially in the Third World.

In Cuba, Trudeau's nonconformity, assuming that it was intended to be deliberately provocative to the United States, was functional. Pictures beamed home showed Trudeau, standing alongside Fidel Castro, wearing a white open-necked shirt without a vest over crumpled brown slacks and casual shoes. Anywhere else it would have been insulting. In revolutionary Havana the message was one of relaxed friendship and lack of inhibition. It implied a radical foreign policy, freed from conventional constraints.

And so the wheel is brought full circle. The leaders of the USSR, born in revolution, supposedly fired by a messianic ideology, are the new establishment, soberly-dressed, preoccupied by status and privilege. Canada, an offshoot of the British empire and subsidiary of American capitalism, acquired a prime minister who bucked convention and yearned for a more free-wheeling, radical role.

REFERENCES AND NOTES

1. Le Bon G 1896 *The Crowd*. T Fisher Unwin, p 149 fn
2. Roach M E, Eicher J B 1979 The language of personal adornment, in Cordwell J M, Schwarz R A (eds) *The Fabrics of Culture*. Mouton, The Hague, pp 7–18
3. Feltham R G 1977 *Diplomatic Handbook*. Longman, pp 30–1
4. Thayer C W 1960 *Diplomat*. Michael Joseph, p 38
5. *Ibid*. p 217
6. Nish I 1982 Japan, in Steiner Z (ed) *The Times Survey of Foreign Ministries of the World*. Times Books, p 329
7. Nish I 1977 *Japanese Foreign Policy 1869–1942*. Routledge and Kegan Paul, p 20
8. Trotsky L 1930 *Mein Leben*. Fischer: Berlin, p 327
9. Carr E H 1966 *The Bolshevik Revolution 1917–1923*. vol 3. Penguin, p 166
10. Von Laue T H 1971 Soviet diplomacy, in Craig G A, Gilbert F (eds) *The Diplomats 1919–1939*, vol 1. Atheneum: New York, p 240
11. Kuper H 1973 Costume and identity, *Comparative Studies in Society and History* **15**: 357
12. Kuper H 1973 *op. cit.*, p 358; Mazrui A A 1970 The robes of rebellion, *Encounter* **34**: 19
13. *Life* 14 Mar. 1964
14. Diop D, The renegade. Quoted in Mazrui A A 1970 *op. cit.*, p 23
15. Nicolson H 1952 *King George the Fifth: his life and reign*. Constable, p 507
16. Lord Butler 1973 *The Art of the Possible*. Penguin, p 40
17. Reid E 1981 *Envoy to Nehru*. Oxford University Press: Delhi, p 58
18. All photographs in Nehru J 1949: **64** *Jawaharlal Nehru's speeches*, 4 vols. Ministry of Information and Broadcasting: Delhi
19. Mortimer E 1982 *Faith and Power*. Faber and Faber, pp 141–2
20. *Ibid*. 1982 p 324

21. *Ibid.* 1982 pp 217–81, 227
22. *The Times* 4 May 1983, 5 Apr. 1983
23. Dore R P 1975 The prestige factor in international affairs, *International Affairs* **51**: 198
24. Brzezinski Z 1983 *Power and Principle.* Weidenfeld and Nicolson, p 230
25. *The Times* 2 Aug. 1983
26. Gilbert M 1974 *Churchill: a photographic portrait.* Penguin
27. *Newsweek* 10 Sept. 1974;   *Life* 30 June 1961
28. *The Times* 2 Mar. 1982
29. Kissinger H 1982 *Years of Upheaval.* Weidenfeld and Nicolson, pp 811, 822, 844
30. Weizman E 1981 *The Battle for Peace.* Bantam Books: New York, p 174
31. De Gaulle C 1971 *Memoirs of Hope.* Weidenfeld and Nicolson, p 80;   Schoenbrun D 1968 *The Three Lives of Charles de Gaulle.* Atheneum: New York, p 278
32. *The Times* 26 Oct. 1982
33. Kyemba H 1977 *State of Blood.* Corgi, pp 247–8. See also photos
34. Mazrui A A 1967 The monarchical tendency in African political culture, *British Journal of Sociology* **18**: 231–50
35. Djilas M 1981 *Tito.* Weidenfeld and Nicolson, pp 92–119
36. Couve de Murville M 1971 *Une Politique Etrangère.* Plon: Paris, p 218
37. *Newsweek* 30 May 1955;   *Life* 6 June 1955
38. Haber E, Schiff A, Yaari E 1981 *Shnat Hayonah* (Hebrew). Zemora, Beitan, Modan: Tel Aviv, p 130
39. Viannson-Ponté P 1964 *The King and his Court.* Houghton-Mifflin: Boston, p 76
40. Sullivan W H 1981 *Mission to Iran.* W W Norton: New York, p 262
41. Aide W A C 1966 Chou En-lai on safari, in MacFarquhar R (ed) *China under Mao: politics takes command.* The MIT Press: Camb. Mass., p 465;   Mazrui A A 1970 *op. cit.*, p 28
42. Menon K P S 1963 *The Flying Troika.* Oxford University Press, p 130
43. Reid E 1981 *op. cit.*, p 136
44. James R R (ed) 1967 *Chips.* Weidenfeld and Nicolson, p 134
45. Nixon R M 1982 *Leaders.* Sidgwick and Jackson, p 220
46. Wapshott N, Brock G 1983 *Thatcher.* Futura, pp 146, 163, 170
47. *The Times* 20 June 1983

Chapter five

'BODY LANGUAGE' IN DIPLOMACY

The human body is the original and also the richest medium of nonverbal communication. Recent research has drawn attention to the wide and subtle repertoire of gestures (or 'markers' as they are called) at man's disposal. Some are involuntary and therefore do not concern us. Others can be manipulated and used for theatrical purposes. They include posture, hand movement, the use of space, facial expression and head movement. The body, in fact, is the source of an entire sign language.

Various terms have been coined to describe the different modes of bodily expression. For instance *kinesics* is the study of body movement, *proxemics* the study of the use of space. Experts dislike the term 'body language' as being vague and popular. In this book, however, I use the term as usefully distinguishing bodily gesture from the other categories of nonverbal communication referred to.

Contrasted with the aridity of diplomatic speech and ceremony, the body language of leaders seems to provide a refreshingly sincere reflection of true feelings. One naturally assumes that gestures and facial expressions are more spontaneous than the stilted formalities of protocol and hence a more genuine index of friendship, pleasure or disapproval. The habit of the media of personalizing power politics, so that international relations are seen as interpersonal relations writ large, reinforces this tendency.

Nothing could be further from the truth. Unfortunately, necessity dictates that the expressions and gestures of the statesman be every bit as contrived as the formalities laid down by protocol. Indeed the more experience leaders acquire in the use of television, the more stylized is their range of personal gestures likely to become. Public behaviour, in the glare of television spot-lights, cannot be permitted the luxury of spontaneity. Politics requires that it be calculated and controlled.

There is now little scope for 'sincerity' in the public gestures of the statesman. The fate of a politician unable to stifle his emotions in public is contempt and failure. Senator Edmund Muskie discovered this to his cost in the 1968 presidential primaries. He shed real tears in front of an audience. It was an unpardonable offence.

But the fact that leadership has its theatrical dimension and personal reactions have lost their spontaneity has strengthened rather than weakened the communicatory value of 'body language'. What gestures have lost in sincerity, they have gained in informativeness. They may no longer be a guide to personal feelings but they are most certainly a sound, because deliberate, indication of the state of political relations. Today officials are as alert in observing the length and warmth of a diplomatic embrace as in attending to the niceties of protocol.

The time may come when guides to diplomatic practice will specify the requirements of 'body language' just as they now define the details of etiquette. When that happens 'body language' will lose its usefulness. Until then statesmen still have at their disposal one means of communication, not regulated by formal protocol (though there are certain conventions of use) able to express the nuances of political substance rather than mere form. For the onlooker 'body language' thus provides an invaluable guide to underlying attitudes. In this sense it does constitute a genuine index of the state of relations – but at the political and not personal level.

'Body language', like dress, is intimately associated, for obvious reasons, with the person of the leader. Both permit him to enact – personify – political abstractions inadequately communicated by words alone. Where 'body language' differs from dress is in the occasion and purpose of its use. To dress is to perform an action continuous through time; clothes are worn either for the duration of an appearance by the actor or habitually at certain kinds of events. In consequence, they are best at making a statement about the self-appraisal of the actor as to his role, identity and status in the international community – qualities that are in themselves continuous.

In contrast, 'body language' is a 'one-off' and discontinuous medium. It consists of discrete acts and not ongoing displays. A gesture is no sooner made than completed; perpetuated, perhaps, on film, but transitory and even subject to subsequent contradiction.

'Body language', then, is not suited to the illustration of an ongoing state of affairs in the way that dress is. Its contribution to political communication comes especially at *threshold* moments, whether, literally, of greeting, parting, etc. or, more figuratively, at the transitional stages of a relationship.

Greeting and parting are crucial points of an encounter because they define the nature of the social relationship between the participants. In general terms, when you greet or part from someone you are recognizing him as socially acceptable. Conversely, to refuse to acknowledge someone is to deny his acceptability as an associate.[1] In addition, greeting and parting provide an opportunity to demonstrate to observers the precise tone of a relationship and the attitudes of actors to each other at a given point in time.

Since they deal with the modalities of relations between states, bodily gestures depend for their meaning on discrimination and variation. To the extent that a particular expression or mannerism is invariant, it cannot be informative. Jimmy Carter's smile was uninformative because it was indiscriminate. (Actually, close associates did learn to distinguish between true pleasure, masked anger and the bland public face on the basis of involuntary cues, but this does not affect the basic point.)[2]

In everyday life 'body language' makes use of a more varied repertoire of 'markers' than is the case in politics. For the diplomat variety is neither possible nor necessary. It is not necessary because the substance of international communication is more restricted than that between individuals and therefore covered by fewer symbols. As we shall see below, however, there is, within the bounds of this rather narrow vocabulary, ample scope for flexibility of expression, especially when combined with other forms of nonverbal communication.

THE HANDSHAKE

The handshake, while an ancient form of greeting, is not indigenous to all cultures: India has the *namaskar* gesture in which the palms are brought together; Ethiopia a gesture in which the right arm is brought across the chest, accompanied by a bow. The handshake has, however, been more or less universally adopted as an international salutation.

According to the sociologist Deborah Schiffrin, the handshake is to be understood as an *access ritual*, an act preceding a period of increased access. It attests, in symbolic form, to the basic regard and respect that the parties hold for each other. Since it requires a coordinated effort by both sides, it constitutes mutual and simultaneous proof that the forthcoming interaction will also conform to convention. What will actually take place can obviously not be foreseen in detail. That the person and dignity of the participants will be respected is assured by the ritual.[3]

Because of its commonness in diplomatic encounters, the handshake tends to be taken for granted. It seems to be no more than the habitual accompaniment to the beginning or end of an encounter, without any particular significance. If Schiffrin is right, though, its significance lies in its very routine predictability – an affirmation that there is nothing untoward in the relationship.

Moreover, in the prelude to occasions, such as tough negotiations, that may generate tension and ill-will, the handshake may be a useful reminder that there is an underpinning of basic courtesies and conventions that will sustain the relationship through momentary squalls. In the aftermath of such an encounter the handshake confirms that this is indeed the case. (It is not self-evident that this should be so. Some particularly stressful meetings are concluded without a handshake, a sign that some kind of rupture has occurred.) When diplomats and leaders meet, after more or less prolonged periods of discontinuity in the contacts of the states they represent, the handshake similarly demonstrates that the relationship has held up in spite of the interruption and intervening strains.

Over and above the basic message of reassurance carried by the handshake, different connotations can be conveyed by particular marks of emphasis or unusual features of its performance.

However, the first variation to be considered is the omission of the handshake as such. This can take two forms: simple avoidance or active spurning. Both convey a sense of disapproval of the rejected party and of a disturbance in the relationship. But whereas the former entails *withholding* the other's social fitness – suggesting that it has been suspended and may later be restored – the latter entails a far more serious *withdrawal* or curtailment of rights.

In the former case disapproval may be quite short-lived. The gesture conveys momentary annoyance and indeed deliberately avoids the formal gravity and therefore greater irrevocability of a diplomatic *démarche* (such as a protest note, breaking off relations, etc.). At a meeting of the consultative assembly of the Council of Europe at Strasbourg in 1951 British delegate Maxwell-Fyfe found himself 'cold-shouldered' in public by other delegates, disappointed at a British refusal to commit forces to a European army. The gesture did no lasting damage. On the other hand the message got through very clearly to the British government. The European Movement 'felt betrayed' by this proof of British aloofness from the Continent.[4]

For states not in diplomatic relations it is customary for their representatives to avoid public displays of greeting, for instance, should they happen to be jointly present at a reception given by a third party. There is no 'relationship' and hence no mutual access to be announced. In most cases, though, the absence of relations is not a permanent arrangement, but rather the expression of a more or less transitory dislocation. Sooner or later, the odds are, relations will be restored. Given the possibility of a change for the better, it is in neither party's interest to humiliate the other. Dramatic snubs would be too hard to forget. In consequence the avoidance of contact is invariably discreet and low-key. In private, indeed, diplomats may well exchange personal courtesies.

Of quite a different order is the calculated snub – the demonstrative refusal to shake hands when the hand is proffered. One author describes this gesture as 'excluding verbal or physical attack, the most rejecting insult one individual can offer another. It is equivalent to spitting on someone'.[5] In terms of Schiffrin's theory, the injured party has offered access to himself in good faith – and has had his personal worth rejected.

For John Foster Dulles, United States secretary of state under President Eisenhower, the Communist world, in a Manichean vision of international politics, was the embodiment of metaphysical evil. His famous refusal to shake Chou En-lai's hand at the Geneva conference on Indochina of 1954 – which rankled for years in Peking – reflected his profound conviction that the Chinese were quite beyond the pale of international society. Dulles succeeded in attending the conference without once acknowledging the existence of the Chinese.[6] His underlying attitude to any kind of physical contact with Communist leaders can be judged from the argument he put forward to oppose a US–Soviet summit in 1955. He believed 'that the spectacle of Eisenhower shaking hands with Khrushchev would destroy the moral image of the United States, have a bad effect domestically, and tend to weaken the Allies' will to stand up to Communism'.[7]

When even the most minimal access has been prohibited over a long period the handshake acquires considerable significance. It is a clear sign that the relationship is about to be renewed; that the partners have again become socially acceptable to each other. Between 1948, when Tito was excommunicated from the Communist camp, and the death of Stalin in 1953, Russian diplomats completely avoided their Yugoslav counterparts wherever they met. Diplomatic relations were formally maintained but all interaction ceased. Most important in a Communist context, no contact took place at the party level. Not once was a handshake exchanged. 'Body language', in fact, was a better index to the state of the relationship than the formal diplomatic position. (It was a hint that in the Communist world, community and true acceptability are only possible between 'fraternal' parties; formal diplomatic relations are a necessary expedient but do not imply shared membership of a single international society.)

Shortly after Stalin's funeral the Yugoslav chargé d'affaires, one of a group of foreign diplomats presenting their condolences, had his hand shaken by a Soviet deputy foreign minister. The envoy considered this such a momentous occurrence that he at once reported home by ciphered telegram.[8] The Yugoslav's judgement was certainly a sound one. Within months it became clear that Moscow was indeed interested in restoring contact with Belgrade, both at state and party levels. The gesture had been finely calculated and accurately interpreted. Reconciliation was at hand.

The handshake can convey various messages. The common sight of international statesmen shaking hands for the benefit of the cameras is a statement, as we have seen, of correctness in political relations. Each is declaring the other acceptable as a partner for diplomatic business. The jostling presence of the media, the officials and the lights in themselves contribute to the charged atmosphere of the occasion. We are left in no doubt that what is taking place is more than an empty formality but is a ceremony, in the full sense of the word, of renewal at a national level.

The *Peking Review*, an English-language publication of the People's Republic of China, explained to its readers the meaning of the ritual in a purported dialogue between Deng Xiaoping and Jimmy Carter in the White House Rose Garden in January 1979. The two leaders had just shaken hands before the press. Deng: 'Let's shake hands again.' They did so. Deng: 'Now the people of both countries are shaking hands!'[9]

Beyond the primary message of correctness, a lesser or greater degree of amity can be conveyed by variations of the basic theme. The demonstrative offer of one's open palm emphasizes trust as well as friendship. Presumably its force derives from the eagerness and confidence it enacts. By initiating the exchange one shows that one is offering access to one's person without fear of rebuff.

An example of this variant appeared at the signing of the Soviet–West German treaty of 1970 normalizing relations between the two parties. As Chancellor Brandt put his signature to the document, Prime Minister Kosygin awaited him with open palm. It is noteworthy that the gesture accompanied the signing of this particular treaty. The 'body language' added a human dimension – an illustration – to the momentous change in relations between the former enemies that the treaty represented.

The duration of the handshake is another way the core meaning can be modified. A brief clasp of the hands clearly lacks warmth, especially if the occasion calls for something more emphatic. The restraint displayed, possibly even hesitation, tells its own story. On the other hand in an atmosphere of crisis or intense negotiations the message may be one, not of coolness but of businesslike expeditiousness and of a close working relationship needing little external embellishment. Exemplified by Secretary of State Alexander Haig in his contacts with British and Argentinian figures in the crisis diplomacy that preceded the Falklands war, it also conveyed a sense of the gravity of the situation. Time was not to be wasted on formalities.

The long, drawn-out handshake is theatrically cordial. A reluctance to let go is supposed to reflect, one assumes, a deep personal attachment between the leaders. It is a simple but effective emphatic device for the benefit of those watching in person or at home on television. As displayed by de Gaulle and Adenauer at the conclusion of the latter's 1962 visit to France it was a genuine indication of the state of special relations between two close allies. Between Sadat and Begin, at the end of the November 1977 meeting, it marked the transformation in relations that had taken place from one of utter disjunction to *de facto* recognition and the beginning of peace negotiations.

Sadat, for one, was perfectly aware of the political significance of his willingness to take the hand of an Israeli leader. In his speech to the Israeli parliament that was the high point of his visit he had cleverly brought out the double meaning of the term *salam*: peace as a condition between states and peace as a salutation as in *al-salam alaykum*. 'We used to meet in international congresses and organizations and our representatives used to and still do not exchange greetings and salutations ... But I say to you today ... I announce it to the whole world ... we accept to live with you in peace, permanent and just.'[10]

Other variants of the handshake involve the manipulation of accompanying features such as facial expression, the proximity of the two parties and the use of the left hand. For instance, the double handshake seems to be a device to stress cordiality and sincerity. It was a speciality of Adolf Hitler and, more recently, of Deng Xiaoping and Ronald Reagan.

Lord Carrington, as British foreign secretary, had the habit, especially on trips to the Third World, of striding towards his counterpart with his arm stuck out in front of him. A rather gauche gesture, its effect was to convey an impression of forced heartiness. It can be included with the various devices drawn upon by British diplomacy in recent years to dispel any post-colonial suggestions of condescension or superiority.

THE EMBRACE

One form of greeting, comparatively rare in Western diplomatic circles ten or fifteen years ago, but now more common, is the embrace. In some cultures, for instance the Latin and Slavic, it has always been a form of public greeting between friends. In others it is reserved for members of the family when meeting or parting. As the 'kiss of peace' between Christians it is an ancient sign of fellowship, found today only in the ceremony of the Eucharist and in meetings of ecclesiastics.

As a diplomatic gesture the embrace has come to express the latter sense of fraternity or fellowship.

Within the Communist world it possesses this connotation and is the conventional greeting between the delegates of fraternal parties. Originating in Russian practice, it was taken up by the European Communist parties and thence spread to Soviet allies overseas.[11] It tends to be used at the commencement and conclusion of a visit. During the course of the visit the handshake is retained. The embrace can therefore be considered as a sort of emphatic and denominational synonym for the latter. Its use is a sign of ideological comradeship. Conversely its omission is an ominous hint of ideological delinquency.

The element of doctrinal endorsement contained in the embrace implies that its absence or presence functions as a quite reliable indication of existing and even forthcoming Soviet policy towards the object of the greeting. In retrospect it can be seen to have been a suggestive omen at turning points of Soviet diplomacy.

Just three days before the Soviet invasion of Hungary in 1956, Khrushchev and Malenkov, desperately concerned to secure Yugoslav compliance with their handling of the crisis, unexpectedly visited Tito on his island of Brioni. Their conduct is revealingly described by a senior Yugoslav official who was present at the meeting:

> They behaved in an extremely cordial manner, as never before. This was a premeditated gesture intended to influence our talks and our whole attitude toward them, because it is simply impossible to behave otherwise toward people with whom one has recently been exchanging kisses as with the closest of friends ... We had not exchanged kisses with the Russians at our previous meetings; we hadn't even talked to them for nearly seven years, but now they had decided that we should kiss each other in the difficult circumstances which had arisen – for them, rather than for us.[12]

It was not possible, on the basis of Soviet 'body language', to predict the invasion of Hungary. What could be deduced, as Micunovic argues here, was that the Soviet leaders were at a critical juncture – hence the unscheduled flight – and that they were engaged in an all-out, indeed unprecedented, effort of flattery and persuasion. Something was about to happen in their treatment of the crisis.

Again, on the eve of the 1968 invasion, Soviet plans for the 'revisionist' Czechoslovak leadership were hinted at with a surprising lack of dissimulation by Soviet 'body language'. The occasion was the crucial Soviet–Czech meeting of 29 July at Cierna-nad-Tisson. Arriving at the border town by train, Brezhnev formally *shook hands* with the assembled Czechoslovak leaders. He thereby effectively refused them fraternal status. The traditional embrace and kiss were reserved for one man alone – the president, Ludvik Svoboda.[13] Following the invasion, the latter was the only member of the Czechoslovak delegation to retain his position.

The Polish crisis of 1980–81, the unprecedented assumption of authority by the military in a Communist state and the imposition of martial law, posed severe ideological and political problems for the USSR. The appointment of General Jaruzelski as prime minister and then first secretary of the Polish Communist party, could hardly have taken place without Soviet consent. Nevertheless it was widely believed that the Kremlin was far from happy with the arrangement and had accepted it simply for want of a better alternative. True or not, it was necessary to disperse doubts about Jaruzelski's legitimacy in Soviet eyes. Otherwise it would be impossible to restore domestic confidence and, no less important, the international credit-worthiness of the Polish regime. The classic solution was to lay on a visit for Jaruzelski, with full honours, in Moscow. The hearty embraces with which he was greeted by Soviet leaders at the airport made quite clear, as was intended, his full acceptability and put an end to doubts as to his permanence.[14]

Influenced by Communist practice the embrace has become the standard emblem of ideological and Third World fraternity – that is, friendship that supposedly goes beyond political expediency. Members of the Socialist International, including the normally inhibited northern Europeans, have adopted it. A photograph on the front page of *The Times* of a fraternal embrace between Harold Wilson and Golda Meir set off ructions among Arab ambassadors in London.[15] The latter understood – correctly – that the gesture was a sign of true regard and fellow feeling between two veteran socialists. Moreover, since Mrs Meir had herself become a symbol of the state of Israel's stubborn struggle to survive, Wilson's gesture also implied a strong degree of sympathy for the Zionist movement. The ambassadors knew what they were protesting about.

For their part Arab, African and other nonaligned leaders embrace on meeting to show off their regional or Third World solidarity. Not for them, they imply, the cold and tawdry manipulation of power but a new brotherhood of man. Bestowed on an outsider the fraternal embrace communicates to watching audiences that the privileged guest is 'one of us' and therefore deserving of especial trust. The embrace between Presidents Eanes of Portugal and Cabral of Guinea-Bissau in June 1978, only five years after Portugal's hasty withdrawal from her African empire, made a strong and lasting impression. It also reflected the profound political point that both men had decided to base their foreign policies on a renewal of the Portuguese–African relationship.[16]

OTHER GESTURES OF SALUTATION

Two other gestures of salutation exemplified in the international arena are, to use Desmond Morris's terms, the *inconvenience display* and the *triumph display*.[17]

The inconvenience display involves putting oneself out for the benefit of a guest. It includes such practices as greeting a visitor at the entrance of a building or seeing him to his car at the end of a meeting. Descending degrees of regard are expressed by waiting inside the lobby, at the door of one's office or by simply rising from one's chair and moving forward. To remain seated may be an implicit snub.

Chou En-lai, by a single gesture of this kind, brought himself to the attention of President Nasser of Egypt. On his way to Bandung for the 1955 Afro–Asian conference Nasser, travelling together with Nehru, stopped off in Rangoon. Chou was also in the Burmese capital. With apparent spontaneity he decided to accompany U Nu out to the airport to meet the plane. Nasser was surprised and flattered. Their subsequent unscheduled meeting proved to be a landmark in the development of Sino–Egyptian relations and, perhaps even more important, in the cultivation of Nasser by the Communist bloc.[18]

It is not far-fetched to assume that in fact Chou's presence in Rangoon and his trip to the airport to greet Nasser were meticulously planned in advance, possibly at Soviet request. China and the USSR were very eager indeed at this time to cultivate the rising force of nationalism in the Middle East as represented by Colonel Nasser. But, as later in the ping-pong initiative, Chou was careful to avoid a rebuff. Thus the gesture was directed towards both Nasser and his travelling companion Nehru and the subsequent meeting took place at a neutral venue. If nothing came of it, there would be no loss of face. It all seemed a most happy coincidence.

The inspired element in Chou's *démarche* was the insight it reflected into Nasser's sensitivity on issues of status. Egyptians and other Arabs, like the members of all group-oriented societies, are intensely concerned as to how they will appear in the eyes of others. There is nothing more painful than to be slighted in public, no greater reward than a compliment to one's pride. Chou understood this precisely because of the analogous importance of 'face' in Chinese culture.

It is one of the ironies of contemporary history that almost at the very moment that a Chinese prime minister was displaying his skill at the manipulation of the personal gesture, an American secretary of state was revealing his own misjudgement. John Foster Dulles had not been at all happy to learn of the projected conference of newly-independent states, fearing that it would adopt an anti-American stance. Nor had he concealed his misgivings from Colonel Nasser, specifically requesting him not to attend. In order to reassure the United States government Nasser broke a personal rule and the night before his departure for Indonesia attended a private dinner with American ambassador Byroade. This was a very gracious, meaningful gesture – an inconvenience display in fact.

But while the Egyptian leader was away in Bandung, Dulles concluded that he was set on a dangerous course and had to be left in no doubt of American disapproval. The secretary of state therefore instructed Byroade to join with his British and French counterparts and to stay away from Cairo airport for the ceremony of officials and members of the diplomatic corps which was to greet Nasser on his return home. When Nasser stepped off his plane the only major ambassador to meet him was the representative of the USSR. Nasser was furious and utterly humiliated.

The contrast between Western arrogance and Communist thoughtfulness was blatant. Where Chou had gone out of his way to honour him, the Western powers had shamed him in public. Byroade, looking back, was of no doubt that the strain in Egyptian–American relations culminating in the affair of the Aswan dam (when, in reaction to the withdrawal of an Anglo-American offer to finance the hydroelectric project, Nasser nationalized the Suez canal) began with this unfortunate incident.[19]

The period between the Bandung conference of April 1955 and the Suez war of November 1956 saw Egypt's shift away from the Western camp and into the Communist orbit. It was only really with Nasser's death in 1970 that the reverse movement got under way. Here again, strangely enough, it was an inconvenience display that signalled the realignment. The episode took place in Washington, one week after the end of the 1973 Yom Kippur war, at the conclusion of a seminal meeting between Richard Nixon and Egyptian Foreign Minister Ismail Fahmy. The American president insisted on accompanying his guest to his car. His explanation left no doubt of his grasp of the profound political significance of the move: 'Normally, I accompany foreign ministers only as far as the Rose Garden, where my daughter Patricia got engaged. But to show the press and everybody my interest and the new US position towards Egypt, I shall escort you to your car.' Fahmy was highly satisfied by this gesture of public deference.[20]

Throughout the Middle East in particular and the Third World in general the subtle signs by which dominance and subordination, honour and disrespect, are communicated, are observed with almost obsessive attention. And, should the tables be turned in a relationship, and yesterday's servants become today's masters, revenge for past indignities will be savoured to the full.

For Saudi Arabia the quest for prestige and recognition has become, in effect, a primary foreign policy goal. Failure to recognize this can cloud even a relationship grounded in substantial shared interest. For the visit to London of their foreign minister on one occasion the Saudis were adamant that he be greeted at the airport by no less a figure than the prime minister himself, Harold Wilson. Although the prime minister's attendance was certainly not required by protocol the Saudis made it clear that his absence would lead to the cancellation of the visit. Eager – perhaps over-eager – for the development of commercial relations, Wilson felt unable to turn down the Saudi demand. Here was an inconvenience display reflecting on both guest and host. On the one hand it certainly exemplified the enhanced status that the energy crisis and astronomical oil revenues had bestowed on Saudi Arabia. On the other hand British compliance in this act of submissive flattery provided sad evidence of the extent to which the government had reconciled itself to the 'facts' of Britain's decline.

The inconvenience display, with its careful attention to the nuances of courtesy, works well at the diplomatic level. However, it lacks a striking visual dimension for the non-specialist observer. The handshake and the embrace are effective ways of displaying friendship and community to a wider audience. An even more dramatic gesture of this kind is the *triumph display*. In its basic form triumph is communicated by thrusting one's arms into the air and proudly showing oneself off to an audience. De Gaulle made the gesture, in which his tall frame formed the letter 'V' for victory, into a personal hallmark, a reminder, if needed, of his role in the liberation of France.

The gesture takes on added significance when it involves more than a single figure. In this case it symbolizes unity and victory, past or prospective, in a common struggle. Nasser liked the pose, both in its solo version and in the company of other Arab leaders. It well caught his philosophy of Arab unity and proclaimed struggle to free the Arab world from 'imperialist' influence. After his nationalization of the Suez canal and the abortive Anglo-French invasion in 1956 it also reflected his triumphant regional status.

Nixon also cultivated the gesture and perhaps the heroic role it suggested. He startled President Ceauşescu by raising the Romanian leader's arm aloft at the end of a visit to Bucharest in August 1969. It may also have been intended to startle the Soviet Union, since the trip was a deliberate intrusion into its East European sphere of influence. But its primary audience was the American public, watching on television.

The Kissinger memoirs make clear just how alert Kremlin observers are to visual and symbolic aspects of diplomacy. Ambassador Dobrynin actually expressed an explicit interest in seeing Chinese-made films of Kissinger's Peking visits.[21] It must have been, therefore, in full awareness of the political implications of his move that Deng Xiaoping took a leaf out of Nixon's book at the White House at the end of January 1979. After an exchange of welcoming remarks Deng grabbed the arm of Jimmy Carter and held it high. He later repeated the gesture at the Kennedy Center.

At the American domestic level it clearly displayed Sino–American solidarity and the attractive spiritedness of the Chinese leader. Just what was implied at the international level may become clearer if we take the gesture together with the text of an interview published in *Time* magazine the same day. 'If we really want to be able to place curbs on the polar bear', Deng told his interviewer, 'the only thing is for us to unite.'[22]

The Carter administration, of course, was well aware of the Chinese wish to sharpen the anti-Soviet thrust of their relationship. Indeed the communiqué published during the Deng visit noted Sino-American opposition to 'hegemony or domination', a euphemism whose meaning would not be lost on the Soviet Union. However, it is doubtful whether President Carter fully realized the full extent to which he was being manipulated.

At meetings between Deng and the president the Chinese leader stated the intention of his government to teach the Vietnamese 'an appropriate limited lesson' – in other words, to attack them. Analysing the various possible Soviet responses to such a move, Deng went on to ask for the 'moral support' of the United States.

It was an outrageous request to which no American president in his right mind would accede, snatching any advantage or initiative in the triangular Sino–Soviet–American relationship away from the United States and converting it into a catspaw of Chinese policy. After discussing the proposal with his advisers Carter urged Deng to reconsider his decision and in a written letter stressed the importance of restraint. The United States, even Brzezinski understood, 'could not collude formally with the Chinese in sponsoring what was tantamount to overt military aggression'.[23]

On the surface, therefore, the Carter administration had avoided giving any commitment to China in the event of a Sino–Soviet confrontation. It is hard to believe that Deng seriously entertained the possibility of American compliance. Nevertheless he had cleverly outmanoeuvred the United States. On 5 February 1979 Deng left for home. Twelve days later the People's Liberation Army launched its offensive against the USSR's ally, Vietnam. In the light of Deng's visit to Washington and the display of Sino–American solidarity, both verbal and nonverbal, who would credit the claim that the United States was simply an innocent bystander? Expressions of disapproval could hardly be taken at face value. Carter had been duped into seeming complicity with the Chinese leader. True, there was no 'formal' public commitment, but there was most certainly the appearance of tacit, informal collusion. What more did the Chinese need? Deng, it is clear, understood the utility of nonverbal communication rather better than had his American host.

CULTURALLY-SPECIALIZED GESTURES

Alongside those few gestures that have acquired some kind of international status in the lexicon of nonverbal communication there is an abundance of body signals of more or less restricted regional application. All societies possess such mannerisms and gestures, which are rooted in cultural assumptions of the most basic kind about kinship, sexuality, space and time.

Tone of voice, for instance, is something we take for granted. But in different cultures there are quite opposing meanings attached to loudness and softness. For the Chinese, overloudness is associated with anger; for an Arab it denotes sincerity; in the United States it may simply reflect cordiality and enthusiasm. Punctuality is another habit which totally differs from one society to another. In the Middle East or

South America an agreed time is often no more than a rough approximation, and a delay of half an hour is not something to be taken personally, as it would be in northern Europe.[24]

For communication between states culturally-specialized gestures and manners pose difficulties; there is always the risk that they will be misunderstood or incorrectly used. Far from facilitating communication, they may actually obstruct it. How can an Arab or, indeed, Argentinian leader be expected to grasp the grave implications of a warning, delivered with British calm and understatement, when his instincts tell him that these cues are evidence of insincerity?

To the extent that such habits and mannerisms are conscious and can be suppressed, they will be avoided in cases of cross-cultural communication. The advantage of protocol and diplomatic convention is that they permit contact and dialogue even in the absence of shared cultural assumptions. When there is a common cultural background, however, local gestures can be a considerable asset. They facilitate communication by providing a symbolic code with the resonance only a shared heritage can evoke; they obviate the discomfort associated with cross-cultural contact; they permit the exclusion of uninitiated third parties.

In the Arab world 'body language' is one of the mechanisms which help to maintain a sense of community over and above particular conflicts of interest – and differentiate Arabs from non-Arabs. It is an important component of that fabric of shared symbols and values, deriving from religion, language and history, which constitute the Arab identity. Ease of communication is a direct consequence of the possession of common conventions and assumptions.

One distinguishing aspect of Arab culture is the use of space. Interpersonal contact is more tactile and proximate than is the case in North America or Western Europe. When Arabs converse, they sit closer together than would Anglo-Saxons, they are more apt to touch each other while talking, look each other more squarely in the eye and talk in louder tones. This has been demonstrated, quite conclusively, in experimental situations.[25] Arab male friends, when they are close together in public, either sitting, standing or out walking, consider it quite proper to hold hands. This has none of the sexual connotations it would have in the West.

Among Arab diplomats touch and proximity, therefore, are key elements in the display of friendship. Films of inter-Arab visits show the leaders walking hand-in-hand or sitting close-up on a sofa, gesturing animatedly, touching and looking into each other's eyes. There is something very wrong in political relations when these signs of endearment are absent. For an Arab statesman it is as natural to employ, even manipulate, such cues, as it is for a Western leader to prolong a handshake or put on an appearance of feigned pleasure. The only difference is in the vocabulary used.

An exceptionally percipient – or well-briefed – Western statesman can exploit such culturally-specialized manners to his great advantage. Henry Kissinger owed at least some of his success in breaking down barriers between the United States and the Arab world to his ability to communicate with its leaders, both verbally and nonverbally, in terms they understood. He had none of the traditional American inhibitions – often mistaken for patronizing aloofness – against prolonged eye-contact, touching, holding hands and embracing.

But it is only rarely that a stranger can accommodate himself, without disclosing some discomfort, to the intimate habits of a foreign culture. Edward Hall, the originator of the study of *proxemics*, the use of space in human interaction, notes that 'the intensity and intimacy of the encounter with Arabs' has been found 'to be anxiety provoking' for Americans.

> The Arab look, touch, voice level, the warm moisture of his breath, the penetrating stare of his eyes, all proved to be disturbing. The reason for these feelings lay in part in the fact that the relationship *was not defined as intimate*, and the behaviour was such that in the American culture is only permissible on a non-public basis with a person of the opposite sex.[26]

There is a very revealing photograph taken during a visit made by Sir Anthony Eden to Cairo in February 1955. It shows the British prime minister almost squirming with embarrassment as an ebullient Nasser tries to hold his hand. This seemingly trivial episode clearly stuck in Eden's mind because he refers to it in his memoirs: 'Before our talks began we were photographed together. As the flashlights went off, he seized my hand and held it.'[27] The distaste is evident.

In another photograph from the visit Eden can be seen uneasily poised at the very corner of a leather sofa. Nasser has clearly edged up to him and *is sitting too close for the Englishman's comfort*. Eden also found himself quite unable to hold the Egyptian's gaze.[28]

The end result of this uncomfortable encounter was that Nasser took away the unfortunate impression that he had been patronized. He had tried hard to be friendly but Eden had rebuffed all his overtures. It was the unsuccessful opening to a tragic relationship; the beginning of a true dialogue of the deaf. Now Eden knew Arabic and was no stranger to the Middle East. Nasser doubtless felt that his reserve was intentionally political and not simply based on cultural ignorance.

It would have been better, paradoxically, for British foreign policy had Eden not been known as an Arabist and not paraded his area expertise. His Arab audience would then have taken his behaviour with a grain of salt. Arabs are well aware that their customs are not those of the West. They have had long experience of the European and his ways. Accordingly they do not read the same implications into a display of physical restraint on the part of a Western leader that they would in the case of a fellow Arab. Eden had actually addressed Nasser in Arabic at their introduction. If he intended, as a matter of policy, to be correct but distant, he should have been more consistent about it.

FACIAL EXPRESSION

Recent research indicates that the same emotions are displayed in different cultures by similar facial expressions. The basic 'faces' – surprise, happiness, sadness, disgust, fear and anger – have been found around the world.[29]

Where people in various cultures do differ is in their *display rules*. First, the same stimulus may provoke quite different emotional reactions in different cultural contexts. Whereas an insect usually stimulates disgust in a Westerner, for someone else it might induce pleasure as an edible delicacy. Second, different cultures disagree about when it is seemly to show off certain emotions, if at all. Some cultures feel no compunction about displaying amusement at others' discomfiture. In Britain and America such a reaction is suppressed – except when it occurs in a theatrical context.[30]

However, the role of facial expression in international relations does not depend upon the universality or otherwise of particular cues or display rules. Nor do we need to know the modalities of such expressions in various cultures. This is the realm of the ethnologist. For our purposes it is sufficient to observe those facial gestures which have been conventionally adopted by the international community as stylized expressions of one's political attitude. To the extent that a national leader wishes to communicate a particular impression of approval, interest, friendliness and so on to a foreign audience, he is obliged to make use of whatever commonly understood cues are available.

As in other areas of nonverbal communication, the 'theatrical repertoire' of the statesman is far narrower than that of the private individual. Fear, disgust, surprise and sadness are not usually expressed at the international level. On the contrary, they tend to be suppressed in case they reveal too much about one's true diplomatic position.

Clearly politicians and officials are not robots and the mask does slip. When it occurs, though, it is invariably by accident and not design. As a general rule, the public display of emotion is intended to communicate political effect and not personal feeling. Facial expressions can be thought of simply as convenient *ideograms* – pictorial symbols that convey an idea or a meaning directly. Statesmen smile not because they are happy, but because they have an interest in conveying satisfaction. Our task, then, is to decipher the code.

The 'diplomatic emotions' most commonly displayed or augmented by facial expression are pleasure, displeasure, agreement, disagreement, equanimity and anger.

The smile is the great cliché of international relations. If a camera is in sight, then the smile is automatically switched on. It is a *social* smile, worn both to signal that everything is fine and under control, and also to wipe off other revealing cues. After all, it is hard to maintain total facial blankness.

Thus the smile as such does not, in public at least, necessarily possess its private meaning of pleasure or happiness. The standard smile, bland as margarine, is the facial equivalent of white noise: it is neutral. To signify pleasure, supplementary features are required – and these do seem to vary from one culture to another. The Russians tend to a rather heavy-handed jocularity; laughter and back-slapping are in order. Others may be more restrained. The basic principle is usually: the wider the smile, the greater the joy.

A surprisingly wide range of expressions are available to the expert practitioner. In this, as in other aspects of the dramatic art of diplomacy, the master was Chou En-lai. According to Chinese author Yao Ch'ien, Chou's 'five smiles' became famous within the Chinese politburo: Writing of the 1950s Yao claims that

> When he meets a Soviet 'elder brother' he gives him a beaming welcome with outstretched arms; when he sees Mao or Liu Shao-ch'i he gives them a broad grin but his hands remain slack at his sides; when he greets diplomats from capitalist countries his smile is a little aloof as befits a prime minister; when he encounters other members of the Politburo or colleagues of some standing, he offers them a half-grin that moves the upper part of his face only; and when he greets lesser members of the Central Committee or leaders of other parties, the facial muscles relax, but only the skin smiles.[31]

Lest it be thought that Yao's story is apocryphal there is a good deal of corroborative evidence about Chou's ability to put his facial expressiveness to political use. At the beginning of the drawn-out 1954 Geneva conference on Indo-China Chou, though charming with other delegates, put on a stern face for the press. Parading his tough negotiating position – in a manner characteristic of Communist diplomacy in general – he was photographed in a determined pose, unsmiling, fists demonstratively clenched at his sides.[32]

The breakthrough in the talks was heralded by a remarkably visual thawing-out of Chou's intransigence: Chou and French delegate Jean Chauvel (who had served in China years before) often used to pass each other – but without acknowledgement – in the corridors of Geneva's Palais des Nations. One day Chou turned his gaze on the French diplomat; the next day he winked; then on the following day he actually smiled. Chauvel understood and reported that a *démarche* was imminent. He was not surprised, therefore, when on the fourth day Chou turned to him and suggested that he meet with French Premier Mendès-France.[33]

Obviously, where a smile is the norm, its absence acquires significance. Once again one must assume that a political point is being transmitted – the personal pleasure that leaders have in each others' company is not for public show. Moreover genuine dissatisfaction with the state of one's relations with another government is more often downplayed than publicized. Why benefit third parties with the information, lose face with public opinion or make it more difficult to restore relations?

There are at least two possible explanations for a show of displeasure. The first entails dissimulation. If one is engaged in profitable ties with an unpopular regime – a Chile or a South Africa – it may be best to make it appear as a grim necessity. 'We are not enjoying this, but we have no choice', is the message. A second motive for the display may be the wish to leave its object in no doubt that his government is in bad odour. As to the implications of such a deterioration, this will depend upon the nature of the relationship and the circumstances. Between a patron and a client the hint that all is not well contains an implied threat of withdrawal of support. Publicizing the sanction is intended to enhance its credibility.

President Reagan neatly encapsulated both moral dissociation and the *implication* of pressure at a meeting with the Israeli foreign minister at the time of the 1982 Israeli siege of Beirut. During the 'photo opportunity' session (that precedes every official meeting with a foreign dignitary) Reagan sat glum and subdued. Hardly a word was exchanged. White House officials let it be known that it was a deliberate gesture intended to contrast sharply with the normal handshakes and smiles.[34]

If the display or absence of pleasure provides a commentary on the general state of relations, the show of agreement or disagreement makes a more specific point about the content of policy. It is true that a substantive issue can be effectively debated in verbal terms. However, facial expression is far from being duplicatory since it unambiguously associates the leader with the political point being made. Careful linguistic formulations are also likely to lack the force of a dramatic enactment. With an inaccessible leadership a personal display by the chief may be the only evidence of his 'true' attitude available to the bureaucracy and outside observers.

Subtlety of this kind appears to be the province of Oriental rather than Western diplomacy. On the one hand Asian cultures have a particular propensity for allusiveness. On the other hand hierarchical political systems tend to make greater use of indirect modes of communication.

A poignant example can be taken from the period just before Pearl Harbor. The context of the episode was the opposition of the Emperor Hirohito of Japan to the intransigent policy of the military clique that was in power. Prevented by tradition from overt intervention in affairs of state, he made his views known in the only way open to him. On 11 November 1940 ambassador Joseph Grew of the United States had the task of presenting the greetings of the diplomatic corps in Tokyo to the emperor. The occasion was a ceremony to commemorate the 2600th anniversary of the founding of the Japanese empire and a large crowd was present. Grew takes up the story:

> The Emperor, who had preserved an almost rigid expression throughout the rest of the program, nodded at each of my points and nodded vigorously when at the end the hope was expressed that Japan would contribute to the general culture and well-being of mankind. Arsène-Henry, the French ambassador, came to see me the next day on purpose to tell me that he had watched the Emperor's face and was convinced that his nods of approval were given to impress the Government and the higher officials of the Empire with his own desire for peace. Arsène-Henry was so impressed with this that he cabled the Government about it as an important political indication. Even the official Court release to the press announced 'His Majesty seemed greatly pleased' with the speech.[35]

Within the Byzantine labyrinth of the Communist world facial expression was one of the symbolic mediums by which the Chinese conducted their esoteric ideological debate with the Soviet Union during the Khrushchev era. Presumably the primary audience was the domestic bureaucracy, which had to be kept up-to-date about the true state of affairs. A secondary audience may also have been the other fraternal parties of the Communist bloc who were being lobbied for their support. Until the first expulsion of Soviet experts from China in 1960 the titanic struggle could be conducted largely out of sight of Western observers. To the uninitiated such visible clues as there were would not necessarily appear intentional. It was only within the framework of the ideological polemic that they acquired significance.

We now know that a crucial stage in the Sino-Soviet split was the failure of Khrushchev's Peking mission of October 1959. Two photographs of his departure, released by the government-controlled New China News Agency, are particularly revealing. (Communist practice would never have permitted their publication without instructions from the very highest level.) One shows sceptical officials listening to the Soviet leader's farewell speech (in which he reiterated the Soviet position on various ideological issues). Another shows the normally serene or smiling Mao grimacing in distaste. A classic artistic device reminds us that this is art, not nature. The photograph itself contains the view of a photographer . . . photographing Mao.[36]

The final emotional display to be considered is that of anger. It has become especially associated, in the twentieth century, with the conduct of totalitarian diplomacy. Three countries have specialized in its use: Fascist Italy, Nazi Germany and Soviet Russia. In all three cases anger has been deliberately put to good effect, in the context of a philosophy of ideological struggle, to induce fear and enhance the credibility of threats.

The personal display of anger is effective for several reasons. In the first place it involves the infringement of the diplomatic convention of imperturbability and good manners. It therefore carries the broader implication that the performer is not prepared to abide by the existing 'rules of the game' at all. He becomes an unknown quantity. And, as Yehezkel Dror has pointed out, an image of 'craziness' – irrationality – can be a powerful asset in a diplomatic confrontation. Since his behaviour is unpredictable, one can never know how far he can be pushed or, indeed, to what lengths of fanaticism he may go.[37]

The second advantage of anger is one shared with other personal gestures. It enacts, in a very graphic manner, the message of the communicator. Carefully drafted speeches and diplomatic notes, however threatening in substance, can never have quite the impact of an outburst of rage. Their form belies their substance. If, moreover, they draw upon diplomatic circumlocution and have been worded to leave a loop-hole for retreat, they are likely to be even less genuinely intimidating. The fact is that declaratory diplomacy – the communication of threat or warning in verbal terms – has been consistently ineffective in the twentieth century. Some more forceful index of credibility has usually been needed. One expedient is gunboat diplomacy or 'sabre-rattling'. Where this is ruled out, or as an additional measure, a personal show of rage can help.

Many cultures severely restrict the public display of anger. It is unpleasant, embarrassing and makes social relationships more difficult. Those brought up with such inhibitions are at a double disadvantage faced with those who are not. Psychologically they are disoriented and intimidated by anger. Moreover they are unable to appraise its authenticity. Pleasure, it is assumed, is routinely simulated; social necessity often calls for it. But fury is not.

Mussolini was the first international figure to exploit his temper for purposes of policy. His habit was then copied by other Italian diplomats and became part of a particular style of diplomatic conduct, the *tono fascista*. The style was characterized by belligerent rhetoric, the glorification of war and a contempt for compromise. Looked at as a rational expedient anger helped to conceal the underlying weakness of the regime and lent greater credibility to Fascist rhetoric than it probably deserved. It also reflected a more profound bitterness at Italy's supposedly disadvantaged position in the world.

Doubtless Hitler's fanatical outbursts had their basic origin in a psychopathic instability. But tactically their effect was well-judged to put maximum psychological pressure on his opponents. There was reason in his madness. Thus he was successful in browbeating such leaders as Chamberlain in September 1938 and Hacha of Czechoslovakia in March 1939. The frenzy of Hitler's speeches convinced observers of his utter sincerity and the credibility of his threats. Nevile Henderson, British ambassador in Berlin, was so terrified of Hitler's rages that he went to considerable lengths during the summer of the Sudeten crisis to avoid 'pushing him over the brink'. The policy of concessions – appeasement – which the British government were inclined to adopt in the face of Hitler's fanaticism, played into the latter's hands. Their approach, though unwise with hindsight, has frequently been the natural reaction of Western democratic statesmen to immoderation. Unfortunately, leaders brought up on the values of moderation and compromise are disarmed and disconcerted by extremism.

It is, surely, insight into this basic vulnerability that has motivated the tempestuous tone of Soviet diplomacy since the Second World War. Believing history on its side, the Soviet Union is an inherently cautious and patient power. Its representatives have well known when their policy stands to be best served by a show of sweet reasonableness. Conversely histrionics of the most brutal kind have been put on when they served Soviet tactical objectives. Exploitation of Western feelings of guilt and the sense that where there is anger there must be injury have gone hand in hand with a philosophy founded on the dialectic and ideological conflict. Anger, in this light, is no more than 'a manifestation of the sincere and principled character of Soviet policy'. If Communists are angry, Soviet diplomats are saying in effect, it is because they have a right to be angry.

Khrushchev, who became notorious for his intemperate outbursts, was never angrier than when adopting the characteristic Soviet guise of the prosecuting counsel (a role originated at the United Nations by Andrei Vishinsky, who had actually played a leading role in the Stalinist show trials of the 1930s). A show of bad temper put on for British Prime Minister Harold Macmillan during his 1959 visit to the USSR took just such an accusatory tone: the West, Khrushchev stormed at his guest, wanted war, was 'preparing for war and choosing [its] own time for war'. This indictment, calculated to throw its target on the defensive, has been the stock-in-trade of Soviet invective in the post-war period.

Rage also accompanied and was intended to reinforce Soviet threats to sign a separate peace treaty with East Germany if the Western allies refused to withdraw from West Berlin. The performance was repeated on many occasions, most notably during Khrushchev's September 1960 appearance at the United Nations. As Macmillan addressed the general assembly the Russian leader snarled in anger, waved his finger in the air and banged on the desk with his shoe. To objective observers it was an ugly and demeaning outburst. But, as Macmillan understood, it 'stole the show' for Khrushchev, left Western audiences dismayed and disoriented and 'shocked and frightened' the smaller countries.[38]

In the short term Khrushchev's Berlin campaign was not successful. In the longer term the chilling bellicosity of Soviet diplomacy, combined with an effective propaganda and the relentless build-up of military power, has intimidated Western opinion, weakened NATO and provoked the United States into ill-considered spasms of retaliation. Used, then, with cool calculation, the display of anger has proved to be a demoralizing weapon against the Western democracies.

REFERENCES AND NOTES

1. Firth R 1973 *Symbols: public and private*. Cornell University Press: New York, ch 9

2. Brzezinski Z 1983 *Power and Principle*. Weidenfeld and Nicolson, pp 21–2
3. Schiffrin 1981 Handwork as ceremony: the case of the handshake; in Kendon A (ed) *Nonverbal Communication, Interaction, and Gesture*. Mouton: The Hague, pp 237–50
4. *The Times* 25 Mar. 1982; Eden A 1960 *Full Circle*. Cassell, p 33
5. Montagu A, Matson F 1979 *The Human Connection*. McGraw-Hill: New York, p 38
6. Kissinger H 1979 *The White House Years*, Little Brown: Boston p 742; Eden A *op cit*. 1960, p 117; Nixon R A 1982 *Leaders*. Sidgwick and Jackson, p 235
7. Bohlen C E 1973 *Witness to History*. W W Norton: New York, p 378
8. Micunovic V 1980 *Moscow Diary*. Chatto and Windus, p 4
9. *Peking Review* 9 Feb. 1979
10. Salem-Babikian N 1980 The sacred and profane: Sadat's speech to the Knesset, *Middle East Journal*, p 17 fn
11. Weit E 1973 *Eyewitness*. Andre Deutsch, p 114; Talbott S (ed) 1974 *Khrushchev Remembers: the last testament*. Little, Brown: Boston, p 479
12. Micunovic V 1980 *op. cit.*, p 131
13. Dornberg J 1974 *Brezhnev: the masks of power*. Basic Books: New York, p 225
14. *The Times* 2 Mar. 1982
15. Rafael G 1981 *Destination Peace*. Weidenfeld and Nicolson, p 345
16. Washington S 1980 Toward a new relationship. *Africa Report* Mar.–Apr., p 18
17. Morris D 1977 *Manwatching*. Harry N Abrams: New York
18. Heikal M H 1978 *The Sphinx and the Commissar*, Harper and Row: New York, pp 57, 59
19. Badeau J 1983 *The Middle East Remembered*. The Middle East Institute: Washington, p 178
20. Fahmy I 1983 *Negotiating for Peace in the Middle East*. Croom Helm, p 51
21. Kissinger H 1979 *op. cit.*, p 1117
22. *Time* 29 Jan. 1979
23. Brzezinski Z 1983 *op. cit.*, pp 408–10
24. Hall E T 1955 The anthropology of manners. *Scientific American* **192**: 84–90
25. Hall E T 1963 A system of notation of proxemic behavior. *American Anthropologist* **65**: 1003–26: Watson O M, Graves T D 1966 Quantitative research in proxemic behavior, *American*

Anthropologist 68: 971–985; Watson O M 1970 *Proxemic Behavior*. Mouton: The Hague
26. Hall E T 1963 *op. cit.*, pp 1005–6
27. Nutting A 1972 *Nasser*. Constable, facing p 173; Eden A 1960 *op. cit.*, p 221
28. Heikal M H 1973 *Nasser: the Cairo documents*. NEL Mentor, photo no. 22; Thomas H 1967 *The Suez Affair*. Weidenfeld and Nicolson, p 13
29. Eibl-Eibesfeldt I 1972 Similarities and differences between cultures in expressive movements, in Hinde R A (ed) *Nonverbal Communication*. Cambridge University Press, pp 297–314; Ekman P 1972 Universals and cultural differences in facial expressions of emotion, in Cole J (ed) *Nebraska Symposium on Motivation, 1971*. University of Nebraska Press: Lincoln, Nebraska, pp 207–83
30. Harrison R P 1974 *Beyond Words*. Prentice-Hall: Englewood Cliffs, p 121
31. Ching P, Bloodworth D 1973 *Heirs Apparent*. Farrar, Strauss and Giroux, p 27
32. *Newsweek* 14 June 1954
33. Devillers P, Lacouture J 1964 *End of a War*. Pall Mall Press, p 251
34. *The Times* 4 Aug. 1982
35. Grew J 1944 *Ten Years in Japan*. Hammond, Hammond, pp 305–6
36. *Life* 19 Oct. 1959
37. Dror Y 1971 *Crazy States*. D C Heath: Lexington
38. Macmillan H 1972 *Pointing the Way*. Macmillan, pp 281, 397

Chapter six

THE LEADER AS *METTEUR-EN-SCÈNE*

In the theatre of power the leader is not only an actor; he must also be, at one and the same time, producer and director of the drama. He (and his decision-making team) provide the underlying political conception and must harness the different elements of the performance – script, choreography, scenery and props – to this ultimate end. Incongruity or dissonance, unless deliberate, can only confuse their overall purpose. Faced with an audience which will seek meaning in the slightest detail, the *metteur-en-scène* strives to leave nothing to chance.

Writers on the dramaturgical approach to human behaviour have all emphasized the importance of *setting*. Erving Goffman, one of the pioneers of the approach, defines 'setting' as the 'furniture, decor, physical layout, and other background items which supply the scenery and stage props for the spate of human action played out before, within, or upon it'. Settings, he continues, tend to be fixed in space 'so that those who would use a particular setting as part of their performance cannot begin their act until they have brought themselves to the appropriate place and must terminate their performance when they leave it'. However, in exceptional circumstances a star performer may take his setting along with him.[1]

A fixed setting for political action might be the entrance to No. 10 Downing St. or an army base in Northern Ireland. A mobile setting might be the American presidential jet and entourage. Like a medieval monarch, modern heads of government are preceded and accompanied by sometimes hundreds of officials and aides. Limousines, communications equipment, even choice foods are sent on ahead. Public relations specialists stake out the planned itinerary and may suggest alterations and improvements to ensure the most politically appropriate settings for appearances of their chief. For his 1955 trip to Moscow Chancellor Adenauer's staff sent a special train on ahead carrying literally everything including sacks of potatoes. True, West

Germany had no Moscow embassy; but the hint that the Russians lacked even potatoes was a thinly-veiled insult. President Nixon's aides were notorious for the high-handedness with which they sought to design the stage for foreign appearances of the president. Before one visit to Canada they infuriated their Canadian hosts by actually proposing that one of the rooms where Prime Minister Trudeau was to receive his mighty guest be refurnished and repainted blue, because this would make for better television. Fortunately for international goodwill, most governments do not go quite so far.

Murray Edelman has provided a near definitive account of the function of settings in the (domestic) political process. Every human act, he points out, takes place in a setting, which is usually taken for granted. Certain kinds of acts, however, involve settings which are painstakingly constructed – 'as if the scene were expected either to call forth a response of its own or to heighten the response to the act it frames'. Such acts include theatrical performances, religious ceremonies and formal political actions. Setting, in these cases, is integral to action.

Though it is with political action that his concern lies, Edelman concludes from observation of religion and the arts that 'settings have a vital bearing upon actors, upon responses to acts and especially upon the evocation of feelings and aesthetic reactions'. For this reason settings must be meticulously contrived: 'They are unabashedly built up to emphasize a departure from one's daily routine, a special or heroic quality in the proceedings they are to frame.'

In essence the contrived setting removes the performance from the realm of everyday life and transposes it into an artificial universe. 'Such backgrounds make for heightened sensitivity and easier conviction in onlookers, for the framed actions are taken on their own terms. They are not qualified by inconsistent facts in the environment. The creation of an artificial space or semblance thus sets the stage for a concentration of suggestions: of connotations, of emotions and of authority.' Disbelief is suspended; the condensed symbolism of the performance acquires a reality of its own, insulated from the alternative logic of the real world.[2]

In contrast to Goffman, Edelman is inclined to associate settings in their contrived sense with mass audiences rather than intimate face-to-face groups. He sees them as a product of the television age, of the televized press conference and not the off-the-record backgrounder. In fact the live performance, Edelman argues, is, paradoxically, less informative and more remote than the discrete, closed meetings of a previous era. Whereas clearly defined rules of quotation enabled presidents such as Franklin Roosevelt to brief newspapermen in full confidence, the intrusion of television has left only a pretence of openness. Fear of error and self-exposure before the cameras has had a paralysing effect on leadership, leaving the field open to the charlatan and the professional actor. Charm and polish are mistaken for true ability.

Television has become *part of the setting*, imposing a logic all of its own on both the content and context of the subsequent performance. It is precisely this point that shapes the nature of communication in the television age – and defines the task of the leader as performer.

Edelman would wish to go beyond Goffman in another important respect, and here I must differ with him. In his view it is insufficient to restrict the meaning of 'setting' simply to physical features of the environment. It must also include, Edelman argues, the social context of action, 'generally accepted assumptions about basic causation or motivation'. In a war, for example, 'a military leader is expected to fight'; against a background of detente he is expected to act 'as an adjunct to peacetime social and governmental activity'.

Edelman is of course right that social circumstances define the scope of role performance. But surely he is detracting from the analytical usefulness of the concept of setting by over-extending the boundaries of its meaning. Many and varied factors affect human behaviour; this is a truism. The utility of the dramaturgical approach is that it focuses on that aspect of the situation which the participants themselves deliberately manipulate. One assumes self-consciousness.

Moreover the remarkable and disconcerting feature of television is that its logic *takes precedence over* the logic of the situation it depicts. A television viewer does not automatically accept that a wartime situation has its own special rules of the game or that government conduct must be judged on its own terms. For him part of the setting of any televized scene is the armchair in which he is sitting and the four walls of his living-room – in short, domestic banality. From this perspective, and this is one lesson of Vietnam and Watergate, he is not prepared to grant the civilian and military leadership any special privileges. The real world in which they are obliged to act, with its moral ambiguities and choices of lesser evils, is not part of the viewer's comfortable setting; hence it does not exist. If anything, he judges war and government by the mythical standards of Hollywood, enacted by John Wayne and James Stewart, to which he has been relentlessly exposed for decades. In the celluloid world people die elegantly, neatly punctured by non-fragmenting bullets.

The logic of television, therefore, does not permit leaders to take for granted that the viewing public will understand the 'assumptions about basic causation or motivation' which underlie government behaviour. Left to itself television deals in effects and not in causes – counter-insurgency and not insurgency, the fire rather than the arson. If it was not filmed it did not occur. Television transforms the one who responds to violence into the aggressor. By the time the forces of law and order react to a provocation the perpetrator may be well away from the scene of his crime. In the mind of the viewer it is therefore the police or the army who become guilty by visual association. Only in the cinema is there a visual symmetry of action and reaction. Television can only catch the reaction. Thus from a propaganda point of view responsive action, which is predictable and can be covered by television crews warned in advance, will always be at a disadvantage to initiatory action, which is unpredictable and inaccessible to television. A bomb is planted; it explodes hours later; the perpetrators are unknown. The army or police react; they search, make arrests, are filmed dragging suspects to a van. Television logic brands them as the violators of human dignity.

Given television's peculiarly fragmented and non-causative image of reality, governments are bound to attempt to restore the balance in a manner that makes clear the original provocation, the cause of their own reaction. Just as the director of a documentary film re-enacts crucial historical scenes that were not filmed at the time, governments have to find some cinematic way to create in the mind of a watching audience the true pattern of cause and effect. States in which the media are simply controlled instruments of propaganda have little difficulty in fabricating their version of events and censoring images that are inconvenient to their case. In countries where the media are not state-controlled, legitimate devices must be found to frame justified reactions in a way that will place any moral responsibility where it belongs. If causes are invisible, they must be dramatized and made visible. Policy assumptions that are self-evident to decision makers must be somehow presented in a visually comprehensible way to viewers.

One way to do this is by the careful construction of settings. Apt staging can in itself help to define the nature of the problem being addressed. In a pastoral context violence is incomprehensible – hence the absurd gratuitousness and horror of the 'search and destroy' operations of the Vietnam war as depicted on television. Military retaliation can only be explained to the spectator sitting comfortably at home, 6,000 miles away, if it can somehow be staged against a backdrop of the bloody consequences of the original provocation. The easy way out was that chosen by the United States in Grenada and Britain in the Falklands in 1982: to restrict access by the media. But this is only possible when operations are in fact being conducted in a geographically remote area. The 1982 campaigns were de luxe operations from this point of view and governments cannot always expect to be so fortunate. What they can do is to stand on their moral right to have the plight of the original victims depicted, provide swift and assisted access by television crews to scenes for which the opponent bears responsibility and insist that causes and not just effects be presented. Altogether governments have to realize that in the modern world television is not an inconvenience to be overcome, a hindrance to the conduct of military operations, but an integral partner in the political processes surrounding war – indeed a voice that can be decisive in determining the legitimacy or otherwise of the campaign from the perspective of the general public.

Rescues are among the most dramatic and popular forcible actions taken by government. In the struggle against terrorism it is the terrorists who have acquired an image of daring and adventure, able to manipulate media scheduling and the content of news broadcasts as they see fit. Very recently television cameras have become available that are not only light and totally portable but are also capable of filming steadily and uninterruptedly even under conditions of intensive movement. It may soon be possible for specially-trained cameramen to be actually attached to rescue missions – thereby presenting legitimate acts of state violence in an authentically causative setting.

An imaginative leadership, skilled in public relations and understanding the power of the modern media, can derive considerable benefit from the creative framing of executive action. Choice of an appropriate setting powerfully affects the reception of the intended message. Where better for the pope to condemn nuclear arms than Hiroshima? Where better to condemn Communism than the Berlin Wall?

Setting can relate to action in three ways. It can amplify it: de Gaulle enacted his policy of *grandeur* on a stage that uncannily resembled a royal court. It can provide a contrapuntal accompaniment; as when the pope in Hiroshima presented a message of non-violence. Or it can modify the accompanied performance; Jimmy Carter, envisaging a less grandiose world role for the United States than his predecessors, sought to minimize pomp and circumstance and on foreign trips was content to be received with relative modesty.

Setting can be divided into venue and decor.

VENUE

At the most general level the very geographical location of an event affects its resonance. A banality in Washington may be a sensation in Peking. Not a few international negotiations have been delayed or even cancelled altogether because of a failure to agree on their venue. Why is it that such great significance should be attributed to this?

First, the choice of venue is thought to reflect on the prestige of the host. Whether what is at stake is hosting an international conference, the work of an international agency or the Olympic games, honour is the spur. And, if Hans Morgenthau is right, a policy of prestige is one way 'of demonstrating the power a nation has or thinks it has, or wants other nations to believe it has'. He also notes that a state enjoying preponderance in a particular area will often host conferences or institutions dealing with that area.[3] Sure enough, Islamic conferences are frequently held in Saudi Arabia, meetings of Communist parties take place in Moscow and many of the world's financial institutions are located in New York. Shifts in the location of recurrent international events provide an index of the changing locus of relative power.

The same principle applies with yet greater force to bilateral talks. A long tradition associates the visitor with supplicant. So failure to provide the venue for bilateral negotiations may reflect on one's relative status. One of the mistakes of the appeasers in the 1930s was to override this principle. Anthony Eden opposed – without success – holding talks with Mussolini in Rome rather than London on the grounds that it would be taken as a sign of weakness: 'We should be regarded as running after the Italian Government, and this would increase Mussolini's value in Hitler's eyes ... [it] would be regarded as another surrender to the dictators.'[4]

Not surprisingly, provided the disparity in power and prestige is sufficiently marked (but not *too* marked) the more powerful partner may find it easier to swallow his pride than the weaker. De Gaulle always found it harder to travel to meet American presidents than they did to come to him. On no account could France be seen to be the *demandeur* – the supplicant. De Gaulle even refused to come to Algiers in 1944 to meet the dying Roosevelt.

On the other hand Khrushchev well understood in 1955 that for the reconciliation with Yugoslavia he would have to journey to Belgrade. The prize would be worth the effort. 'We were a big country, a big party', he notes in his memoirs, 'with great authority and prestige in the world communist arena.' In other words, the USSR was big enough to admit its error. Had the Yugoslavs come to Moscow (which was unlikely) 'it would have looked as though they had come begging, with their hats in their hands'. For this very reason Molotov, then Soviet foreign minister, opposed the trip.[5] Let Tito come to Canossa.

The classic compromise, when neither side is prepared to concede the venue, is the choice of a meeting place in some third country. The superpowers have often opted for Geneva. It possesses the advantages of extensive conference facilities and, above all, a location in neutral Switzerland. Helsinki and Vienna have also, for similar reasons, become centres of international activity. In all these cases the host is an incidental beneficiary: he acquires both prestige and a reinforcement of the neutral status on which his security rests. (Former chancellor of Austria Bruno Kreisky was so impressed by these considerations that he was prepared to go to considerable expense to build an international conference centre in Vienna. 'A large army would cost us more and bring us less', was his claim.[6])

Where there is no conveniently neutral venue available another expedient for sidestepping issues of prestige is the choice of a border location or some point equidistant from the two states. Mexican President Portillo first shook hands with the incoming President Reagan on the Friendship Bridge over the Rio Grande. Even more melodramatically, Dr Kaunda of Zambia and South Africa's Botha actually conducted discussions in 1975 in a railway carriage on the Victoria Falls Bridge (between the then Southern Rhodesia and Zambia; representatives of the Smith regime and the black nationalist movement also met). Both these settings were effective in actually symbolizing the equality of status of the two parties rather than merely avoiding a loss of face by one side or the other.

A second factor in the choice of venue is its historical or cultic connotations. In the history of a nation certain sites – of decisive battles, great achievements, the seat of past power and glory (real or imagined) and so on – become infused with memories and associations. At some period in the past they may have been picked out, because of their resonance, as places of celebration or memorial. They then become symbols encapsulating the resounding events surrounding the site.

Thus, Masada, the scene of the last stand and believed collective suicide of Jewish zealots against Rome, has become a place of Zionist pilgrimage – a symbol of national resistance and a preference for self-sacrifice over submission to tyranny. For the Polish nation the monastery of Jasna Gora at Czestochowa, the home of the icon of the Black Madonna, the queen and succour of Poland, performs a like function. For Zimbabweans it is the mysterious ruins of Great

Zimbabwe from which their country takes it name and aspirations of national renaissance.

Places such as these naturally suggest themselves as settings for both domestic ceremony and international theatre. For the culmination of the 1962 visit of Chancellor Adenauer to France, General de Gaulle chose the setting of the cathedral city of Reims. The place of baptism of the Frankish King Clovis in 492 and hence a shrine of the French monarchical tradition, the town was seriously damaged in both world wars. De Gaulle explains his *mise-en-scène* in his memoirs:

> The journey ended at Reims, the symbol of our age–old traditions, but also the scene of many an encounter between the hereditary enemies from the ancient Germanic invasions to the battles of the Marne. In the cathedral, whose wounds were still not fully healed, the first Frenchman and the first German came together to pray that on either side of the Rhine the deeds of friendship might for ever supplant the miseries of war.[7]

Thus a place sacred to French history and the scene of past conflict with Germany was used as an evocative backdrop to an historical act of reconciliation.

Dramatic suggestiveness of a more sinister kind was implicit in the presence of President Brezhnev of the Soviet Union in Prague in April 1981. Faced with the disturbing unrest of the Polish people, the foundation of the Solidarity movement and the disintegration of the power of the Polish Communist party, Brezhnev could hardly have chosen a more pointed forum to remind Eastern Europeans of historical and geopolitical realities. For, only thirteen years before, Soviet tanks, on his orders, had entered the Czechoslovak capital to crush the 'Prague spring' of liberalization. By the mere act of coming to Prague Brezhnev had told his story – without any need for unseemly threats. The USSR would, in the last resort, use force to preserve the unity of the Soviet empire – the so-called 'Brezhnev doctrine' enunciated in 1968 – as well as its own authority.[8]

It can be seen that a fitting choice of venue for political action may not only provide a suitable setting but actually make a statement in its own right. When Pope John Paul II visited Hiroshima in 1981 he ensured the attention and comprehension of a worldwide audience for his appeal for international peace and nuclear disarmament. It was the stuff of drama for the pontiff to stand at the very epicentre of the 1945 explosion and tell the crowd: 'To remember Hiroshima is to abhor nuclear war. To remember Hiroshima is to commit oneself to peace.'[9]

Recognition of the 'memory of Hiroshima' obliged French President Mitterrand to exclude the city from the itinerary of his 1982 official visit to Japan. A visit there would have misrepresented French policy. On the contrary, M. Mitterrand used his presence in the only country to have suffered nuclear attack to reaffirm that France would remain a nuclear power and would not desist from nuclear tests in the South Pacific. Seen in this light Mitterrand's avoidance of Hiroshima was as eloquent of his purpose as John Paul's actual visit there was of his. It discomfited his Japanese hosts, for whom Hiroshima is a national shrine. Otherwise it effectively underlined French realism. The message could not have escaped the attention of Japan's neighbour, the USSR.[10]

Finally, a venue may be insisted on to achieve recognition of its controversial legal status. Most states do not recognize Jerusalem as the capital of Israel and maintain their embassies (if at all) in Tel Aviv. To site them in Jerusalem would imply approval of Israel's claims to that city over those of her Arab rivals. Practical problems arise during the visits of foreign leaders. Since Jerusalem is the seat of Israel's government, it can hardly be ignored. Nor would an Israeli leader receive a guest in Tel Aviv at the expense of Jerusalem. This would then be tacitly acknowledging the problematic status of his own capital. And, as in all cases of violation of sacred symbols, would lead to public uproar.

In the day-to-day conduct of diplomatic business foreign representatives do routinely come up to Jerusalem without fuss (though they decline, in their official status, to visit annexed East Jerusalem). For visiting statesmen inobtrusiveness is less easily ensured. The commonest solution is simply to downplay their presence in the city. Meetings are restricted to anonymous, bureaucratic locations. Famous landmarks, recognizable to an international audience – and Jerusalem is full of them – are avoided. At a press conference given in Jerusalem by President Mitterrand even a sign bearing the name of the city was removed at the insistence of French officials. President Mubarak of Egypt, reversing the symbolism of his predecessor in order to edge back into the Arab fold, declined either to visit Jerusalem or to send his envoys there to negotiate.

Another city long a focus of international contention is Berlin. An almost overwhelming burden of symbolism attaches to it and has long since obscured any substantive issues involved in its status. Until the 1948–49 crisis the city, it is true, was peripheral to Western consciousness. After all, the Russians had got there first. With the blockade Berlin became a test case of Western determination to resist Soviet 'aggression'. Since then it has frequently provided the backdrop for affirmations of the American and wider NATO commitment to the defence of West Germany in general and West Berlin in particular. The 1963 Kennedy visit, on which he made his 'Ich bin ein Berliner' speech, is the best-known of a long series of similar episodes. (Incidentally, the memorable quality of the occasion is clear proof of the dramatic importance of correct staging. Set in Washington, Kennedy's ringing message would surely have fallen flat.)

For the USSR Berlin symbolizes something else entirely. During the course of the Great Patriotic War (Second World War) the Nazi capital was very much the tangible goal of the Russian armies. Its capture represented victory achieved after enormous sacrifice. So the city is a symbol of both the agony and the triumph. The 'taking of the Reichstag' and the 'raising of the flag' on that building are, in countless illustrations, the visual token of the culmination of the war for Soviet citizens.

The Soviet Union, then, sees itself in Berlin by unchallengeable right of conquest. True, Stalin was bound by the Yalta agreements to concede zones of occupation to his allies in Berlin. But these were rights granted for political expediency and not won, in Soviet eyes, on the field of battle. The allied presence, in short, was an anomaly. Once the division of Germany had become an irreversible fact, the absorption of the Western zones, with their vast industrial potential, into the American camp, boded ill. Berlin then came to stand for the threat of the resurgence of the old Reich and revanchist German ambitions.

Only after 1973 was East Berlin accepted by the West as the capital of the (East) German Democratic Republic. Until then the West German view that East Germany was not a legitimate entity held sway. Reunification was seen as the ultimate goal. In opposition to this alarming doctrine East Berlin was held up by the USSR as an embodiment of the irreversible political transformation that had taken place in East Germany and in the status of its capital. Accordingly it was there that Socialist Unity (Communist) party was established (in 1946) and the German Democratic Republic proclaimed (in 1949). The central organs of the East German state were concentrated in Berlin and those few states which maintained diplomatic relations had their embassies there. International congresses, conferences and gatherings – usually of Communist states – were pointedly held in the city.[11]

Finally, Berlin provided the setting, not, of course, by chance, for some of the most serious challenges posed by the Soviet Union to the West in the Cold War. From the Soviet point of view Berlin was the fulcrum where military and moral superiority over the West combined. Ironically, by the very fact of the challenge Berlin was transformed into a symbol for the West and retreat from it became impossible. Benign neglect by the Russians would almost surely have been a more successful approach.

DECOR

By 'decor' is meant the physical appearance and layout of the stage. It includes external architectural features and interior fittings such as furniture and decoration. Decor can be permanent or varied for each individual performance. From the former we can learn about the 'philosophy' and fixed principles of foreign policy of the regime. From the latter we can learn about the objectives it has set itself in a given situation in relation to a particular international actor.

President de Gaulle was acutely conscious of the role played by dramatic effect in government. Given France's objective weakness at key points in his career, he cultivated an extraordinary genius for transmuting the dross of symbolism into the gold coin of power. 'The great leaders', he wrote prophetically long before achieving office, 'have always carefully stage-managed their effects.'[12]

Throughout his public life de Gaulle laid great stress on the influence of the visual image on a mass audience. A photographic section was one of the first units of the Free French forces set up in London in 1940 and quickly set to work to project a politically favourable image of the leader. Photographs of de Gaulle were widely distributed by clandestine means in wartime France to counteract the cult of Marshall Pétain, whose portrait was displayed everywhere.

Of all de Gaulle's wartime portraits the most famous, a masterpiece of artifice, shows the General in soaking oilskins and holding binoculars, apparently on active naval patrol. The image was of the energetic and resolute man of action, on duty with his forces off the coast of France. Actually he was on a brief and quite danger-free trip off the south coast of England . . . again and again de Gaulle showed himself adept at self-presentation.[13]

For the design of the setting of the glittering theatre that was the Fifth Republic de Gaulle called upon the assistance of the distinguished man of letters, André Malraux, who became his minister of culture. Not since Albert Speer's work for the Nazi regime was so much concerted effort expended on the decor of power. The basic theme was simply that of *grandeur*, the key concept in de Gaulle's philosophy of France. 'France cannot be France without grandeur'.

The elegance, splendour and prestige of the Gaullist court were to provide the harmonious backdrop for a 'great national ambition': the economic and social regeneration of France and the establishment, throughout the world, of French power and influence.[14]

According to Philip Cerny, the classical settings of the Fifth Republic were much more than tasteful embellishments. Settings 'create expectations about content'; de Gaulle's primary political aim, the necessary condition for everything else, was to create a symbolic universe for the French which would bind them together in shared endeavour. 'The dramatic function of grandeur, then, was to provide a viable foundation for the development of a consensus which French society had previously lacked ... [de Gaulle] became an expert at the necessary symbolic *bricolage*' (a Levi-Strauss word meaning a symbolic synthesis put together by a myth-maker).[15] Seen in this light Gaullist symbolism was not at all marginal to government but a central means of social control.

The atmosphere surrounding the presidency of the Fifth Republic under de Gaulle (and to a greater or lesser extent ever since) was that of 'a royal court' – Harold Macmillan's phrase.[16] However, the style and panache with which this outrageous anachronism was carried off bore absolutely no resemblance at all to the tawdry and pretentious charade referred to by Ali Mazrui as the 'monarchical tendency'. After all Paris and the sort of settings de Gaulle exploited – the Elysée, the Champs-Elysécs, the Places de la Republique, l'Etoile and la Concorde, Versailles, Fontainebleau and so on – were either the 'real thing' or sufficiently old for this not to matter.

Every official act carried out by de Gaulle was carefully staged in conformity to an overall design. His press conferences, set in plush, chandeliered elegance (and prearranged to avoid surprise questions), proclaimed a lofty dignity and sweeping historical vision. They were the fitting occasion for the announcement of some of his most momentous decisions. (Compare with the easy informality and sparse decor of an American presidential press conference.)

Even something as comparatively routine as the reception of a foreign envoy was meticulously choreographed. The following description is that of a former United States ambassador, Charles E. Bohlen:

> On July 11, a month after the six-day war, I went to see de Gaulle. As in all my calls at the Elysée, the visit was almost liturgical in form. I arrived at the entrance of the Elysée, walked up a flight of stairs, was greeted by an aide, and then taken to an outer office guarded by a military aide. I waited in a chair for a few moments until a buzzer

sounded. The military aide then escorted me into the office, which was furnished like a salon of the eighteenth century, big windows looking out on lawns, flower beds and chestnut trees. De Gaulle came around the table that served as his desk and greeted me in the middle of the room. Then he motioned me to a chair, returned to his desk, sat down, folded his hands over his stomach, and said, 'Monsieur l'ambassadeur. J'écoute.'[17]

The most memorable examples of Gaullist *mise-en-scène* were the splendid state pageants at which an image of renewed French stability, power and prestige could be projected. It was on these occasions that André Malraux came into his own. 'The ideal ceremony,' one observer wrote, 'takes place in a setting replete with esoteric significance and historical memories that are linked, however artificially, with the occasion; it borrows the spirit from tradition, whereas the rites have to be invented. It must inflame the imagination of the masses, and, at the same time, have meaning for officials, prominent citizens, diplomats, and foreign governments; thus it serves as a link between propaganda and political strategy, between the past and the future.'[18]

Just how this worked in practice can be seen from the 1959 visit of President Eisenhower, told in de Gaulle's own words:

> Our conversations began at the Elysée and ended at
> Rambouillet ... Housed in the medieval tower where so many of our kings had stayed, passing through the apartments once occupied by our Valois, our Bourbons, our emperors, our presidents, deliberating in the ancient hall of marble with the French Head of State and his ministers, admiring the grandeur of the ornamental lakes stretched out before their eyes ... our guests were made to feel the nobility behind the geniality, the permanence behind the vicissitudes, of the nation which was their host.[19]

It was, in the discriminating opinion of a veteran diplomat, 'an astonishing production, of which de Gaulle himself was the theatrical promoter'.[20]

It is on the great state occasions that all the elements of political theatre are woven together into a rich tapestry of sites, sounds, colours and actors. Drawing on history and heritage the production powerfully reaffirms national values and the legitimacy of the regime. The total impression rather than any single effect is of the essence. Nevertheless here, as elsewhere, genius is an attention to detail and it is of interest to disentangle some of the interwoven threads and note their contribution to the overall design.

When it comes to staging a diplomatic show the first detail that the planners must consider is the itinerary. Where, when and for how long will the participants meet? What routes will be taken and by what means of transport? How are the media to be handled? Technical factors such as security, prior engagements and problems of traffic control and access obviously play a key role. Still, the scope for creative design remains considerable. And, since purposiveness will be anyway assumed, no prop or item of scenery can be allowed to go by default.

The itinerary of a visit is a very clear expression of its underlying theme and purpose. Contrast two visits by Asian leaders to the United States – one seeking to portray ideological harmony, the other technical cooperation.

In May 1955 President Sukarno of Indonesia was invited on a two-week state visit. His aim was to mobilize American support in his country's conflict with the Netherlands over Dutch New Guinea; the United States sought a valuable ally against Communism. Both sides struck a common chord of anti-colonialism – well calculated to place the autocratic ruler in the most favourable light. Vice-President Nixon likened Sukarno to George Washington and told him: 'You led your people to independence from colonial rule.' In his turn the Indonesian president shrewdly played the role of 'a pilgrim of democracy' at such national shrines as Monticello and Springfield – the homes of Jefferson and Lincoln. Summing up, James Reston correctly remarked that 'a visit like this is essentially a public relations exercise in which Sukarno is compared with George Washington and Thomas Jefferson and the image is created of an attractive leader fighting like our founding fathers for similar goals'.[21]

In complete contrast was the 1979 visit of China's Deng Xiaoping. In his case a note of ideological affinity could obviously not be sounded. Nor was much available in the way of an historical link. Too many of the associations were unhappy ones. The solution was to skirt both dimensions entirely and concentrate on the modernistic and ideologically neutral theme of technological cooperation. In Atlanta Deng was taken to the Ford motor company plant; in Houston he visited the LBJ space center and toured the Hughes tool company – one of the world's largest manufacturers of oil drilling equipment; in Seattle he went round the huge Boeing aircraft complex where China had several jumbo jets on order. Thus both sides could emphasize their own understanding of the relationship. For the Chinese, exploitation of capitalist technical expertise in the task of internal development; for the Americans, the opening up of a vast and profitable market.

The Deng visit was most exceptional in lacking an historical dimension. Normally it would be difficult to plan an itinerary which totally avoided sites of historical interest. Nor would one wish to insulate a guest from one's heritage – invariably a theatrical asset for a host trying to make a political point. Framing a current episode in a wider historical perspective is a classic device for elaborating on its meaning. At its most skilful an itinerary can create a changing symbolic environment of great cumulative impact.

A remarkable example of this was Pope Paul VI's tour of Israel and Jordan in 1964. Every stopping-point along the meticulously planned route was associated with some event in the life of Jesus and possessed symbolic relevance for current concerns of the Church. Nazareth was used as the setting for a pronouncement on family life; Bethlehem for an appeal for Christian unity and inter-faith respect; Jerusalem, with its enormous vibrancy, for among other things, the first meeting of a Roman Catholic pope and an Orthodox patriarch since 1439.

Only the Holy Land could have provided the series of settings from which Paul could proclaim, in word and gesture, the revolutionary changes in Church policy and doctrine that were his aims for the second Vatican council then in progress. From where else could a pontiff signal, at one and the same time, his support for oecumenicism, reconciliation with Judaism, peace among men, a return to Christian first principles and a redefinition of the Vatican's place in the world? This was theatre of the most concentrated kind. And, indeed, the practical consequences of the visit, looking back over two decades, can be seen to have been immense.

Few statesmen can achieve the denseness of symbolism attained by a Paul VI or a de Gaulle. Yet every leader who sees himself as a link in the chain of his people's history is bound to relate, in symbolic action, the present with the past. If he cannot evoke the echoes of a nation or a faith's heritage he should not be its leader.

What of the buildings and structures within which political theatre is enacted? Baldwin Smith has written on the link between politics and architectural symbolism in the Roman and Medieval periods. Beyond its utilitarian and aesthetic rationale, he argues, classical architecture had a 'persistent expressive intent'. It reflected, in symbolic form, spiritual beliefs and values, provided a setting for sacred ritual, and expressed the claims of rulers to 'universal and divine authority'. The ordinary man was dependent upon the arts for his conceptual imagery; symbolism in architecture 'was always most effective at a popular, instinctive, and illiterate level'. Smith then goes on to remark how modern totalitarianism has turned back to this tradition.[22]

Both Fascism and Communism followed the example of Rome. Civic pageantry, so central to these societies, required the construction of great triumphal avenues and places of concourse. Little is left of Hitler's conception of Berlin. But the political philosophy behind Speer's blueprints is clear enough. 'The new Reich', Hitler declared in 1938, 'will create new spaces for itself and its own buildings. I will not move into the old palaces ... we will enshrine the prestige of the Reich in buildings born of our own times.' The Nazi regime would build its own legitimizing structures, just as it had created its own rituals and legends. It would not look to the architecture of a discredited epoch to house the new civilization.

Hitler's schemes were on a grandiose scale. A grand boulevard was to be built which, passing under a huge victory arch, would lead up to a cluster of great buildings of state. Over them would tower a gigantic domed hall, its volume sixteen times that of St Peter's, Rome, to hold between 150,000 and 180,000 people. Nine hundred and fifty-seven feet in the air a German eagle, the globe in its claws, would crown the hall. Looking back, Speer saw in this plan a reflection of Hitler's lust for world domination. In its florid and decadent style were intimations of the Führer's eventual downfall.[23]

Stalin and Mao succeeded where Hitler failed. Both have left an indelible stamp on their respective capitals. The same monumentality found in Hitler's schemes can be seen in such completed edifices as the Moscow hotels *Moskva* and *Ukraina* and Peking's Great Hall of the People. For their construction irreplaceable historical sites were demolished. Curiously, one of Stalin's projects drew Hitler's personal, chagrined attention – plans for an enormous assembly hall (never built) at least 1,300 feet high and surmounted by a statue of Lenin a further 300 feet high.

Nothing could be more eloquent of the Communist dictators' purpose than the immense expanses of Tienanmen and Red Squares, still used as settings for the gigantic parades at which the myths and rituals of Communism are acted out. The human beings who participate in these processions in homage to omnipotent leaderships are reduced to miniscule proportions, dwarfed by vast acres of pavement and bordered by enormous, tasteless buildings.[24]

Communist 'diplomatic' architecture reflects these same megalomaniac tendencies. At the 1938–39 New York World Fair the Soviet pavilion towered above all others (stirring up some indignation in the United States). Vnukovo airport, near Moscow, built about the same time as the port of entry for foreign flights was bigger and more ornate than all contemporary American and European airfields, though it lacked basic technical facilities.

The Soviet authorities have also made great efforts over the years to provide their delegations with accommodation consistent with what they see as their prestige and status. One example is the Soviet embassy in East Berlin, rebuilt in 1951 at a reported cost of $3million, with a 69-foot-high lobby and scores of rooms decorated in precious marble, woods, murals and mosaics. It was used as the venue for a meeting of the 'big four' foreign ministers in 1954. In Warsaw the USSR has a converted palace at its disposal; in Washington the mansion built by railroad sleeping car magnate George Pullman.[25]

Not to be outdone, the People's Republic of China has spent a fortune on its overseas missions. One curious aspect of its clandestine rivalry with the USSR at the end of the 1950s was the Chinese attempt to outshine the Russians in the scale and luxury of their embassy facilities. The Chinese embassy in Kabul, for instance, was not only grander and better cared for than its Soviet counterpart but also had the finest swimming pool in the Afghan capital. In Ulan Bator, the capital of Mongolia, where the two Communist giants were in vigorous competition, China built an enormous embassy including an 800-seat cinema and room to entertain 2,000 people.[26]

The obsession with size seen in Communist architecture reflects several purposes: the wish to overawe onlookers with the sheer, irresistible might of the regime; the need to project an impression of opulence and material success (myths central to Communism but never attained in practice); the theatrical desire to create suitable settings for political action. Communist delegations are larger and their diplomatic receptions on a grander and more generous scale than those of other governments. For this, lavish facilities are needed. Finally, negotiations and diplomatic contacts must take place in surroundings redolent of power and status.

But not only totalitarian regimes lay stress on the symbolic function of architecture. Every government, within the limits of its purse, tries to project a style that matches the purposes of its diplomacy. West Germany, notwithstanding its economic strength, has consciously sought to live down the ignominy of the Nazi period and opted for a foreign policy that avoids independent initiatives and leans upon the collective decisions of international organizations such as NATO and the EEC. Accordingly its embassies are functional and unobtrusive. France, in contrast, seeing itself as a great power with an active foreign policy in the fields of defence, trade and culture, lays stress on an appearance of dignity and refinement – a perfect foil, in effect, for the governing style of the Fifth Republic.

Britain, passing through the discomfort of decolonization, its foreign policy buffeted by pendular changes of government and an absence of national consensus, has undergone an erosion of self-confidence and prestige. National decline has taken substantive form in a loss of export markets, military retreat and a diffident diplomacy. As power has drained away public pressure has increased for a reduction in Britain's overseas representation and the disposal of some of her heritage of diplomatic property.

Under the Conservative governments of the 1950s the ministry of works was still building in the grand style: an expensive embassy in Georgian pastiche was put up in Rio de Janeiro; a large new chancery was added in Cairo; and a fine new embassy on the Tigris was planned for Baghdad.[27] Since then a succession of committees and commissions has sought to trim budgets by economizing on foreign accommodation. The foreign office, perceiving that more modest residences would result in a loss of face and effectiveness, has fought a rearguard action to oppose the trend.[28] It knows that outward appearances do count. If a nation's own self-estimate is a low one, others can hardly be expected to take it more seriously.

The interior decoration of embassies and public buildings is also commissioned with political theatre in mind. Furniture, art, ornaments and other artifacts serve as props in an overall design or as explicit symbols. French diplomatic scene-setting is marked in interior decoration as in architectural form by classic elegance. President Mitterrand has followed his predecessors in a penchant for the decor of the seventeenth and eighteenth centuries, the age of French supremacy in diplomacy, war and the arts. As host to the eighth world economic summit in Versailles (1982) he supplied a splendid setting, lavishly refurbished but also equipped with the most up-to-date communications equipment. It left a glittering impression.[29]

Soviet furnishing echoes, in its massive Victorian ornateness, that obsession with power and status already mentioned (as well as a dislike of innovation in all art). However, a sharp distinction must be drawn here between Soviet and Chinese taste. Alongside the bombastic decor copied from Stalinist Russia must be set the exquisite heritage of Chinese pre-revolutionary civilization. In the early years, and then during the cultural revolution, many priceless treasures were lost for ever. At other times greater efforts at conservation and exhibition were made.

Chou En-lai, that refined product of the mandarin tradition, certainly realized that the Western world's admiration for his country's art could be put to good political use. At the 1954 Geneva conference Chou rented a sumptuous villa which he furnished with the most beautiful ornaments. In these surroundings Chou 'comported himself', in French Prime Minister Mendès-France's phrase, 'like an aristocrat from the world's oldest civilization'. Anthony Eden also admired the elegance of the villa's decor, especially its priceless porcelain. After a difficult conversation with Chou some complimentary remarks about the ornaments helped to thaw the chill between them. Eden 'thought it a mark in [Chou's] favour that he understood the importance which his country's art could have for his visitors'. Chou doubtless thought that Eden's admiration was a way of intimating his genuine interest in progress.[30]

Almost 20 years later, when Richard Nixon and Henry Kissinger came to the Middle Kingdom, like so many awed foreigners before them, they too were struck by the wonder of its art and culture. And like Eden they grasped the message that the proud display of China's past was meant to convey: 'The Chinese wanted to use the majesty of their civilization and the elegance of their manners to leave an impression that nothing was more natural than an increasingly intimate relationship between the world's most avowedly Marxist state and the embodiment of capitalism.'[31]

Furniture has sometimes arisen as an issue in the staging of negotiations. For instance, where the bone of contention is the legitimacy of one of the parties, his very right to sit at the negotiating table is necessarily an object of fierce controversy. By extension the shape of that table acquires acute significance. Should it be square, each negotiator having a side to himself, suggesting equality of status? Or should it be round, blurring any disagreement over identity? Might not separate tables be appropriate?

At the 1959 four-power conference on the German question (held in Geneva) gruelling preliminary negotiations focused on the seating of the West and East German delegates. The 'real issue', as Britain's Harold Macmillan realized, was the recognition of East Germany. The United States, refusing recognition, demanded a square table at which only the four occupying powers would be seated. The USSR wanted a round table with room for all. While they argued, the conference proper had to be delayed, Swiss carpenters awaiting instructions. The ingenious compromise was a round table for the big four – and two adjacent tables for the Germans.[32]

The shape of the table came up again in Paris during the Vietnam 'peace' negotiations. This time the question was the status of the

National Liberation Front, which North Vietnam insisted had the right to one side of the table, South Vietnam naturally disagreeing. 'This was not a trivial issue', Dr Kissinger writes, 'it was of great symbolic significance to our South Vietnamese allies ... Hanoi sought to use the beginning of the negotiations to establish the NLF as an alternative government.'[33]

At the December 1973 opening of the Geneva conference on the Middle East symbolism and substance overlapped in baffling complexity. There were supposed to be seven participants: the two superpowers, the UN and the regional contestants – Syria, Egypt, Jordan and Israel. Gromyko, for the USSR, suggested a seating plan placing the USSR, Egypt and Syria on one side of the UN chairman, the United States, Israel and Jordan on the other. The implication was that Jordan had no place in the Arab fold, while the Soviet Union appeared as the Arabs' true champion. The United States rejected this.

Once this was sorted out a further problem arose: Syria, unwilling to acknowledge Israel in any shape or form, refused to attend. In the hope that she might join the conference at a later time, an empty table was left. But where was this to be situated? Egyptian Foreign Minister Fahmy insisted that it be placed between the Egyptian and Israeli delegations. And at this point Israel threatened to walk out. How ridiculous, her foreign minister expostulated, 'to open a "peace conference" with a visual message that the two countries which were supposed to make peace with each other could not even sit normally around a table? I told [UN Secretary-General] Waldheim that I would refuse to accept a seating arrangement with a hint of Israeli ostracism, as if we were afflicted with leprosy. For one thing the quarantine table would get all the media coverage and the conference would be a public failure before it began.'[34]

In the classic European tradition – still taken for granted – bilateral negotiations take place across a long negotiating table. The set-up is familiar from TV coverage of both industrial and international bargaining. However, there is nothing sacred about this format. Students of proxemics point out that in other cultures quite different seating arrangements may be customary. Indeed in the Far East the division of delegations in the Western manner, seated in symbolic confrontation on opposite sides of a table, is felt to be conducive to neither communication nor compromise. The very format is evocative to the Oriental mind of tension and conflict.

It was, then, an inspired improvization on the part of US Secretary of State William Rogers when, during negotiations with Japan on the future of the Okinawa bases, he suggested abandoning the familiar seating arrangement. The negotiators, he proposed, should sit alongside one another, in alternation, as though for a meal. The Japanese delegates were 'delighted' by the idea. For them, as for the Chinese, the mixed informality of the dining-table is precisely the setting they find most convivial for negotiation and compromise.[35]

Art can be used decoratively, to complement the style of furnishing. Or it can be used as explicit symbolism, indicative of ideological and political purpose. Observers of the Communist scene have long paid careful attention to the images and icons displayed in public and in the media. But even non-Communists use portraiture to make a point. If history is used to legitimize and illustrate present policy, clearly pictures of past episodes and heroes can serve the same purpose. Syria perceives its conflict with Israel as a repetition of the wars against the Crusaders. Even if it takes generations, the Jews will be expelled in the end. President Assad was hinting at this in 1974 when he received Dr Kissinger opposite a painting depicting the conquest of the last Crusader strongholds by Arab armies.[36] Egyptian Foreign Minister Kamal Hassan Ali, in Israel for talks on autonomy for the West Bank, showed his loyalty to the Palestinian cause by holding a press conference at the Egyptian embassy in front of a large picture of the Harem es-Sharif – the sacred Moslem site in annexed East Jerusalem that has become a symbol of Palestinian hopes.[37]

Statuary is another art form readily amenable to political manipulation. Robin Jeffrey, in a study of symbolic politics in the Indian city of Trivandrum, describes how important political debates focused on the apparently marginal issue of which historical figures were to be commemorated in stone. The decision to put up a particular statue reflected the rise or decline of social groups and political movements whose heroes' artistic fate was in fact a metaphor for their own position in the community.

Jeffrey sees statues as serving several political functions: the embodiment of desired values, such as unity, patriotism or virtue; the legitimization of the government in power; or the tangible celebration of the victory of a new political force.[38] Analogous principles can be seen to be at work in international as in domestic politics.

When Salvador Allende came to power in Chile in 1970 one of his first symbolic acts was the unveiling of a statue to Ché Guevara, the Marxist revolutionary and guerrilla fighter killed in Bolivia in 1967. A number of South American militants, including the secretary-general of the Cuban workers federation, were present, giving the ceremony its international complexion. The event did not go unnoticed in Washington. Allende was making a ringing declaration about his accession to power, the ideology of his government and its external aims and orientation.[39]

Where statues can perform a specifically diplomatic role is as symbols of friendship. They are effective because they are both prominent and permanent. In extreme cases they can, it is true, be pulled down. Nevertheless, to erect a statue in a public place in honour of another country is to assert one's pride and faith in the long term viability of the relationship. One has given a hostage to posterity.

Examples of this practice can be found in many countries. The United States has its memorial to Lafayette; China commemorates the revolutionary contribution of the Canadian doctor Norman Bethune. Such statues serve a twofold purpose. The ceremony of their unveiling is in itself a most resounding act of friendship – perhaps the truest compliment one government can pay to another. Second, the site is subsequently available as a fitting setting for those rituals of reaffirmation that states stage on occasion in order to renew their friendships.

REFERENCES AND NOTES

1. Goffman E 1971 *The Presentation of Self in Everyday Life*. Penguin, pp 32–3
2. Edelman M 1964 *The Symbolic Uses of Politics*. University of Illinois Press, Urbana, pp 95, 96
3. Morgenthau H J 1967 *Politics Among Nations*, 4th edn, p 73
4. The Earl of Avon 1962 *Facing the Dictators*. Cassell, p 589
5. Talbott S 1970 *Khrushchev Remembers*. Little, Brown: Boston, p 379; Micunovic V 1980 *Moscow Diary*. Chatto and Windus, p 23
6. Stadler K R 1981 The Kreisky phenomenon, *West European Politics* 4: 14
7. De Gaulle C 1971 *Memoirs of Hope*. Weidenfeld and Nicolson, p 180
8. *Financial Times* 19 Apr. 1981
9. *The Times* 26 Feb. 1981
10. *The Times* 19 Apr. 1982
11. *Great Soviet Encyclopedia* vol 3 1973. Macmillan: New York, pp 198–9
12. Schoenbrun D 1968 *The Three Lives of Charles de Gaulle*. Atheneum: New York, p 97
13. Borge J, Viasnoff N 1979 *De Gaulle et les photographes*. EPA, Paris

14. De Gaulle C 1971 *op. cit.*, p 19
15. Cerney P G 1980 *The Politics of Grandeur*. Cambridge U.P., pp 81, 84, 88
16. *The Times* 25 Feb. 1982
17. Bohlen C E 1973 *Witness to History*. W W Norton: New York, p 510
18. Viannson-Ponté 1964 *The King and his Court*. Houghton-Mifflin: Boston, p 29
19. De Gaulle C 1971 *op. cit.*, pp 210–1
20. Alphand H 1977 *L'étonnement d'être*. Gaillard: Paris, p 315
21. Harsano G 1977 *Recollections of an Indonesian Diplomat in the Sukarno Era*. University of Queensland Press: St Lucia, pp 127–40
22. Smith E B 1956 *Architectural Symbolism of Imperial Rome and the Middle Ages*. Princeton University Press: Princeton, pp 3–9
23. Speer A 1970 *Inside the Third Reich*. Macmillan: New York, pp 210–22, 666
24. Auty R, Obolensky D 1980, *Russian Art and Architecture*. Cambridge University Press, p 169
25. Barghoorn F C 1960 *The Soviet Cultural Offensive*. Princeton University Press: Princeton, p 51; Myaradi N 1952 *My Ringside Seat in Moscow*. Thomas Y Cromwell: New York, p 15; *Life* 22 Feb. 1954
26. Kaznacheev A 1962 *Inside a Soviet Embassy*. J B Lippincott: Philadelphia, p 132; Micunovic V 1980 *op. cit.*, p 354
27. Trevelyan H 1973 *Diplomatic Channels*. Gambit: Boston, pp 33–4
28. *The Times* 6 Apr. 1983
29. *Ibid*. 5 June 1982
30. Mendès-France P 1974 *Choisir*. Stock: Paris, pp 58–9; Eden A 1960 pp 121–2; Randle R S 1969 *Geneva 1954: the settlement of the Indo-Chinese war*, Princeton University Press: Princeton, p 284
31. Kissinger H 1979 *The White House Years*. Little, Brown: Boston, p 1066; Nixon R M 1982 *Leaders*. Sidgwick and Jackson, pp 222–3
32. Macmillan H 1972 *Pointing the Way*. Macmillan, p 63
33. Kissinger H 1979 *op. cit.*, p 52
34. Eban A 1979 *An Autobiography*. Futura, p 547; Kissinger H 1979 *op. cit.*, pp 795–6
35. Meyer A H 1974 *Assignment Tokyo*. Bobbs-Merrill: New York, p 32; Harrison R P 1974 *Beyond Words*. Prentice-Hall: Englewood Cliffs, p 153
36. Kissinger H 1982 *Years of Upheaval*. Weidenfeld and Nicolson, p 779

37. *The Times* 29 Oct. 1981
38. Jeffrey R 1980–1 What the statues tell: the politics of choosing symbols in Trivandrum, *Pacific Affairs* 53: 484–502
39. Kissinger H 1979 *op. cit.*, p 680

Chapter seven

DIPLOMATIC SIGNALLING

No study of nonverbal communication in international politics would be complete without a survey of some of the specialized procedures and devices used within the diplomatic community for the purpose of tacit communication. At issue here are the conventions which a professional group has developed for its own internal use rather than the theatrical effects intended to impress a wider public. They are not, on the whole, visual or histrionic and not, therefore, geared to television. If anything, they are understated. For this reason they serve to transmit precise, unemotive information which will remain within the 'magic circle' of the initiated.

Diplomatic convention is not an esoteric code, though participants in the business of diplomacy would find it difficult to grasp what was happening were they ignorant of its principles. Experienced diplomatic correspondents and other observers are usually well aware of its working and significance. It does tend to puzzle outsiders, as do all in-group semiologies, but its main justification is functional: to enable the transfer of comprehensible information between professionals on those particular subjects that concern them.

There is, of course, a quite detailed lexicon of specialized diplomatic and legal terms at the disposal of the diplomatic community. Nonverbal expedients are in no sense a replacement but rather an accompaniment to this verbal code. In fact there is a close integration of the two codes with much cross-referencing. For instance, the breaking-off of diplomatic relations is an unmistakable gesture of displeasure. But its implementation is unlikely to take place in isolation and will be prefigured and accompanied by appropriate verbal exchanges. Unlike some of the more theatrical gestures seen so far, which can stand on their own, diplomatic practices are part and parcel of an overall system of linguistic and social behaviour.

The special contribution of diplomatic signalling is a three-fold one.

First, it provides the irrevocable reinforcement of action to mere speech – 'acts speak louder than words'. As one former career diplomat points out, 'statements of protest are not taken at their face value. What counts is the strength of the retaliation, which is calculated in the light of the effect on the offended government's interests'.[1]

Second, various nonverbal diplomatic cues can help to indicate the precise weight to be attached to a verbal message. The same message can acquire quite different connotations of urgency, menace or benevolence depending on the manner in which it is conveyed.

Finally, since diplomatic practices are, by definition, bound up with the sheer technical conduct of diplomacy – contact and communication between representatives of different governments – they inevitably reflect mutual attitudes. They can, therefore, be used as fairly discreet, prompt and direct indicators of the current state of diplomatic relations.

DIPLOMATIC RELATIONS

Without diplomatic recognition there can be no exchange of envoys between states and so this act must be considered fundamental to international relationships. According to classic British and American custom (not always adhered to in practice, particularly by the latter), recognition of a new state was not supposed to be a political concession but a straightforward acknowledgement of the facts: a particular community was recognized to have acquired certain defined qualifications of statehood – including the prospect of permanence, independence of any other existing state and the capacity to observe the obligations of international law. In fact, as even Oppenheim grudgingly admits, 'political considerations may from time to time influence the act or refusal of recognition'. Most contemporary writers put it even more strongly.[2]

When a state achieves its independence by a due and orderly transfer of authority from the colonial power, then recognition is likely to be no more than a formal act. In the more controversial circumstances of secession or revolution, however, recognition may well carry profound political implications, including a willingness to support the fledgling entity in its struggle, whether it has achieved 'the prospect of permanence' or not. Moreover, it is also tantamount to an affirmation of hostility against the existing state whose integrity is threatened – a momentous step indeed.

In such a situation the legal form of the act is no more than a convenient medium or metaphor for something eminently political. Take, for instance, Zambia's recognition of Biafra after the latter had seceded from the Nigerian federation. It had very little to do with legal considerations. On the contrary, President Kaunda, who was outspoken in deploring a legalistic approach to world affairs, believed that legal issues were quite beside the point. His decision, rather, stemmed from concern at the suffering consequent on Nigerian prosecution of the war against breakaway Biafra and was meant as a symbolic affirmation of justice and human rights.[3]

The converse of this principle is equally true: the refusal to grant recognition to a new state which does fulfil the established criteria of statehood may signal a wish to encompass its downfall. The declaration of the State of Israel in May 1948 was immediately followed by American and Soviet recognition, although it was far from certain that Israel would survive the simultaneous invasion launched by her Arab neighbours. Recognition, granted for political reasons, was the prelude to diplomatic support and indirect arms aid. Great Britain, in contrast, not at all convinced of Israel's viability and assisting the armies of Egypt, Jordan and Iraq in the war, withheld *de facto* recognition until the beginning of 1949. And the Arab states themselves, even after the conclusion of armistice agreements, declined to accept Israel in any shape or form, denying Israel's right either to sovereignty or existence as a national community.[4]

Distinct from the recognition of statehood is the recognition of the new head or government of an existing state. The purely legal test of recognition has been defined as follows by a British government minister: Whether or not the new government enjoys 'with a reasonable prospect of permanence, the obedience of the mass of the population, and ... effective control of much of the greater part of the territory of the state concerned'.

Here again political considerations intrude on occasion. In an age when subversion and covert intervention in the internal affairs of others have proliferated, domestic rivalries have frequently become arenas for ideological or geostrategic competition between outside powers. Communist states are swift to recognize left-wing seizures of power, while the United States is equally prompt to recognize the successes of its own clients. Recognition may be equivalent in such cases to approval, and acknowledgement of 'paternity' or even a commitment to assistance of one kind or another. Non-recognition, especially of a well-established authority, is a clear sign of disapproval.[5]

After the Ne Win coup in Burma in 1962, for example, the USSR delayed recognition for some time, regarding the new regime 'with mistrust'. The People's Republic of China, seeing it in a friendly light, granted recognition right away.[6] American non-recognition of the MPLA government of Angola (in contrast to most of its NATO allies) was accompanied by a refusal to grant direct or indirect aid or loans, and covert assistance to the regime's enemies. Even Britain declined for years to recognize the governments of the Yemen Democratic Republic, North Vietnam and North Korea, although they were all undeniably in effective control over their respective states.

Under international law a breach of diplomatic relations may occur when 'acute disagreement' has arisen between two states or when one of them is felt by the other to be abusing its diplomatic privileges. Whatever the precise circumstances, a rupture of relations is the severest expression of dissatisfaction that one state can make to another in peace-time. In practical terms a diplomatic rupture is self-defeating, since it precludes negotiation between states just when it is most needed. Nor is it much use as a penalty and may actually entail the initiating state in the greater material loss. Clearly the act is first and foremost a gesture rather than a sanction.[7]

In 1967 the USSR broke off relations with Israel to signal its support for the Arab side in the Six Day war. It then found itself excluded from diplomacy to resolve the conflict for years afterwards. Given Arab attitudes in the dispute, the absence or rupture of relations with Israel has always had wider implications for a state's position in the Middle East. Breaking off relations with Israel has been a low-cost way of obtaining Arab gratitude. It is noteworthy that at the time of the 1956 Sinai campaign the USSR also broke off relations with Israel – but not with France and Britain, also involved in the attack on Egypt.

Apart from its conventional sense of emphatic disapproval, a diplomatic breach has also been used as a gesture of ideological affiliation. This particular interpretation must be placed upon the 1981 decision of Jamaican Prime Minister Edward Seaga to break off relations with Cuba. Seaga had already expelled the Cuban ambassador the year before as part of his rejection and reversal of the pro-Cuban orientation of the previous Labour government. His later move resoundingly identified Jamaica with the more militantly anti-Communist policies of the new Reagan administration in Washington.

Because of the difficulty in restoring relations once they have been broken off states often prefer a less irrevocable way of communicating their disapproval. One stratagem is to recall one's ambassador 'for consultations' or to prolong an existing leave of absence, whilst the embassy as such continues to function normally. This was the policy adopted by the Australian government towards Argentina in 1982 to express its 'deep concern and condemnation of the Falklands invasion'.[8]

Another possibility is a downgrading of relations, the policy of the People's Republic of China towards the Netherlands in 1981. Despite repeated Chinese protests and warnings, the Dutch government had gone ahead and approved licences for the construction and export by a Dutch company of two submarines to Taiwan. The Dutch ambassador was then asked to leave Peking while the Chinese announced the recall of their own ambassador. Relations would be reduced to the level of chargé d'affaires, the situation before 1972.

But there was more to the Chinese move than resentment at the decision of the Netherlands. Observers were in no doubt that a warning was also being given to other countries supplying or intending to supply arms to Taiwan. Prominent among these was the new Reagan administration, which was on record as supporting the resumption of arms supplies to Taiwan, cut off by Jimmy Carter. With typical finesse the Chinese government had chosen 19 January 1981, the day before Reagan's inauguration, to make their move. It was on that day that they informed the Dutch of their intention to reduce the level of bilateral relations – while using the *People's Daily* of the same date to warn unspecified other countries about arms deliveries to Taiwan. Here we see a perfect example of the combination of verbal and nonverbal diplomatic signals.[9]

PROTOCOL

Protocol is basically a body of rules governing diplomatic conduct at official functions and other encounters. It provides a framework within which the representatives of different countries can meet in harmony. After all, the substantive causes for abrasion between states are real enough without adding unnecessary disagreement about the external forms of intercourse. Knowing that issues of procedure and prerogative have been decided in advance on an invariant and impersonal basis, no participant need feel that he is being snubbed or discriminated against.

At one time protocol paid particular attention to social hierarchy. Although precedence is still allotted on the grounds of age, rank and position, privilege in the old-fashioned, aristocratic sense remains in residual form only. In the modern international system protocol is about the efficient organization of human contact and not preferential treatment because of an accident of birth.

Present-day diplomatic reality is, in consequence, somewhat duller than the glittering show of pomp and circumstance that existed before 1914. The world of the contemporary head of protocol is functional, cluttered and homogeneous. States big or small, old or new, will settle for nothing less than equal and reciprocal treatment. The surest way to give offence is to infringe this principle.

States are fiercely sensitive to the slightest aspersion on their status and honour. Jean Serres, the international authority on protocol, wisely warns against 'undue sensitivity', pointing out that 'an anomaly can often be the result of negligence or inexperience'. Only a systematic pattern of discrimination, clearly emanating from a qualified authority, should be grounds for protest.

While doubtless very true, it takes a mature and poised diplomatic service to overlook even occasional and inevitable error. Malice aforethought, as Serres sadly realizes, is invariably assumed. 'A deliberate breach of etiquette is always interpreted as a calculated manifestation of distrust [by] the diplomat who is the victim of it, and never fails to affect the relations between the two governments concerned.' To avoid disaster Serres recommends close adherence to the rules. 'One should not depart from them without good reason.'[10]

When even 'a couple of inches missed off a red carpet' may generate outrage it clearly becomes impractical to manipulate protocol, in its strict sense, to communicate a message. (Hospitality and ceremonial, though, which are less rigidly defined by diplomatic protocol, can take up some of the slack, as we shall see.) Protocol, then, is, on the whole, too rigid and uniform to constitute an effective sign system. Like Jimmy Carter's smile, by being bestowed upon everyone, it ceases to have any meaning.

A grotesque example of the invariance of protocol is provided by the following description, by an American diplomat, of the arrival in Moscow of Hitler's envoy Ribbentrop on 23 August 1939 for the negotiation and signature of the Nazi–Soviet pact. The reader should bear in mind that until this meeting these two powers had been the most virulent enemies, each representing, to the other, the embodiment of evil:

> The Soviet government's about-face after six years of opposition to Hitler caused considerable confusion in the welcoming ceremonies for Ribbentrop. The Russians had no Nazi flags available to greet the German Foreign Minister and had to get them at a studio that had been making anti-Nazi films. These were the only flags with the hakenkreuz on them that could be found in Moscow. A Russian band hastily had to learn the 'Horst Wessel Lied', which it played at the Moscow airport with the 'Internationale'. Surely no more contrasting situation could have been devised.[11]

If breaches of protocol are infrequent, a privileged guest may receive honours beyond his official due. To make an especial impression on a prime minister a twenty-one-gun salute (usually reserved for a head of state) may replace the expected nineteen guns; a foreign minister may be greeted as a head of government; a red carpet may be laid for an unofficial guest. It now seems to be the exception, rather than the rule, for Saudi ministers to be received with the protocol due to their formal rank. They have come to consider supplementary marks of favour as their natural right.

Most pointedly, honours may be bestowed where none are due at all. One established practice is to continue to treat a deposed government *as though it were still in power* as an indication of continuing recognition and even of active support for its restoration. During the Second World War various governments-in-exile, their countries occupied by the Nazis, received full protocol honours in London. Prince Sihanouk, the deposed president of Cambodia, has been treated as a head of state by the government of the People's Republic of China in every way since his fall in 1970. On his arrival in exile in Peking he found that Chou-En-lai had convoked the entire diplomatic corps to greet him. 'You remain the Head of State', he was told. 'The only one. We will never recognize another.' According to Sihanouk, 'There is not a hairsbreadth deviation in the treatment, including respect for protocol, which I have always been accorded during visits as Head of State.'

China's conduct has not just been ritualistic but has implied and been perceived by the diplomatic community to constitute a political commitment to Cambodian resistance against Vietnamese occupation. Both at the United Nations and on the ground in Indo-China this moral support has taken active diplomatic and military form. Even today, over 15 years after Sihanouk's overthrow, the Peking press still publishes material intended to indicate his undiminished status in Chinese eyes.[12]

Another interesting contemporary development has been the acquisition of diplomatic privileges by the Palestine Liberation Organization. Strictly speaking there is no provision in international law for the recognition or otherwise of insurgent movements as such, whatever their merits. Where an insurgent is in control of part of the territory to which he lays claim and conducts his military operations according to the laws of war, he may acquire belligerent rights.[13] But this is quite separate from diplomatic recognition, nor does it apply to the PLO. The PLO has also, so far, avoided setting up a government-in-exile, precisely because it fears widespread non-recognition.

Nevertheless the PLO has acquired an established, if anomalous, position in the international community: it is a member of the Arab League, an observer at the United Nations and other international bodies and has offices throughout the world. Many governments associate themselves with its aims, sometimes out of genuine sympathy, but also for extraneous reasons: as a mark of Third World solidarity, to find favour in the Arab world or to thumb a nose at Israel's patron, the United States.

Since diplomatic recognition in a formal sense is out of the question, the most effective symbolic way of expressing sympathy with the PLO has turned out to be the granting of those protocol privileges that the movement would be entitled to were it a fully-fledged government. Thus the chairman of the PLO, Yassir Arafat, is received with the honours due to a head of state; in many capitals PLO representatives and their offices are entitled to the benefits accorded to other diplomatic missions. Since these gestures are 'in the gift' of the host government they can be made without legal implications. Protocol, usually an accoutrement of statehood, is used here as surrogate for it.

Just as protocol can be manipulated to imply some degree of support for an insurgent, so it can be withheld to suggest a denial of the legitimacy of an incumbent. One example can be found in the unique relationship between the two Germanies. When Willy Brandt, as West German chancellor, first initiated a dialogue with East Germany, he faced an awkward dilemma. On the one hand he wished to arrive at a *modus vivendi* which would relieve tension, promote human and cultural contacts, and pave the way for a new, more stable order in Europe. On the other hand he did not consider that there were two separate states on German soil. In his view the German nation was indivisible and the government in Bonn was the only legitimate authority freely voted into power by German citizens. East Germany was a temporary, artificial entity, set up by the Soviet occupying force.

The East German position, naturally enough, was diametrically opposed. This was that East Germany was a separate state alongside West Germany, enjoying full sovereign rights and prerogatives. Where Willy Brandt would withhold recognition, formal or implied, his East German counterparts were most anxious for such a reinforcement to their legitimacy. If full scale legal recognition were not to be obtained, they would do their best to win, by ruse if necessary, some of the marks implying indirect recognition.

Now the whole question of implied recognition is a difficult one in international law. Whatever common sense might suggest, jurists argue that the representatives of states can communicate unofficially with each other, meet informally, sit together in international forums and even arrive at understandings without this necessarily constituting *de facto* recognition.[14]

When the two Germanies entered into dialogue it was, unquestionably, a momentous political step. West Germany had begun psychologically to adjust itself to the reality of the post-war division of Germany. But acceptance of the existence of East Germany was not synonymous with legal recognition of its sovereign status. After all, not even John Foster Dulles, while ostracizing Communist China in every way possible, had ever denied its physical existence.

Negotiations between the Federal and Democratic Republics rapidly focused on the recognition issue at both the semantic and procedural levels. Chancellor Brandt was to visit East Germany early in 1970 as the first, dramatic sign of human contact. The protocol that was to govern his trip became a central bone of contention. As the tangible, outward sign by which one state honours the sovereign status of another, East Germany strove to insert every possible element of formal protocol into the programme. Equally vigorously, the Bonn government sought to exclude all such pretensions. Brandt's train would stop at the frontier, the East German authorities insisted, where an East German engine and crew would take over. At Erfurt, the venue for the meeting, Brandt would be greeted by Prime Minister Stoph. On these issues the East German view prevailed. With great reluctance, however, the demand was dropped that Brandt inspect an East German honour guard or listen to the playing of the two national anthems.

Ideally, the West Germans would have liked to exclude formal protocol altogether, in order to stress the unofficial nature of the encounter and to avoid any concession on the recognition issue. But as the visitors they were in no position to foresee all the ingenious expedients resorted to by the East Germans to create the impression that their sovereignty was being acknowledged. On arrival at Erfurt station the West German delegation discovered that the platform had been completely covered with an enormous red carpet. On the conference table miniature national flags were displayed. At Buchenwald (the site of a former Nazi concentration camp), where Brandt laid a wreath to the victims of Nazism – to enact the shared suffering and moral responsibility of all Germans – his hosts, thwarted at the station, had a military band play the East German national anthem. It was a tasteless intrusion, but the political opportunity was not to be missed – victims or no victims of Nazism.

CEREMONY AND HOSPITALITY

On the whole though, protocol is not a convenient medium for communication between governments. In its place they tend to turn to those aspects of diplomatic activity not covered by convention in order to signal their view of the state of a relationship. While protocol provides a minimal framework of courtesy and fixed ritual for a visit or meeting it does not define in detail the nature and warmth of surrounding ceremony and hospitality. These then become the appropriate vehicles for conveying the overall political theme of a diplomatic occasion.

Hence the care, Jean Serres explains, which governments invest in the preparation of international gatherings:

> The attention that any two governments give to the visit of a head of state, minister or ambassador, a warship or a delegation, the signing of a treaty or the celebration of an event of common interest, shows the degree to which they desire to manifest the state of their relations, the direction in which they see them progress and the improvements they also wish to bring to them. The solemn ceremonies, the unstinted hospitality, the speech-making, the liberal exchange of gifts and the decorations awarded by some states on such occasions, indicate the degree to which both governments desire to make known their sympathy, their friendship and their collaboration.[15]

The meticulous orchestration of diplomatic 'atmosphere' is both the cause and the result of the latter being looked to as an authoritative guide to official attitudes. Professional diplomats, moreover, trained to be sensitive to changes in the diplomatic climate, are expert at deciphering the evidence about policy contained in ceremony and hospitality. They know that the warmth of a welcome is not the personal whim of the chief of protocol – but the theatrical dimension of high policy. At the same time the involvement of the protocol department of the foreign office in arrangements is an assurance that political attitudes have been ingested by the bureaucracy. It cannot always be assumed that officials and their political masters have identical views.

Ceremony – or its absence – has often been the first straw in the wind of changing attitudes. In June 1967, for instance, on the outbreak of the Six Day war, General de Gaulle curtailed France's 'special relationship' with Israel and came out strongly in support of the Arab states. (His ringing denunciation of Israel for 'firing the first shot' was, in itself, symbolic politics of the first order.) However, the war simply provided a propitious moment for a shift in policy already decided upon; the writing had been on the wall for some time.

Since early in 1966 Abba Eban, the Israeli foreign minister, had drawn the attention of his officials 'to signs of exaggerated French discretion and reserve'. The special cordiality that had previously existed was now absent; visits had tapered off; there was coolness at the United Nations and at the French embassy in Tel Aviv. 'On the other hand, an increasingly ceremonial atmosphere now surrounded French–Arab relations.' All this was a sure index of a shift in French policy. The change of course received presidential sanction later. But the sails had already been set.[16]

Clearly ceremony is more than just showy extravagance. It is understood to signify political purpose and hence, by the familiar reflexive logic of assumed intentionality, must in fact do so. But this is not to say that ceremony may not acquire a psychological weight going beyond its real importance. Norodom Sihanouk, as prime minister of Cambodia, declined an invitation to visit Britain – with some irritation – because it would have been unofficial, that is, without the full-blown panoply of pomp and circumstance he considered his due. Western powers, Sihanouk fulminates in his memoirs, fail to understand the importance of ceremony for the Asian mind: 'Questions of honour for Asians of standing are much more important than those of money.'[17]

Sihanouk's point is well-taken. Unfortunately it threatens to lead, if taken to its logical conclusion, to a situation where the substantive business of diplomacy becomes seriously impeded by unnecessary pageantry. Ceremonial extravaganzas have their place but they are expensive and time consuming.

On occasion, it must be admitted, a harmless ceremonial charade can help to solve a real problem. A drawn-out diplomatic embarrassment resulting from a British refusal to receive an Arab League delegation containing a PLO representative was solved at the procedural level by a compromise which permitted the inclusion of a distinguished Palestinian not formally a member of the PLO. Damage to Anglo-Arab relations caused by the dispute was mended by a colourful ceremonial reception laid on for the delegation. A meeting with Her Majesty the Queen was included as well as a splendid show by the Grenadier Guards. Since the practical purpose of the mission had long since been overtaken by events in the Middle East it was clear that this time the packaging was more important than the content. King Hussein of Jordan, who headed the delegation, commented afterwards that 'the guard of honour welcome by Mrs Thatcher had healed Britain's relations with the Arab world after the disputes which had long delayed it'.[18]

The visit by one leader to another can take various forms. On a *private* visit a leader travels as a private citizen and requires no protocol. A *non-official* visit, laying the emphasis on the conduct of business, minimizes protocol and eschews all public display. An *official working* visit maintains protocol and ceremony within a modest framework, similarly emphasizing the substance rather than form of relations. In none of these cases does the circumscription of ceremony necessarily reflect unfavourably on the state of relations. On the contrary, between close partners it would be ludicrous, not to say impractical, to encumber ongoing contacts with an excess of ceremony.

It is only the official *state* visit that provides full scope for ceremonial display. By its very nature the state visit is a special, and therefore infrequent, event, intended to mark a turning point in relations or reinvigorate a continuing partnership. Designed as a public display of friendship and esteem, the days and nights of a gala visit are filled by formal ceremonies of all kinds, processions and glittering state dinners.

The underlying political message of the occasion is to be found in its itinerary and ceremonial symbolism. Just as a leader creates a symbolic system which reflects and dramatizes his view of his role and mission, so does the state visit conjure up a mythical world in which the nature of a relationship is enacted in the form of pageant and ritual. The dominant theme may be a simple statement of warm friendship. Or it may be more subtle and complex. But the ceremony by which it is conveyed is no more gratuitous than the design of a theatrical performance or religious service.

The artistic motif of the ceremony may draw upon history, legend, religious tradition, folklore or pure fantasy. It is the task of the leader as *metteur-en-scène*, advised by his protocol people, to strike the right note.

For the 1981 visit of President Mitterrand to the United States the theme was 200 years of Franco–American accord. The American War of Independence predictably provided the leading motifs and settings. On his arrival in the old colonial town of Williamsburg, M. Mitterrand was greeted by a redcoat fife and drum band. Among various colourful ceremonies and tableaux was a re-enactment of the surrender of Lord Cornwallis's force to the joint American–French army under George Washington.[19]

Given the record of disagreement and abrasion that has frequently marked relations between the two countries in recent years, the appeal to history was an imaginative way of stressing shared ideals and more permanent sources of alliance. It was also calculated to flatter France by placing the United States in the role of debtor – in opposition to the painful reality for France of American wartime aid and the post-war Marshall plan.

Between the United States and Britain a unique 'special relationship' has evolved of a rather different kind. Grounded in a common culture and language, Anglo–American ties since the Second World War have been marked by a degree of governmental consultation and cooperation in the fields of intelligence and defence rarely found between separate sovereign states. If the Franco–American relationship is celebrated at the level of ideology and historical alliance, the Anglo–American relationship is celebrated at the level of personal and institutional community.

When President Nixon visited London in 1969 he was allowed in on a session of the British cabinet. Business was conducted as though for a routine meeting. It was an unprecedented gesture of the utmost mutual ease and trust. The following year Prime Minister Harold Wilson was invited to attend a Washington 'session' of the National Security Council. President Reagan, for his part, was honoured by being invited to address members of both Houses of Parliament in Westminster Hall, a gesture both of affection and bipartisan support for the NATO alliance.[20]

In all these cases the ceremony reflected a profound familial intimacy, all the more impressive for eschewing the strident pomp that usually marks official visits. The very formality and contrivance of the Mitterrand visit (echoed on the other side of the Atlantic by French receptions for American presidents) hint at the more distant correctness, together with a lack of personal warmth, in French ties with the United States as compared to those of Britain.

In the United States ceremony naturally exploits the Hollywood tradition. Elsewhere more indigenous customs and motifs are drawn upon. In the Middle East a guest is traditionally received with bread and salt or, in the Maghreb, with dates and milk. In the Far East a presentation of fruit and flowers may be used to convey a welcome. In both Eastern and Western Europe one may receive a guest with a bouquet of flowers. Each of these greeting rituals proclaims the acceptability of the visitor and the host's symbolic commitment to his comfort and safety. The ritual also lends colour and warmth to the occasion.

In a similar manner different nations express their esteem and appreciation using different cultural forms. Western European democracies lay strong emphasis in their ceremonial on a sense of order and historical tradition. In contrast, the Communist and Asian nations display a propensity for mass rallies and extravagant spectaculars. The ceremonial of Muslim and Buddhist states invariably reflects their own particular religious vocation.

Newly-independent states may follow local custom or invent their own political ritual. One imaginative and effective ceremony was conceived by the late Kwame Nkrumah of Ghana. Seeking to bring Upper Volta into the union of Ghana, Guinea and Mali – as part of his pan-African vision – Nkrumah invited Voltaic President Maurice Yameogo to Accra in May 1961. Both leaders announced 'the necessity of removing customs barriers and any other barriers which impede contacts between their peoples'. But how was this political concept to be given a tangible form comprehensible to the people?

Nkrumah's inspiration was to have a short stretch of wall specially built at Paga on the two countries' common border. The two presidents met there again a few weeks later and, declaring their determination 'by concrete measures to achieve the total independence and effective unity of Africa', solemnly demolished the wall. Neither legal nor physical barriers were henceforth to 'impede contact between their peoples'.[21] Doubtless inspired by the contemporary episode of the Berlin Wall, Nkrumah had found a striking ceremonial metaphor for a complex and abstract political process.

In relations between the representatives of different cultures care must be taken to avoid well-meaning rituals that do not possess a significance common to both peoples; otherwise serious misunderstanding may result. The *Astoria* affair can serve as an instructive warning:

In October 1938, at a time when relations between Japan and the United States had already seriously deteriorated, Hirosi Saito, the Japanese ambassador in Washington, died. President Roosevelt, at his own initiative and as a mark of respect to the deceased, ordered the United States Navy to convey the ambassador's remains home to Japan. The cruiser *Astoria* was chosen for the mission.

What Roosevelt had not taken into account, as area experts subsequently pointed out, was 'the extraordinary importance' attached by the Japanese 'to the paying of respect to the dead.' Against the background of this cross-cultural confusion Roosevelt's gesture acquired a political significance in Japanese eyes going far beyond the administration's intention. In the context of the time it did, in fact, totally misrepresent the attitude of the United States to Japanese policies and the possibility of an accommodation between the two great Pacific powers. It signalled pliability rather than resolution.

In Japan, however, the move was acclaimed both in the *Diet* (parliament) and in the press. The Japanese foreign minister commended it as a 'graceful act ... an opportunity for the restoration of good relations'. As an expression of their appreciation the Japanese government immediately began to plan an intensive programme of ceremonies and banquets for the cruiser's officers.

The reaction of the State Department to Roosevelt's misleading initiative was one of dismay. In a stream of telegrams to the Tokyo embassy ambassador Grew was instructed to do all he could to play down the episode and avoid excessive publicity. The *Astoria* voyage, he was informed, was intended as 'a gesture of courtesy' but nothing more. 'Any efforts to affix a political or social significance to the visit ... should be discouraged.' By then, though, it was too late to alter the basic character of the mission. The *Astoria*, the Emperor Hirohito later told its captain, 'had performed a great service which was deeply appreciated by himself and the nation'.[22]

A sequel to this unfortunate case of mistaken communication occurred just after the war in 1946. This time the United States government conveyed home the body of the deceased Turkish ambassador in an American warship, the giant USS *Missouri*, in full awareness of its political implications. The United States had never been a Mediterranean power, but in the face of Soviet pressure on Turkey sought a striking demonstration of its new-found interest in the area.

In this the *Missouri* visit was a triumphant success. Moreover the *Missouri*, unlike the *Astoria*, was permitted by the administration to enjoy the full grateful outpouring of Turkish hospitality and ceremonial. Encouraged to believe that the United States would be prepared to exert its power in defence of Turkish independence, the Turkish government made a major effort to magnify the impact of the visit. The result was, as the US ambassador in Ankara reported, 'one of [the] most remarkable demonstrations of friendliness on [the] part of [the] government and people of a foreign country towards US Naval officers and men that has ever occurred in connection with [a] US Naval visit'.[23] In this case, at least, the United States had learnt from its original error.

THE APPROPRIATE CHANNELS

During the course of its long history the diplomatic profession has developed a comprehensive body of terms and procedures for the accurate communication of information. Diplomatic language, though it may appear stilted and anachronistic to the outsider, has been honed down to a fine cutting edge of precision. Every word and phrase in a diplomatic message can be assumed to carry a carefully weighted burden of meaning.

But it is not only the verbal content of a diplomatic communication that has to be considered. Its form and the channel through which it is transmitted also have a significance defined by convention. 'Attention to detail', Satow emphasizes, 'must be scrupulous. Even the size and type of paper to be used, for instance, in different kinds of correspondence are important inasmuch as they lend an appropriate degree of gravity to the matter they contain.'

Satow goes on to describe the various kinds of written communication in use. The most common form is the *note* – a formal personal letter. While different countries have their own practices as to drafting, the important thing from our point of view is that a note is addressed, signed and dated. This implies that the views it contains constitute a permanent record of the official position of the government in question. After it has been communicated in this form it can hardly be denied, since the original note can always be produced. Accordingly a note is a weighty record of policy; its terms are assumed to have been drafted in full seriousness and to deserve serious attention.

Various other forms of communication are in use: The *note verbale* is traditionally an unsigned letter or record of a conversation and less formal than a note. The *memorandum* or *aide mémoire* is usually a detailed statement of facts. The *collective note*, now rare, represents the joint position of its signatories and therefore contains the implicit suggestion of joint action to enforce the views expressed. *Identic notes*, in contrast to the collective note, are messages worded in similar terms by two or more cooperating powers but presented separately. They therefore bear a somewhat less minatory complexion.

One distinction, still of major importance, is that between the formal note and the informal *bout de papier*. This is an unaddressed and unsigned sheet of paper carrying brief notes to be read from or referred to and may be left with one's counterpart as an aid to memory. It is not the record of a conversation. Its status is that of the spoken word and, since it cannot be attributed, is disavowable.[24]

In the context of a negotiation a *bout de papier* – slipped across the table in complete informality – can be a useful medium for conveying a tentative suggestion to break a deadlock. On the one hand, it avoids pushing one's partner into a corner and, on the other hand, can be disclaimed, if rejected, without loss of face. During the Korean armistice negotiations the device was effectively used by both the United States and the USSR.[25]

After the written message in all its forms comes the spoken word. On the whole the oral delivery of a message is thought to indicate a lower level of gravity than its transmission as a formal, written note. The political implications of this distinction vary: one may wish to avoid the definitive irrevocability of a written communication. Or the motive may be to warn – or promise – in a general sense without a precise commitment to action.

A legal point may also be involved. A written *Protest*, that is an official objection by one state to the conduct of another, has a defined legal role. It 'serves the purpose of preservation of rights, or of making it known that the Protesting State does not acquiesce in, and does not recognize, certain acts'.[26] Not to protest may entail, in legal terms, the renunciation of one's rights. Now while a verbal protest conveys the same general sense of dissociation or dissent, it does not carry the same legal implications. One may 'protest' verbally even though one knows the other party to be acting within his rights.

The oral transmission of a message may altogether call its seriousness into question. Just before the Nazi attack on Poland of September 1939 the British ambassador was called to the German foreign office where Minister Ribbentrop read out to him, at breakneck speed, his country's 'final terms' for a 'peaceful settlement' with Poland. However, Ribbentrop declined to leave ambassador Henderson with any form of written document for the benefit of the British government or even against which to check his memory of the conversation. Since there was no way substantive negotiations could be conducted under these conditions it was clear that the proposal was not being made in good faith, but for the record only.

Insincere negotiation reaches its nadir in exchanges conducted through the public media rather than at the negotiating table itself. Directed at influencing public opinion and not at achieving serious compromise, a published proposal will invariably be a proposal that is rapidly rejected. Discretion may not guarantee the successful resolution of talks but is at least a fair index of good faith. Lord Carrington's famous plea to eschew 'megaphone diplomacy' derived from a measure of despair at the seeming inability of the United States and the Soviet Union to avoid scoring propaganda points off one another at the expense of substantive progress in nuclear disarmament talks.

'Going public' is often a sign that serious negotiation is actually at an end and the game is now simply one of achieving propaganda advantage. In a conflict situation it can mean that disagreement is now so profound that one side is ready to condemn the other in public whatever the consequences.

Routine communication between governments is channelled either through one's representative in the host capital or through the representative of the target government in one's own capital. Variations on this basic theme can affect the significance to be attached to the core message.

Clearly communication at the very highest level – between heads of government or their equivalent – is a good sign of the overriding importance of the message in question: it has received and is being brought to the personal attention of the highest possible authority. Unusual in every way, leader-to-leader communication tends to be reserved for only the most intimate relationships or for moments of either grave danger or great cordiality.

The best-known personal correspondence of this kind was that between the Big Three allied leaders, Churchill, Roosevelt and Stalin, during the course of the Second World War. It was instrumental in facilitating mutual understanding and decision-making during a wholly exceptional period.

Churchill had begun writing to Roosevelt even before becoming prime minister in May 1940. His initiative certainly derived from an acute awareness of the central role of the White House in the American system of government and of the vital need to cultivate the personal sympathy of the president of the United States. On his appointment to the highest office Churchill then made use of this invaluable connection to ensure that detailed and authoritative information about the gravity of Britain's position was available to the president of the United States. Anybody reading through the Roosevelt papers is struck by the entirely different level of response to a prime ministerial assessment or request as compared to that of an official or minister, however senior and well-informed. Subsequently the Churchill–Roosevelt channel became such an effective mechanism of prompt allied decision-making in the conduct of the war that Churchill had carefully to guard against its being taken over by the bureaucracy.[27]

Since the time of Roosevelt American presidents have often mistakenly believed that diplomatic logjams could be best cleared by the personal intervention of national leaders. (In fact experience indicates that leaders can best symbolize and set the seal on agreements already reached, while leaving substantive negotiations to the painstaking efforts of the experts.)

When Jimmy Carter first became president in 1977 he decided, at the instigation of National Security Adviser Zbigniew Brzezinski, to write directly to Soviet President Brezhnev. The gesture, he hoped, would convince his Soviet counterpart of American sincerity and enable the establishment of a personal relationship based on mutual trust. Brezhnev's response was cold and rigid. Carter was therefore rapidly disabused of the misapprehension that dealing with the USSR was even remotely similar to working with a friend and ally of the United States. Unfortunately the episode did clearly expose, if only in a minor way, the inexperience and naivity of the American president. Worse, he had been rudely rebuffed, a practice small states can afford but not superpowers whose diplomatic reputation and military credibility depend on an image of strength, seriousness and steadiness.

Another of Carter's diplomatic lapses was the misuse of the 'Hot Line' – a teleprinter link established between Moscow and Washington after the 1962 Cuban missile crisis and intended for use only in situations of the utmost urgency. Contrary to popular belief, the 'Hot Line', until very recently when it was improved, worked more slowly than other available channels of communication. But it did serve to symbolize the two superpowers' grim responsibility for preventing the outbreak of nuclear war by accident or miscalculation. To the Soviet leadership, moreover, it has been seen as a token of equal status with the USA. For the American public it has provided some kind of token reassurance.

There were certainly occasions in his presidency when Carter would have done well to underline his grave disapproval of Soviet conduct by resort to the 'Hot Line'. In neither of the two recorded situations in which he resorted to its use was this so, however. In March 1977 Carter communicated certain disarmament proposals to Brezhnev, using the 'Hot Line' both to personalize the message and to bypass the State Department. In September 1978 he sent a request to the Soviet president to use his influence with Syria to obtain a cease-fire in the Lebanon. In neither case did Carter receive satisfaction. Once again he had invited a rebuff, further contributing to his reputation for inconstancy and weakness. All he had achieved by the inappropriate use of the crisis medium *par excellence* was to pander to Soviet self-importance and emphasize American over-eagerness.[28]

Rarely used, the 'Hot Line' should be reserved only for messages of the very highest import, when it is necessary to stress the gravity and danger of a situation, such as an impending superpower confrontation. For instance, it was called upon by the USSR during the June 1967 Arab–Israel war to warn against American intervention. 'If you want war', Soviet Premier Kosygin threatened, 'you'll have war.' The

United States, for its part, used the 'Hot Line' during the 1971 Indo-Pakistan war in order to restrain India from action in Kashmir. 'It conferred a sense of urgency', Henry Kissinger writes, 'and might speed up Soviet decisions.'[29]

(In parenthesis it is worth remarking that after it was first introduced the 'Hot Line' became something of a status symbol for third parties. De Gaulle wanted one; the Japanese got one as a 'symbolic expression' of 'common concerns'.)[30]

At a level just below that of the summit a government may choose to underline the importance of a communication by insisting on contact at the foreign ministerial level, rather than through officials. The next stage, still indicating weighty importance, is to summon an ambassador to receive a message from the foreign minister in person.

Conversely one may reduce the gravity of a communication by delivering it at a progressively less senior level. When Kuwait was granted independence by Britain in 1961 Her Majesty's Government wished to minimize any possible provocation to Iraq, which had an historical claim to the area. The British ambassador decided to avoid the Iraqi foreign minister, 'since I did not want to suggest that the agreement was of any great importance. We regarded it as merely regularizing the existing position ... I therefore gave the text to the senior official in the Foreign Ministry'.[31]

The principle, common to all hierarchical structures, that the higher the level of attention, the greater the importance imputed to an issue, extends beyond the mere transfer of information to the whole question of diplomatic representation. One state indicates its evaluation of another by the level at which it conducts its relations. Disapproval or coolness is communicated by a lower than expected level of representation. Raising the rank of representation is taken as a mark of respect and esteem.

This tendency can be particularly noted in the composition of visiting delegations. The despatch of a small, low-level delegation to a conference or some kind of national occasion is usually a clear sign of reserve if not an actual snub.

At the Sadat funeral in October 1981 Arab representation was weak, as a demonstration of continuing disapproval for Egypt's policies towards Israel. President Numeiry of Sudan was the only Arab leader present; Sudan, which was closely aligned with Egypt, had been the only Arab League member not to sever relations as a result of Camp David. The dilemma of Arab moderates was well stated by a Jordanian official after his country had sent a middle-ranking delegation to the funeral: 'The murder of Sadat was a tricky business for us', he mused. 'We had to show the conservative states that we were alarmed by the killing of an Arab brother by extremists, but we had to show the radicals that we understood what lay behind it. It's not easy walking a tightrope.'[32]

In contrast to Arab ostracism of Sadat, even in death, was the impressive attendance of Western statesmen. The American contingent alone included the secretary of state and three former presidents. Clearly the United States was concerned to demonstrate in unmistakable terms its continuing endorsement of Sadat's policies and its support for his successor in the face of possible domestic unrest.

With Sadat's departure from the scene Egyptian policy began a slow process of readjustment. President Mubarak's government was particularly concerned to end its isolation in the Arab world. A timely opportunity was presented by the funeral of King Khalid of Saudi Arabia in June 1982. Although the Saudis had expressed their dissociation from Egyptian policy by sending a minor delegation to Cairo a few months before when Sadat was assassinated, President Mubarak, in an unexpected gesture, did come to pay his last respects to the late king – and to pay his condolences to his successor, King Fahd. In diplomatic circles the manoeuvre was widely interpreted as a first public step by Egypt and Saudi Arabia to mending fences with one another.[33]

Not only funerals can be exploited for displays of approval or its reverse. Inaugurations, party conferences (especially in the Communist world), national day celebrations and negotiations all provide similar opportunities.

THE TREATMENT OF ENVOYS

As the heart of relations between states in peacetime is the contact of their representatives and officials. Neither state visits nor funerals make up the bulk of a relationship. It is in the daily round of diplomatic meetings that most business is conducted. To gain a comprehensive picture of nonverbal communication in diplomacy we must look to the treatment meted out by diplomats to each other.

The first appearance of an ambassador on the diplomatic scene occurs when his name is put forward by his government for the approval (*agrément*) of his future host. In most cases the appointment carries no particular significance; the candidate is a professional moving from one career posting to another. Sometimes, though, the opportunity is taken to appoint someone known to be particularly appropriate or acceptable. David Ormsby-Gore (later Lord Harlech), a young family friend of the Kennedys, was a most suitable choice for Britain's Washington embassy during the presidency of John F. Kennedy. The Reagan administration appointed an old personal friend of Prime Minister Papandreou of Greece as ambassador to Athens as a conciliatory gesture. The appointment of a woman ambassador to a government headed by a woman is another thoughtful touch: Austria did it with Golda Meir; Tunisia did it with Mrs Thatcher.

On arrival at his (or her) new post the first task of an ambassador is to present his credentials – the documentary proof of his appointment – to the host government. Until he has done this, tradition deems that he may not enter into the full exercise of his functions. Usually this is a routine matter of a few days. It can be readily grasped how inconvenient and embarrassing it is for a new ambassador to be kept waiting beyond the normal period. Such delay, albeit in a minor way, can be a quite cutting mark of disapproval or disdain.

Britain made use of this ploy implicitly to condemn the declaration of martial law in Poland. When the new Polish ambassador arrived in London in mid-December 1981 he was informed that the Queen would not be available until mid-January to accept his credentials. Buckingham Palace then announced that because of the royal holidays he would not be received until February. Meanwhile the poor man was left cooling his heels, unable to make official calls as an accredited envoy.[34]

Duly accredited and installed, the ambassador can begin work. Among his various duties he will wish to meet and exchange views with officials of the host government in both formal and informal settings. Here again opportunities for preference or discrimination arise.

The most important privilege that an envoy can be granted is simply that of access to the highest echelons of the host government. Since information is the life blood of his profession the closer he is to the sources of policy the better able he will be to perform his role. To be received on a regular basis by the local leadership is a mark of favour indeed.

Where the relationship between two states is one of patron and client the ambassador of the dominant power invariably becomes very much 'at home' in the counsels of the host government. This was the case with the British ambassador to Egypt between the wars and still is the case of the American ambassador to Israel or of Soviet ambassadors in Eastern Europe.

One of the indices of American status in Teheran before the

Khomeini revolution was the privileged position of the US ambassador. Not only was he frequently called into the presence of the Shah and his chief ministers, he was also a prominent figure at official entertainments. William H. Sullivan, the last US ambassador to Iran, describes this intimacy. On one occasion he was invited to a military exercise as the special guest of the Shah. While others sweltered outside, Sullivan had the honour of sharing with the monarch the latter's air-conditioned trailer.

A sure sign of a poor or deteriorating relationship is official neglect of an ambassador. According to Sullivan, even he was 'banished' from the imperial presence for some time after he had dared to raise the awkward subject of the Iranian economy.[35] Following de Gaulle's veto of the British application to join the EEC in January 1963 (which was also a blow aimed at the United States) French ambassador Hervé Alphand, otherwise a well-liked and respected figure, found the White House closed to him. Through his brother Bobby, President Kennedy let M. Alphand know that it would be better if he were not received for the moment.[36]

When relations have been strained in this way an improvement in the atmosphere is likely to be heralded by the reappearance of the envoy on official guest lists or at government briefings.

Official ostracism, and therefore displeasure, can take many forms. Among the first signs of the 'cold peace' – meaning an absence of war without friendly relations – between Egypt and Israel was the social isolation of the Israeli ambassador in Cairo. Neither he nor his wife were invited to official receptions, officials and even private citizens were discouraged from meeting him and he and his staff found great difficulty in renting apartments in Cairo. Though President Sadat had called the exchange of ambassadors between Israel and Egypt a 'living symbol' of peace, an Egyptian foreign ministry document, deliberately leaked to the foreign press, instructed officials to keep their contacts with Israel to a minimum. 'If the Israelis appeared sufficiently isolated', one observer reasoned, 'this would demonstrate that the peace process was an illness the Egyptians had been forced to undergo in order to regain captured territory and to secure valuable American support.'[37]

Other indignities that an ambassador in bad odour may be subjected to are to be kept waiting before an appointment, to be received, if at all, in an ungracious manner, to have his communications left unanswered or, worse still, to have embassy property physically damaged. Unfortunately this latter barbarity, once unthinkable, has become increasingly common. Attacks on embassies, with a greater or lesser degree of government connivance, have occurred in Moscow, Peking, Djakarta, Benghazi and elsewhere.

The ultimate outrage is actual violence against the person of the ambassador. During the cultural revolution in China the British chargé d'affaires and his staff were attacked and beaten by the crowd while army detachments looked on. When the Japanese government announced the impending visit of their prime minister to Peking in 1972, the car of the Japanese ambassador in Taipei (Taiwan's capital) in which he was travelling to the foreign ministry for talks, was pelted with bread by the crowd. It was explained by one 'protester' that bread was used 'to make sure the Japanese official would not be hurt.'[38] These days diplomats must be grateful for even small mercies.

Faced by the possibility of such indignities – which are, one hastens to add, exceptional to the essentially measured tread of routine diplomacy – must the ambassador always remain on the defensive? What means does he possess for expressing displeasure?

Short of submitting an official Protest, or actually being withdrawn from his post, irrevocable acts with serious consequences, the envoy has few sanctions that he can impose on the host government. His principle gambit, in various permutations, is to decline to grace an official occasion with his presence. In diplomacy to celebrate with is to identify with. Absence therefore constitutes a mark of dissociation and hence of dissatisfaction. Sir Humphrey Trevelyan, a British envoy of many years experience, confirms that 'whether to attend an official party or not is a political decision'.[39] Among diplomats there is no such thing as disinterested merry-making.

Disgruntlement can take one of three forms: first, the ambassador can send along a junior official; second, he can stay away altogether; third, he can go and then walk out.

The first alternative is obviously the mildest expression of dissatisfaction. Rarely noticed beyond the circle of the informed, it is a subtle way of downgrading relations, hinting at worse to come, without humiliating the host. This was the measure chosen by Syria after the 1982 Lebanon war to complain about the cautious posture adopted by the USSR. While in Damascus the Syrian government pointedly ignored the second anniversary of their friendship treaty with the Soviet Union, in Moscow the Syrian chargé d'affaires and not the ambassador attended the reception organized to celebrate the event.[40]

The second alternative, the 'diplomatic boycott', has different connotations, depending on circumstances. One may refuse to attend a party for a representative of a state with which one has no diplomatic relations; avoid a function felt to possess unacceptable political implications; or stay away from all official events over a continuous period in order to signal a more generalized disapproval of the host government's policy.

The heyday of the diplomatic boycott was in the mid-1950s when for several months Western governments chose this manner of marking their revulsion at the Soviet invasion of Hungary. There was little else they could do. Nevertheless the gesture seems to have annoyed the Soviet authorities more than one might have expected. Governments are surprisingly sensitive to diplomatic slights.[41]

In recent years the boycott weapon has tended to be used more sparingly. One exception came in 1981 when repeated Soviet violations of Swedish territorial waters culminated in a Soviet submarine running aground close to the Swedish shore. As a consequence, Swedish ambassadors throughout the world boycotted all celebrations of the October revolution and also subsequent Soviet festive occasions. Denmark and Norway joined the boycott as a sign of Nordic solidarity.[42]

Whether to boycott or not can be a difficult and controversial decision whose political implications must be carefully considered. In the above example it was clearly felt by the Danish and Norwegian governments that Soviet misconduct against Sweden could not be permitted to go by default, especially as it was believed that Soviet submarines were equally active in their own waters. On the contrary, to break step, even though Sweden was not a NATO member, would have signalled a dangerous degree of Nordic disunity. Nor would it have been acceptable to public opinion.

On the other hand NATO members, while drawing appropriate strategic conclusions, felt it right to attend Soviet celebrations – notwithstanding such episodes of delinquency as Afghanistan, Poland and now the Swedish incident – for fear of a still further deterioration in Soviet–Western relations. Dialogue had to continue, not as a favour to the USSR, but as an imperative of coexistence in the nuclear age.

The delicacy and importance of the decision whether or not to boycott came to the fore during the Falklands war. On 2 April 1982, the very night of the Argentine invasion, Dr Jeane Kirkpatrick, the US representative at the United Nations, attended an Argentine embassy dinner. The British government expressed their dismay at the gesture. From their perspective it must have looked like a menacing omen that at least some people in the Reagan administration would favour the vital US relationship with South America over that with Britain.

In defence of her action Dr Kirkpatrick put forward the argument that 'a very public gesture by not attending would have damaged our ability to mediate the dispute'.[43] True or not, the controversy is in itself proof that diplomatic decisions of this kind are very far from being trivial matters.

The third variant of the non-attendance gambit is to walk out during the course of a reception. Since this takes place in full view of the other guests, perhaps in the middle of a speech, it is the most theatrical of all the options mentioned so far. It is also a most difficult decision which has to be made by the man on the spot without recourse to his home government (though presumably he will be under general instructions as to his conduct).

Walk-outs tend to occur when something untoward happens during the course of a reception. Either there has been a breach of protocol, an unacceptable guest has been invited, or something unpleasant said. In all three cases the envoy has to consider the possibility that his continued presence, if only to avoid a scene, may be misunderstood to imply a change in the policy of his government.

As far as a breach of protocol is concerned, the ambassador will obviously have to decide whether the lapse is an honest error or a malicious slight on the reputation of his country. Unwarranted sensitivity may expose the ambassador to ridicule.

In the case of the unexpected guest the point of a walk-out is to emphasize one's non-recognition of the country represented. One notorious example occurred in 1954 when the Burmese ambassador in Moscow thought he might contribute to international understanding by organizing a dinner for all the heads of mission without exception. Unfortunately the American ambassador was seated at the same table as the envoy of the People's Republic of China, and the British ambassador with the representative of East Germany. Concerned that their continued presence might be construed as a movement towards recognition, the American and Briton decided to leave. Just as they were on their way out, the Soviet foreign minister arrived. So the gesture acquired overtones of discourtesy not intended. Perhaps the Russian comforted himself with the thought that, as Satow points out, in these matters the question is not personal but political.[44]

REFERENCES AND NOTES

1. Trevelyan H 1973 *Diplomatic Channels*. Gambit: Boston, p 59
2. Lauterpacht H (ed) 1955 *Oppenheim's International Law*, 8th edn, Longman, pp 127-9; Starke J G 1972 *An Introduction to*

International Law. Butterworths, p 140; Kaplan M A, Katzenbach N DeB 1961 *The Political Foundations of International Law*. John Wiley: New York, ch 5

3. Anglin D G 1971 Zambia and the recognition of Biafra, *Africa Review* 1: 102–36
4. Eytan W 1958 *The First Ten Years*. Simon and Schuster: New York, pp 9–16
5. Shaw M 1977 *International Law*. Hodder and Stoughton, ch 6
6. Talbott S (ed) 1974 *Khrushchev Remembers: the last testament*. Little, Brown: Boston, p 322
7. Lauterpacht H 1955 *op. cit.*, p 775; Lord Gore-Booth (ed) 1979 *Satow's Guide to Diplomatic Practice* 5th edn, Longman, pp 187–91
8. *The Times* 7 Apr. 1982
9. *Keesing's Contemporary Archives* 1981 pp 30831–2
10. Wood J R, Serres J 1970 *Diplomatic Ceremonial and Protocol*. Macmillan, pp 19–20
11. Bohlen C E 1973 *Witness to History*. W. W. Norton: New York, p 82
12. Sihanouk N, Burchett W 1973 *My War with the CIA*. Penguin, pp 29, 211; Kissinger H 1979 *The White House Years*. Little, Brown: Boston, p 462; *The Times* 19 Feb. 1982
13. Lauterpacht H 1955 *op. cit.*, p 128
14. Shaw M 1977 *op. cit.*, pp 177–80
15. Wood J R, Serres J 1970 *op. cit.*, p 18
16. Eban A 1979 *An Autobiography*: Futura, pp 339–40
17. Sihanouk N, Burchett W 1973 *op. cit.* pp 204–5
18. *The Times* 19 Mar. 1981, 21 Mar. 1981
19. *Ibid.* 18 Oct. 1981
20. Kissinger H 1979 *op. cit.*, p 417; Wilson H 1971 *The Labour Government 1964–1970*. Weidenfeld and Nicolson and Michael Joseph, pp 621, 755; *The Times* 9 Mar. 1982, 10 Mar. 1982
21. Dei-Anang M 1975 *The Administration of Ghana's Foreign Relations 1957–1965: a personal memoir*. The Athlone Press, p 59; Mazrui A 1977 *Africa's International Relations*. Heinemann, p 51
22. Grew J C 1944 pp 240–3; *Foreign Relations of the United States 1939* vol iv 1955 United States Government Printing Office, Washington, pp 455–62
23. *Foreign Relations of the United States 1946* vol vii 1969. United States Government Printing Office: Washington, pp 822–3
24. Lord Gore-Booth 1979 *op. cit.*, pp 38–54
25. Bohlen C E 1973 *op. cit.*, pp 350, 351

26. Lauterpacht H 1955 *op. cit.*, pp 874–5
27. Churchill W S 1949 *The Second World War* vol ii: *Their finest hour*. Cassell, pp 21–2
28. Brzezinski Z 1983 *Power and Principle*. Weidenfeld and Nicolson, pp 151–6, 161; Carter J 1982 *Keeping Faith*. Bantam Books: New York, p 233
29. Kissinger H 1979 *op. cit.*, p 909
30. *Ibid.* p 334
31. Lord Gore-Booth 1979 *op. cit.*, p 14; Trevelyan H 1970 *The Middle East in Revolution*. Macmillan, pp 185–6
32. *The Times* 13 Nov. 1981
33. *Ibid.* 15 June 1982
34. *Ibid.* 29 Dec. 1981
35. Sullivan W H 1981 *Mission to Iran*. W. W. Norton: New York, pp 71, 84
36. Alphand H 1977 *L'étonnement d'être*. Gaillard: Paris, p 393
37. Legum C (ed) 1981 *Middle East Contemporary Survey* vol iv *1979–80*. Holmes and Meier: New York, pp 114, 115, 116, 558; *Yediot Ahronot* (Hebrew) 26 Mar. 1980, 6 Apr. 1980; Ben-Elissar N 1982 *Parting of the Red Sea* (Hebrew). Edumim and Yediot Ahronot: Jerusalem
38. Lord Gore-Booth 1979 *op. cit.*, pp 192–8; *Japan Times* 18 Sept. 1972
39. Trevelyan H 1973 *op. cit.*, p 125; Lord Gore-Booth 1979 *op. cit.*, p 164
40. Dawisha K 1982 The USSR in the Middle East: superpower in eclipse? *Foreign affairs* **61**: 439–40
41. Bohlen C E 1973 *op. cit.*, p 419
42. *The Times* 6 Nov. 1981, 10 Nov. 1981
43. *Ibid.* 16 Mar. 1982, 11 May 1982
44. Parrott C 1977 *The Serpent and the Nightingale*. Faber and Faber, p 75; Lord Gore-Booth 1979 *op. cit.*, p 453

Chapter eight

SOVIET DIPLOMATIC SIGNALLING

Once the Soviet Union abandoned its initial rejection of 'bourgeois' diplomacy and decided to join the international community in the 1920s, it simultaneously adopted the outward forms of Western diplomatic practice. A regular foreign service was set up, diplomatic relations, where possible, were established, and treaties were concluded in conformity with international law. Soviet failure to maintain its obligations – for instance, the terms under which diplomatic relations were established with both Britain and the United States – the use of its embassies for espionage and propaganda, and the harassment of Western diplomats in Moscow, combined revolutionary militancy with Byzantine traditions.[1] But they were not a rejection of diplomacy as such.

In the conduct of day-to-day relations with other governments the USSR has always insisted upon punctilious attention to established protocol and lavish, almost Victorian ceremonial.[2] We read from the Khrushchev memoirs of his concern, on the eve of a 1959 visit to the United States, 'that we might encounter discrimination, that our reception might not correspond to the requirements of protocol in keeping with our rank'. Later Khrushchev expresses satisfaction at the impressive welcome he received at the airport, 'strictly according to what protocol required for the arrival of a head of government'.

His sensitivity derived in part from the inherent ambiguity of his rank. Although the most powerful man in the Soviet system he was not, unlike his American counterpart, head of state. His main concern, however, was political. 'Here was the USA, the greatest capitalist power in the world, bestowing honor on the representative of our socialist homeland – a country which, in the eyes of capitalist America, had always been unworthy or, worse, infected with some sort of plague.' Yet Khrushchev had given evidence of almost equal trepidation on matters of protocol on a visit to Egypt.[3]

Nor was Khrushchev's successor Brezhnev any less sensitive. Observers concluded that his adoption of the title of president in addition to that of general secretary was primarily for ceremonial reasons, since the office carries no real power in the Soviet system of government. As president he then became entitled by right to the protocol honouring a head of state, thereby bringing himself into line with the president of the United States. Clearly protocol is something of great importance to the Soviet leadership.

In its relations with non-Communist countries the Soviet government fully conforms to convention. Of interest is the special character of Soviet practice in two areas: the protocol governing relations between the USSR and other 'fraternal' Communist states, and some unusual features of Soviet ceremonial and hospitality.

The first point to remark about Soviet protocol (indeed Communist protocol in general) is that it draws a careful distinction between inter-party and inter-government or inter-state relations. Relations between fraternal parties are conducted within a framework of protocol every bit as clearly defined as that found in the classic pages of Satow or Jean Serres. But where inter-state protocol is based on the principle of equality of status, protocol between Communists can be seen to be underpinned by three quite different themes.

First is the maintenance of a hierarchy in which the USSR enjoys the predominant position. Second is the idea that between ideological comrades relations must necessarily be warmer, more intimate and franker than between ideological rivals. Third is the emphasis placed on the outward forms of 'international proletarian solidarity' and revolutionary discipline.

The simultaneous and parallel existence of two sets of protocol obviously entails that in any given situation a decision must be made as to which is to have priority. If the occasion is a meeting of two party or two government delegations, no conflict arises. Where both party and state elements are involved, the problem becomes more complex.

Soviet–Yugoslav relations have persistently exemplified this ambiguity, accentuated by the fact that although the Yugoslav Communist party was run from Moscow in the 1930s, it came to power largely as a result of its own extraordinary efforts and sacrifices against the Nazis – rather than those of the Red Army.

The ambiguity first emerged in 1945 when Tito arrived in Moscow with a Yugoslav *state* delegation to sign a treaty of mutual assistance with the USSR. Since many of the Yugoslav delegates were senior party officials this 'state' designation was both arbitrary and confusing. The logic of the move, according to Milovan Djilas, a member of the Yugoslav delegation, was to emphasize for the benefit of the Soviet Union's Western allies that Yugoslavia was being treated 'as an independent nation' – just as Stalin had assured Churchill it would be in 1944.

Accordingly, at a dinner given in the Kremlin for the visitors, state protocol was maintained in all its formality. The atmosphere was stiff and although all were Communists 'they addressed one another as "Mister" in their toasts' (rather than 'comrade'). But 'apart from the toasts and protocol', Djilas continues, 'we acted like comrades towards one another, that is, like men who were close to one another, men who were in the same movement, with the same aims.'[4]

Afterwards, as Soviet hegemony was extended over Eastern Europe without resistance from the West, the Soviet leadership dropped its insistence on state protocol in contacts with Yugoslav delegations. Then, ironically, with Yugoslavia's expulsion from the Cominform in 1948 – basically over the right to conduct its own affairs as it saw fit – the pendulum swung the other way entirely. Not only was Stalin unwilling to acknowledge Tito's fraternal status, but Tito himself came to insist that Yugoslavia be treated, both in form and substance, with the consideration and respect due to a fully independent state.

After the death of Stalin the Soviet leadership decided to resume friendly relations with Yugoslavia and the old ambiguity reasserted itself. While Tito was not opposed to receiving the benefits of fraternal treatment he would, at the same time, reject any hint of subordinacy in Yugoslavia's position in the world Communist movement.

When Bulganin and Khrushchev came to Belgrade in 1955 to mend fences, Tito insisted that the talks were essentially of a state-to-state nature in order to emphasize Yugoslavia's formal equality of status. The final communiqué was signed by Tito and Prime Minister Bulganin – rather than First Secretary Khrushchev. And, a subtle point of scene-setting, although government buildings in Belgrade were decorated for the occasion, that of the Communist party remained starkly unadorned. This was not a party occasion.

On Tito's return visit to Moscow in May 1956 the ambivalence was maintained at Yugoslav insistence. At Moscow's Kiev station Tito was greeted by Khrushchev, representing the party, Bulganin the government and Voroshilov the state. Lest the point be missed, Tito was accompanied in the open-topped limousine by both Khrushchev and Voroshilov.[5]

The principle that Yugoslav–Soviet relations are based on state-to-state equality rather than inter-party hierarchy has been vigorously maintained by the Yugoslavs ever since. Thus the issue of whether party or state protocol is to have effect has been an indubitable litmus-paper of Yugoslav independence of Soviet hegemony. An apparent question of form has in fact concealed a matter of very real substance.

As far as the USSR is concerned, party relations are considered to have priority over government ties. The Soviet idea of punishment for a recalcitrant party is to downgrade relations from a party to a government level. It was, therefore, an important step along the long road of Sino–Soviet reconciliation when party-to-party contacts resumed, if only symbolically, in March 1985 after a break of almost 20 years. Li Peng, a Chinese deputy prime minister, acted as the bearer of an exchange of greetings between Soviet First Secretary Gorbachev and his Chinese counterpart Hu Yaobang. Moreover Li, when referring to Gorbachev, used the loaded appellation 'comrade'. By further sending fraternal greeting to 'comrades' of the Hungarian Communist party at their congress in Budapest, the Chinese demonstrated that the change of tone was more than a momentary compliment but augured the re-entry of the Chinese party into the mainstream of Communist relationships.[6]

Party-to-party agreements are also viewed by Communist states as being inherently superior to those arrived at between governments. Khrushchev, in his time, was quoted by the Yugoslav ambassador in Moscow as having explained that 'a party agreement [is] more lasting and more binding, because "government" agreements can be concluded with a different ideology and a different social system'. By this he was presumably implying that these latter agreements are more transient because subject to considerations of Leninist expediency, and the dictates of the 'class struggle' – whereas party agreements are not.[7]

Tito's main quarrel with the concept of fraternal relations was that they – then as now – implied the primacy of the Soviet Union. This is fully reflected in Communist protocol. At meetings of the Communist camp the superior status of the USSR is clearly acknowledged. The Soviet delegation heads the published list of guests, enjoys pride of place in treatment and accommodation and comes second only to the host delegation in seating and speaking arrangements.

At the seventh party congress of the East German Socialist Unity party held in East Berlin in 1967 the privileged position of the Soviet Union has been described by one of the Polish participants. Whereas most of the delegates from the sixty Communist parties attending the congress ate in a communal dining room, top Soviet officials took their meals in the separate building where they were lodged.

(Another interesting point of protocol mentioned in the same account was the privilege accorded to the Polish delegation of receiving its food in a private dining room off the main hall. 'According to the strict tenets of Communist party protocol this was both a mark of special favour to the Poles and an indication to the representatives of all the fraternal parties that the Polish visitors were regarded as the second most important delegation after the one from Moscow.' A similar practice has been observed at Communist diplomatic receptions where the guest of honour is entertained together with the party hierarchy in an exclusive salon set apart from the main reception rooms.)[8]

The characteristic deference to the USSR adopted by other Soviet-bloc states has also been noted at international conferences. At the 1954 Geneva conference on Korea and Indo-China, a quite invariable protocol was seen to be in operation. At the afternoon break in the Korean plenary sessions Soviet Foreign Minister Molotov went first to the side of Chinese delegate Chou En-lai, then to the North Korean representative. The order of speechmaking was always (1) North Korea, (2) the People's Republic of China and (3) the USSR, giving Molotov the diplomatically privileged final word. But for the Indo-China sessions the order was (1) the Vietminh, (2) the USSR and (3) the People's Republic of China, conceding to the Chinese primacy in what was recognized as their own sphere of influence. At the close of meetings Molotov always left first, a sign of respect by the others, followed by Chou En-lai and then the North Korean or Vietminh delegate.[9]

What is noteworthy here – though Soviet domestic practice should perhaps prepare one for it – is both the rigidity of the procedure and the insistence that it should be strictly adhered to in important and trivial matters alike. It indicates not only a characteristic Soviet preoccupation with hierarchy but also an apparent fear that the slightest deviation will spell disaster. In the light of the momentous consequences of the Yugoslav and Chinese repudiation of Soviet hegemony there was some substance to this fear.

Given the distinction in the Communist system between government and party, it is natural that careful attention should be paid to the external, protocol signs of the latter's primacy. One index of the priority of fraternal countries is the infinitely superior access to the higher levels of leadership granted to Communist ambassadors as compared to their non-Communist counterparts. A Western ambassador must consider himself extremely fortunate to be granted even a rare call on the Soviet foreign minister. Most encounters simply take place at official functions. Some envoys have gone through their entire posting without meeting other than second-rank foreign ministry officials on a personal face-to-face basis. To be permitted an audience with the party leader himself is quite a rarity. Apart from the war years, the only non-Communist ambassadors Stalin ever received were those of Britain, France, the United States and India – and then for a single meeting only.[10]

Communist ambassadors, as befits the entirely different nature of their relations with the USSR and other fraternal states, are far more likely to see, on a current basis, government ministers and can also expect to have access to politburo members and even the first secretary. We can read in the diaries of Yugoslav ambassador Micunovic of the relative frequency of his meetings with Khrushchev. When relations became strained, one of the Soviet devices for making this known was to restrict contact to routine diplomatic channels.[11]

It goes without saying that the Soviet ambassador to countries of the Soviet bloc has virtually the access of a politburo member to the client leadership. Tito testifies that during the 1948 crisis in Soviet–Yugoslav relations Soviet ambassador Lavrentyev saw him personally almost continuously. One of the features of the relationship bitterly resented by the Yugoslavs was that coordination tended to blur into blatant interference. When Tito complained about this, Stalin refuted him. In the latter's view a Soviet ambassador 'not only has the right but is obliged, from time to time, to discuss with Communists in Yugoslavia all questions which interest him'.

On occasion this 'right' seemed to entail the virtual grant of pro-consular status. Ana Pauker, Romanian foreign minister in the late 1940s, was actually called to the residence of the Soviet ambassador, together with other members of the Romanian politburo, at two o'clock in the morning. And during the 1956 Hungarian and Polish, and 1968 Czech crises the respective Soviet ambassadors acted as autonomous sources of authority.

Admittedly these were exceptional times but they do demonstrate a totally different tone in ambassador–host relations to that customary between independent, sovereign states. Vernon Aspaturian argues that Soviet ambassadors really act in a dual capacity – as envoys and also as official Soviet party representatives.[12]

To the outside world the most characteristic mark of the priority of fraternal relations (as well as the Soviet delight in protocol and ceremonial) is the Soviet treatment of visiting delegations. Except in exceptional circumstances non-Communist visitors are greeted by their government or state counterparts. Party representation is not in evidence. Crowds and other signs of official warmth tend to be strictly rationed.

Quite different is the standard reception for a Communist figure. At the airport to greet him will be his opposite number in the party. If he is the leader he will be met by the first secretary of the party and members of the politburo – the real powers in the land. The guest will receive a comradely embrace and other outstanding marks of 'fraternal good will', in Khrushchev's phrase, such as an impressive military parade, welcoming members of the young pioneers and large and enthusiastic crowds lining the roadside into the capital.

Deviations from this pattern are an ominous sign of tension in relations. In 1963 Khrushchev chose to parade his contempt for the People's Republic of China by missing a welcoming reception for a delegation led by senior politburo member Deng Xiaoping. Instead, Khrushchev was 460 miles away in Kiev to greet, of all people, Belgian Foreign Minister Paul-Henri Spaak. It was an extraordinary demonstration of the peaceful coexistence doctrine, so vigorously opposed by China. Not to be outdone, Mao Tse-tung ensured that he was on hand at Peking airport to greet the returning party, thus setting his seal on the Chinese position and implicitly rebuking Khrushchev's unpardonable lapse.[13]

So deeply ingrained is this important tenet of protocol that when President Brezhnev visited Belgrade in 1976 and was not met at the airport by President Tito Moscow Radio felt itself obliged to explain to its listeners that this was 'in accordance with the protocol customary in Yugoslavia'. (What it did not mention was that on his 1971 visit to Yugoslavia Brezhnev *had* been greeted at the airport by Tito.)[14]

As in some sense an international commonwealth or brotherhood the Communist camp lays great emphasis on spectacular national party congresses customarily attended by fraternal delegates from all over the world. Formally these gatherings are the occasion for such domestic party activities as elections to the central committee and other organs, the announcement of party appointments and the report of the central committee presented by the first secretary. But they also provide an opportunity to demonstrate the solidarity of the Communist movement and air current ideological and practical issues. Behaviour at these meetings is finely regulated by protocol.

Since attendance is a mark of the universalism central to Communist ideology, it is customary for the host party to issue invitations to all fraternal parties, whether in power or not. Not to be invited is rare and a serious slight to the excluded party. It was yet another of the signs of Yugoslav ostracism in the early 1950s, and that of China (and its ally Albania) in the late 1960s and 1970s. In the case of the major parties, to be invited and not to attend constitutes a severe snub to the host party.

A typical gathering was the 25th congress of the Communist party of the Soviet Union held in 1976. In attendance were 103 Communist party delegations. Not represented (besides the schismatic Chinese and Albanian parties) were those of Japan and Egypt. The Japanese party's absence was attributed to its support for the return of the Japanese islands occupied by the USSR since 1945; that of the Egyptian party to the recent deterioration in Soviet–Egyptian relations.[15]

Protocol is specific about the rank of the visiting delegation. According to Gomulka's interpreter Erwin Weit, 'the unwritten protocol governing communist meetings lays down that each delegation must be headed by leaders of equal rank'. Thus in 1959 a disgruntled Khrushchev was obliged to fly straight to the 10th anniversary celebrations of the People's Republic of China, although he had only just returned from an exhausting tour of the United States. Leadership of the delegation by a lesser figure would have been understood as a snub by the Chinese – the last thing the USSR wanted at that particular juncture.[16]

At congresses of the ruling East European Communist parties the custom is to send a high-ranking delegation headed by the party leader. At the congresses of non-ruling or minor Communist parties honour is satisfied by a lower-ranking delegation. For instance, at the 1981 18th congress of the Mongolian People's Revolutionary party, held in Ulan Bator, the major foreign delegations, following the Soviet example, tended to feature a secretary of the party's central committee who would also be a politburo member. Non-ruling Communist parties would not necessarily be present on an occasion such as this, though the absence of a delegation from a ruling party would carry political significance.[17]

One of the recurrent indices of the state of Soviet–Romanian relations is the attendance or absence of the party leader at the head of a visiting delegation. At the end of 1969, following President Nixon's visit to Bucharest (which offended against Soviet bloc protocol in that Nixon had not yet been to Moscow, nor had the visit been 'cleared' with the Soviet authorities), First Secretary Brezhnev cancelled his planned attendance at the impending Romanian party congress. His place was also taken by Soviet Prime Minister Kosygin in 1975 at the 30th anniversary celebrations of Romania's liberation.

To emphasize his own independence within the Warsaw Pact

President Ceauşescu of Romania not only adopted an individual stance on world issues but also kept away from such gatherings as the December 1975 congress of the Polish United Workers' party. However, he did make a point of attending the Soviet party congress two months later. In the first place it was simply too important to miss; second it would be inexpedient to challenge the USSR directly; finally it was advantageous to use Moscow as a platform to put forward his view of 'the right of each party freely to define its own political line', while demonstrably remaining within the Communist fold. The whole point of the exercise was to remain balanced on the tightrope of national independence without crossing over the red lines of Soviet tolerance.

Just such a loss of equilibrium appeared to have occurred in April 1976 with the publication in Bucharest of a book referring to the Romanian character of Bessarabia (now Moldavia), annexed by the USSR after the Second World War. On this occasion Ceauşescu had gone too far. Within a short time a series of ominous Soviet, Hungarian and Bulgarian publications broke surface questioning Romania's own right to certain of its territorial acquisitions.

A clearly shaken Ceauşescu was then obliged to deny that he had any 'territorial or other problems with the Soviet or the other neighbouring socialist countries'. Further assurances seem to have been given at a meeting with Brezhnev at an East Berlin conference of European Communist parties to which the Romanian leader had hastened. Now was not the time for gestures of independence.

After this perilously near loss of balance by Ceauşescu the restoration of Soviet–Romanian relations was marked by a pilgrimage he made to Brezhnev in the Crimea. In the resultant communiqué the need for 'proletarian internationalism' was affirmed – a code phrase meaning Soviet leadership of the world Communist movement. En route to the Crimea Ceauşescu pointedly stopped off at the Moldavian Soviet Socialist Republic. ... Satisfied by Ceauşescu's reassurances, Brezhnev paid a 'visit of friendship' to Romania, for the first time as a guest of the Romanian president, in November 1976.[18]

Party congresses follow a general pattern laid down by convention. Surprises are not welcomed. According to custom, visiting delegations, however small, have the opportunity to address the plenum, conveying their fraternal greetings and expressing the position of their party. Usually these speeches are not controversial. On occasion – during the Sino–Soviet split or the emergence of 'Eurocommunism' in the mid-1970s – they may be very controversial indeed.

In 1981 a critique prepared by the Italian Communist party for the

26th Soviet party congress was considered so unacceptable that the right of address was withdrawn altogether. Apparently no less insolent was the refusal of the Spanish delegation to speak at the same gathering, since this was understood to imply disagreement over intervention in Afghanistan. The next party congress that year was held five weeks later in Prague – and this time the Spaniards were not invited at all.[19]

Controversy is most unwelcome at a party congress since this infringes the basic rule of class discipline and ideological solidarity. The display of unity is all important. However long and boring the speech of a fraternal delegate, his colleagues must always appear to be listening attentively. Erwin Weit explains:

> It is an unwritten rule of protocol that everyone should listen with 'great interest' when the representative of a fraternal party speaks. And when one of the most powerful men in the mighty Soviet Union makes a speech then the audience must be all ears. Only occasionally, when the speaker pronounces a sentence in a loud voice and then pauses briefly, do they know that it is their duty to provide 'stormy applause'.[20]

This norm of congress decorum, intended to demonstrate consensus, has been manipulated to display precisely the reverse. Two practices can be observed: one, to maintain a disapproving silence in the face of others' applause; alternatively, to applaud at the wrong moment.

The silence stratagem has been used by the Soviet Union in its ideological campaigns with Yugoslavia and China. At a 1957 conference of world Communist parties an early indication of troubles to come was the 'glacial silence' with which the Soviet delegation received the speech of Mao Tse-tung.

Chou En-lai was the one to introduce the inappropriate applause stratagem. At a 1964 congress held in Moscow Chou ostentatiously avoided applauding references in the Brezhnev speech urging peaceful coexistence with the West. Instead, photographs show him, with his head resting on one hand, sitting in demonstrative boredom amongst applauding delegates. However, at another passage in the speech praising the Soviet army Chou, in the words of an observer, 'startled onlookers by clapping wildly before even the seasoned cheerleader Mikhail Suslov could get his hands above the table'. And when Defence Minister Malinovsky sharply attacked the United States, Chou broke into delighted acclamation. Presumably on the principle that what China approved could not be right, next day's *Pravda* edited out this part of the speech.[21]

Like other states, the USSR has its national shrines at which it is the custom for visiting delegations to lay commemorative wreaths as a mark of respect. Communist visitors will lay a wreath at the massive Lenin mausoleum in Red Square, while non-Communists usually content themselves with the more recent Tomb of the Unknown Soldier, unless they choose to make a special gesture.

For many years, before the latter memorial was built, some visitors were placed in a dilemma. One Hungarian minister, before the Communist take-over of his country, totally refused to lay a wreath on Lenin's tomb on the grounds that he had no wish to pay homage to the 'father of Communism'. With the Soviet opening to the West under Khrushchev a state rather than party memorial was erected to avoid just such embarrassments.[22]

After Stalin's death and the inclusion of his body in the Lenin mausoleum, another kind of problem arose. Not everybody prepared to honour Lenin's memory would do the same for Stalin. When Tito was in Moscow in 1956 he got round the difficulty by attaching an inscription to his wreath saying it was for Lenin.[23]

With Chou En-lai this apparently trivial issue acquired positively theological proportions. In 1957 Chou dedicated wreaths to both Lenin and Stalin. But his wreath to Stalin read: 'To the great Marxist-Leninist J V Stalin', thereby asserting the Chinese view of Stalin as one of the four great names of Marxism-Leninism. In 1961, at the 22nd congress of the Communist party of the Soviet Union, Khrushchev orchestrated a collective denunciation of Stalinism, much to China's disgust. In retaliation Chou left the assembly with his delegation in order to place a wreath on Stalin's tomb in symbolic defiance of the Soviet position. Whereupon Khrushchev then pushed through a resolution to move Stalin's remains from the Lenin tomb to under the Kremlin wall. To this Chou responded by walking out of the conference altogether.

Now that Stalin had been banished from the central shrine of Communism, what were the Chinese to do? Chou found an answer even to this. Back in Moscow in 1964 (for the last time) Chou first laid a wreath on Lenin's tomb. He then insisted on walking around behind the mausoleum to stand reverently at the as-yet unmarked plot where Stalin now lay.[24]

Punctilious in matters of protocol, the USSR, like many other countries, exploits ceremony and hospitality for making political points. A number of unusual practices are in evidence.

The most characteristic of these is the adoption of an inflexible hierarchy in its treatment of foreign guests. Commenting, as have many observers, on the rank-consciousness of Soviet society,

Mohamed Heikal, a frequent visitor to the USSR, has argued that 'the Russians grade countries, as they grade party members, because it is alien to their nature to do otherwise'.[25]

This system of grading is based on three factors: the ideological complexion of the regime in question; its power and importance; and the Soviet wish to make a political impression. Heikal discerns four separate categories of treatment.

'Five-star' treatment is reserved for the leaders of ruling Communist parties and major Third World leaders. The latter are few and, in recent years, increasingly far between. They have included such giants of the 1950s and 1960s as Nasser, Nehru and Sukarno. About the only contemporary figure who approached this stature was Mrs Indira Gandhi.

The five-star welcome is truly sumptuous. A flight of Migs escorts in the arriving plane (more often than not a special Soviet jet placed at the disposal of the guest). Present at the airport is the entire party leadership and diplomatic corps. Massed bands, a large honour guard and twenty-one-gun salute fulfil protocol requirements in more than ample measure. Characteristically, several hundred pioneer children are on hand with flowers to brighten the formality. On the entry into Moscow the guest, escorted in an open limousine by the first secretary, is applauded by enormous crowds waving miniature flags of both states. Rose petals may be flung in front of the cavalcade and native folk music played over loudspeakers. Welcoming banners, giant portraits of the visitor and crossed national flags adorn the route.

In Moscow itself and on tours around the USSR the guest can expect to be entertained with unrivalled luxury – planes and holiday homes put at his disposal. And there is no doubt that if such treatment is intended to trumpet Soviet esteem and to build up the status of the recipient, it works. Together with diplomatic support, economic and military aid, and the development of cultural relations, such receptions have been an effective means for the expansion of Soviet influence in the Third World.[26]

The role of the crowd in Communist practice is worth pausing over. While protocol and ceremony are doubtless impressive, it is the presence and behaviour of a mass audience that makes all the difference for a guest. Communist crowd orchestration is based on a shrewd insight into leadership psychology. But the deeper significance of the crowd is ideological: its presence is a manifestation of the popular will supposed to underpin Communist power. An enthusiastic popular welcome is 'proof' that relations between host and guest go beyond the pragmatic and express true 'fraternity between peoples'.

Nothing is left to chance. We know from Communist and other sources that 'popular enthusiasm' is highly organized, from the exact number of workers and children transported in from factories and schools, to the warmth of their applause and the slogans they will chant (led by an inconspicuous cheerleader reading from a card), and even to the size and number of flags to be waved.[27]

Western leaders can never hope to be honoured with a five-star welcome, whatever their power and importance in the Soviet scheme of things. Since they are neither fraternal nor nonaligned they are ideologically disqualified. However, only one or two degrees less rapturous than the five-star welcome was the four-star show put on for General de Gaulle in 1966 – the only one of its kind accorded a Western dignitary.

Absent from the reception was the ultimate accolade of a personal welcome by party leader Brezhnev. Nor were there such sycophantic embellishments as folk music, pioneer children, giant portraits or a flower-strewn progress. Nevertheless there were several unprecedented features, including a seven-jet flypast, a thousand workers assembled at the airport to shout 'Vive la France' and an estimated 800,000 people along the route into Moscow.

It was undoubtedly intended as a unique homage to the only remaining wartime leader (Tito excepted), a statesman of world stature and moreover one who had just withdrawn the last French forces from NATO. In French eyes it was 'a brilliant reception in every way. The authorities had sought to multiply their marks of favour and to introduce innovations into the display in order to underline the exceptional character of the visit'.[28]

The standard three-star welcome for a Western leader entails strict adherence to protocol, is restricted to government and state officials as appropriate, and avoids extravagant manifestations of acclaim. Points of detail may be calibrated to project an appropriate message of approval and status: the size and enthusiasm of the crowd on the way into Moscow can vary, as may the decorations. After a more or less successful visit bonus points can be awarded or subtracted. Harold Wilson noticed on the way out to the airport after one visit that 'every lamp standard bore the British and Soviet flags, and the streets were lined with thousands of flag-waving "factory workers who had come to cheer", which always spontaneously happens when the Kremlin is pleased with the way the visit has gone'.[29]

The two-star welcome, while following protocol with typical punctiliousness, avoids any display of warmth. No crowds are present to symbolize popular consent. The visit is bared back to its strictly business-like essentials. This was the reception awaiting President Nixon in Shanghai in 1972. There were no formal diplomatic relations; the visit followed years of hostility; in Chinese eyes Nixon was a supplicant to the Middle Kingdom, bearing tribute as had China's vassals in times past.

A lone US flag flew in front of the airport terminal. An honour guard was present and a red carpet had been laid, as befitted a head of state. But apart from Chou En-lai and forty-three officials, no one else was present. There were no crowds. In Peking itself Tienanmen square lay 'vast in its emptiness'. The greeting, in Kissinger's words, was 'stark to the point of necessity'. It 'reflected the truth that only the most dire necessity could bring together countries whose other relations warranted none of the joyful ceremony usually associated with state visits'.[30]

Fortunately, perhaps, for guests subjected to such minimal celebration, the welcome is certainly not the only opportunity Communist states (which all follow Soviet practice) have to express their esteem. There are all sorts of ways open to a host to make his guest feel more – or less – at home, and the Communists know and manipulate most of them. 'Hospitality', a former British ambassador in Moscow has no doubt, is used 'as a political instrument'.[31]

Certainly the Soviet Union is the last country one could accuse of being niggardly in its entertaining. On the contrary, it has always astonished its guests with the Oriental scale and opulence of its official feasting. 'So it must be', one admiring guest was told by the Soviet ambassadress. 'Only the finest is worthy of a great nation.'[32]

Apart from this obvious prestige dimension, hospitality is regulated with subtlety as an index of progress in the course of diplomatic negotiations. During the Moscow talks towards the Soviet–West German treaty of 1970, hospitality was repeatedly used by the Soviet authorities at moments of deadlock to induce a sense of optimism and hint at the possibility of flexibility in their negotiating posture. At one point, in February, 1970, West German Foreign Minister Walter Scheel landed at Moscow for a one-hour stopover en route to India. Waiting to greet him was Soviet Deputy Foreign Minister Semyonov who insisted on entertaining him to a late supper of caviar, roast chicken and ice cream. Toasts were drunk to the two countries' relations and as the atmosphere grew animated Semyonov held his glass aloft and declared: 'We shall continue to talk until we reach an agreement.'

A few weeks later chief German negotiator Egon Bahr returned to Moscow armed with new instructions for a fresh round of talks. The improvement in atmosphere was palpable. At the airport a more impressive welcoming delegation than ever before awaited him. And when he arrived at his hotel Bahr discovered that he had been moved from cramped quarters on the twenty-ninth floor to a plush suite on the third.[33]

Such calibration of hospitality works both ways. Besides encouraging or auguring a breakthrough it can also be used to warn of a breakdown. One Hungarian negotiator discovered that after being lavishly cultivated, his rejection of the Soviet position ushered in a period of frigidity: 'From then on we were given the cold shoulder. ... Having once been given almost too much attention, we were now being totally ignored. No invitations to the opera, the ballet, to state receptions or long sight-seeing tours arrived. ... '[34]

Anthropologists have often pointed out the social and cultic significance of the shared meal. To break bread with a stranger is a powerful symbol of peaceful intentions and mutual trust. Presumably this is also the underlying meaning of the diplomatic feast, the origins of which are lost in antiquity. When former enemies come together in this way they are in effect enacting a 'rite of passage' from one status to another. During the secret Paris talks on ending the Vietnam war American and North Vietnamese negotiators symbolized their gradual diplomatic convergence by a changing social relationship.

At the outset of the talks, little food was served. As the negotiations got under way the North Vietnamese laid out modest snacks and there was some social conversation during breaks. During the course of 1972 the two sides moved closer to agreement. On 1 August, as talks appeared to approach fruition, more generous refreshments were served by the Vietnamese hosts, including fruit and biscuits. On 14 August wine and rice cakes made their auspicious appearance. Following the hiatus of the American presidential election, an agreement was finally concluded. For the first time, on 13 January 1973, the two delegations actually ate a meal together as a group; before this, meals had always been taken in separate dining rooms. Now Vietnamese and Americans sat alternately around the one dining table and toasted their future peace and friendship.[35]

Ironically, the Paris peace was, as we now know, the prelude to a serious deterioration in relations between Peking and Hanoi. As long as the war had lasted the North Vietnamese had scrupulously avoided taking sides between the USSR and the People's Republic of China. They needed all the aid they could get. But with the withdrawal of

American forces the imperative need for such caution was removed and a number of serious differences emerged, culminating in the China–Vietnam border war of February–March 1979.

Among the early signs that indicated to observant analysts that something had gone badly wrong was a breakdown in *social* relations between Chinese and Vietnamese diplomats. It proved to be an unerring index of a profound political dislocation. In September 1975 a Vietnamese delegation visited Peking. At first all seemed to be going well. The delegation was received by Mao Tse-tung. Then in the middle of unfinished business, the Vietnamese got up and left. There was no joint communiqué, which was a break with normal diplomatic practice suggesting an inability to agree. But worst of all was the Vietnamese failure to give the customary return banquet for their hosts – knowing what notoriously high store the Chinese set by diplomatic feasting. If the two sides could no longer eat together 'in peace', could they continue to live together in peace?[36]

All Communist states can be observed, in gastronomic as in other aspects of diplomatic choreography, to follow Soviet precedent. The USSR was first on the scene and was naturally looked to by its satellites as a paradigm. One quite distinctive Soviet practice, though not copied by the others, is the diplomatic picnic.

Under Stalin it was quite inconceivable that Soviet and Western diplomats could relax together or even meet in an informal setting. Privileged fraternal colleagues could hope to join the Soviet dictator at his *dacha* outside Moscow, carousing until the small hours, but nobody else.

Once the Cold War had ended, the Soviet leadership looked around for a striking way to demonstrate the new atmosphere of detente and their own far greater accessibility. They began turning up at Moscow embassy receptions. But their most ingenious expedient was to throw a splendid garden party at a *dacha* in the countryside outside Moscow for foreign diplomats and their families and foreign journalists.

It was a remarkable occasion, doubly astonishing for those who remembered Stalin's last paranoid years and the intolerable atmosphere of segregation and suspicion that had surrounded envoys in the Soviet capital. Suddenly all was sweetness and light. There was rowing on the lake and fishing. At a sumptuous two-hour lunch Soviet Prime Minister Bulganin toasted his guests and told them how glad he was that the end of the Cold War made such a function possible. As intended, the Western press was full of stories and photographs to prove Bulganin's point. *Life* magazine had a lively account of the proceedings:

Naturally there was champagne and vodka for all. At a Russian party there always is. But it was the gregarious behavior of the hosts that made the picnic memorable. Bulganin helped Avis Bohlen, daughter of the US ambassador, catch fish, played with the Italian ambassador's son, visited the deer preserve and praised the journalists ('we have become good friends'). Marshals Zhukov and Konev showed guests where to pick berries ... Towards sundown there was a song fest. ... [37]

Since 1955 the Soviet leadership has reserved the picnic stratagem for only its most favoured guests. (The hunting party is a de luxe version of the same idea, by the way.) Laureates have included Paul-Henri Spaak, Henry Kissinger and Willy Brandt. For the two latter statesmen the hospitality was basically a prize for business well done. [38] In the case of Spaak the political message was more subtle and is worth recounting in greater detail.

Spaak's visit to the Soviet Union took place in July 1963, in other words not long after the Berlin and Cuba crises had convulsed East-West relations. The Belgian foreign minister was taken to Khrushchev's *dacha* in the depths of the Ukrainian countryside where the two men spent an idyllic day while discussing world issues. They ate, reminisced, strolled through the woods and then went for a trip down the Dnieper joined by Khrushchev's grandchildren (Khrushchev frequently made use of his family to soften his image). As the sun set all joined in a sing-along.

Following the visit Spaak reported back to his NATO colleagues. The conclusion to be drawn from the talk in the woods was clear: 'we had entered a phase when both the two great camps facing one another were quite happy to maintain the status quo, and this confirmed us in our decision to leave well alone'. [39]

On a number of occasions throughout this book it has been noted how Communist states manipulate the presence or absence of the party leadership to make a political point. To some extent all governments control access to their highest authority as a sign of esteem or displeasure. In Communist regimes this behaviour acquires even added prominence. Since there are no electoral rallies, parliaments with real power or regular press conferences, appearances by the leadership are strictly limited. Nor is the party's first secretary – the pinnacle of the pyramid – obliged by protocol to meet visiting government visitors from outside the Communist world.

There have been periods in Soviet and Chinese diplomacy when months have passed without the leader showing himself in public. Only on a handful of regular occasions throughout the year – May Day, meetings of the party central committee and so on – is an appearance positively expected. Such displays as there are are carefully staged. If we add to this picture the practice of the personality cult – which seeks to depict the leader as a larger than life paragon of wisdom and virtue – it is easy to see why leadership appearances acquire such political significance.

Whether or not a visitor who is not a fraternal leader is received by the party leadership involves a decision at the highest level. We specifically learn from Khrushchev's memoirs that he never received foreign guests without first consulting his comrades.[40] To be received by the leader, then, is a particular accolade intended either to legitimize or celebrate a relationship. It will hardly ever be arranged in advance but will be 'awarded' during the course of a visit or negotiation as a mark of approval.

At the signing in the Kremlin of the Soviet–West German treaty of 1970 by Chancellor Brandt and Prime Minister Kosygin, Brezhnev and his politburo colleagues turned up unannounced to place the full weight of the party behind the reconciliation. In films of the occasion Brezhnev can be seen hovering in the background and leaning benevolently over the two signatories. Characteristically, at the signing of the Polish–West German treaty a few months later, party secretary Gomulka also turned up 'unexpectedly'.[41] The East European allies of the USSR can be observed to imitate the example of their senior partner in the most minute details of choreography.

An appearance by the party leader is not only a compliment for non-Communist visitors but is also an eagerly sought-after privilege within the 'camp'. When Brezhnev invited Gomulka to travel with him on his special train, the East German leader Willi Stoph is reported to have been furious at this sign of discrimination. Having worked to undermine Gomulka's position at the just concluded East German party conference (of April 1967) Stoph clearly understood that Gomulka had been awarded a vote of confidence. The fact that the German was *not* invited could be seen as a rebuke.[42]

Under Nikita Khrushchev the embassy reception became a major tool of diplomatic communication. Just which members of the presidium (politburo) would attend was a major point of speculation by the diplomatic community. According to a British diplomat three factors determined attendance: 'the importance of the country in Soviet eyes, the degree of friendship existing with that country (this takes second place) and, in addition, the attitude the government of the country has taken towards any receptions which the Soviet Ambassador has held there.'[43]

Both in the case of Britain and the United States Soviet friendliness began in 1954 when members of the presidium first turned up at national day receptions, peaked in 1955 and 1956 before and after the Geneva summit and then fell off in 1957 and 1958 after the Suez and Hungarian crises. By 1959 only the odd senior party figure was attending.[44]

The Chinese and Yugoslavs were subjected to a similarly regulated campaign of official approval on the part of the USSR during this period. With hindsight we can see that yet another early straw in the wind of Sino–Soviet discord was the failure of the top Soviet leadership to attend the Chinese national day celebrations of September 1956. The reception at the Moscow embassy itself was attended by a large number of Soviet citizens – but this only served to emphasize the absence of key party figures. Moreover the Chinese ambassador Liu Siao was significantly away in Peking.[45]

The 'body language' of Soviet leaders at parties like this was also a focus of attention at this time. It became possible, by observing Khrushchev's behaviour from one reception to the next, to plot the development of Soviet foreign relations. Here he would ostentatiously sit down with the US ambassador; there he would cross the room to take the Chinese ambassador by the arm and lead him to the top table. Observers learned to take careful note of Khrushchev's interlocutors, the length of conversations and the range of expressions that flitted across the old trooper's face. Not everybody approved of these public performances, often played out not just for the benefit of the diplomatic corps, but for foreign journalists as well. 'Such scenes', one Communist envoy remarked, 'organized by the Russians in public places when they think it can benefit them, are becoming more unpleasant every time they occur.'[46]

Unfortunately for us, Khrushchev's pantomimes were rejected by his successors. The Brezhnev style was deliberately different: formal, dignified, removed from the public view. Members of the politburo ceased to enliven embassy receptions (though they might well attend a closed lunch or banquet as a gesture of favour). Access to the top grew very much more restricted. Significantly, at the annual Kremlin reception for the diplomatic corps ambassadors would now be separated from their hosts by a table of caviar and refreshments dividing the hall into two. From Brezhnev on Soviet leaders began to behave in a manner they believed more befitting a superpower.[47]

REFERENCES AND NOTES

1. Thayer C W 1960 *Diplomat*. Michael Joseph, ch 1

2. Kohler F D 1970 *Understanding the Russians.* Harper and Row: New York, p 253

3. Talbott S (ed) 1974 *Khrushchev Remembers: the last testament.* Little, Brown: Boston, pp 370, 376, 377; Heikal M H 1978 *The Sphinx and the Commissar.* Harper and Row: New York, p 135

4. Djilas M 1963 *Conversations with Stalin.* Penguin, pp 82–3

5. Micunovic V 1980 *Moscow Diary.* Chatto and Windus, pp 57, 58; *Le Monde* 17 Aug. 1977

6. *The Economist* 13 Apr. 1985

7. Micunovic V 1980 *op. cit.*, p 288

8. Weit E 1973 *Eyewitness.* André Deutsch, p 114; Dewhurst C H 1954 *Close Contact.* Houghton-Mifflin: Boston, p 148

9. *Life* 28 June 1954

10. *The Daily Telegraph* 20 Mar. 1981; Kelly D 1952 *The Ruling Few.* Hollis and Carter, pp 430–1

11. Micunovic V 1980 *op. cit.*, pp 26, 32, 151

12. Dedijer V 1953 *Tito Speaks.* Weidenfeld and Nicolson, pp 315, 318, 339, 340, 341; Aspaturian V V 1971 *Process and Power in Soviet Foreign Policy.* Little, Brown: Boston, pp 658–9

13. *Life* 19 July 1963

14. *Keesing's Contemporary Archives 1977*, p 28171; *New York Times* 23 Sept. 1971

15. *Keesing's Contemporary Archives 1976*, p 27733

16. Weit E 1973 *op. cit.*, pp 49–50; Talbott S (ed) 1974 *op. cit.*, p 307

17. *Keesing's Contemporary Archives 1981* p 31025

18. *Ibid.* 1975 p 26888; *Ibid.* 1976 pp 27642, 27736, 27785; *Ibid.* 1977, p 28163

19. *Ibid.* 1981 pp 30837, 30909

20. Weit E 1973 *op. cit.*, p 207

21. Micunovic V 1980 *op. cit.*, pp 197, 284, 322–3; *Life* 20 Nov. 1964

22. Nyaradi N 1952 *My Ringside Seat in Moscow.* Thomas Y Cromwell: New York, p 87

23. Micunovic V 1980 *op. cit.*, p 296

24. *Ibid.* p 199; Hsu Kai-yu 1969 *Chou En-lai: China's grey eminence.* Doubleday Anchor: New York, p 175; *Life* 20 Nov. 1964

25. Heikal M H 1978 *op. cit.*, p 25

26. *Ibid.* pp 89, 143; Harsano G 1977 *Recollections of an Indonesian Diplomat in the Sukarno Era.* University of Queensland Press: St Lucia, pp 141–65; Menon K P S 1963 *The Flying Troika.* Oxford University Press, pp 111–6

27. Weit E 1973 *op. cit.*, pp 42–3; Haines J 1977 *The Politics of Power.* Jonathan Cape, p 84; Trevelyan H 1973 *Diplomatic Channels.*

Gambit: Boston, p 128; Bohlen C E 1973 *Witness to History*. W. W. Norton: New York, p 403

28. *Time* 1 July 1966; *Newsweek* 4 July 1966; Couve de Murville M 1971 *Une Politique Etrangère*. Plon: Paris, p 219
29. Wilson H 1971 *The Labour Government 1964–1970*. Weidenfeld and Nicolson and Michael Joseph, p 213
30. Kissinger H 1979 *The White House Years*. Little, Brown: Boston, pp 1054–5; Trevelyan H 1973 *op. cit.*, p 128
31. Hayter W 1966 *The Kremlin and the Embassy*. Hodder and Stoughton, p 41
32. Jackson G 1981 *Concorde Diplomacy*. Hamish Hamilton, p 168
33. *Newsweek* 23 Feb. 1970, 16 Mar. 1970
34. Nyaradi N 1952 *op. cit.*, p 241
35. Kissinger H 1979 *op. cit.*, pp 1315, 1466
36. *Keesing's Contemporary Archives 1976* p 27909; Fraser J 1980 *The Chinese*. Fontana, pp 76–9
37. *Life* 22 Aug. 1955; Parrott C 1977 *The Serpent and the Nightingale*. Faber and Faber, pp 68–74; Menon K P S 1963 *op. cit.*, pp 120–1
38. Brandt W 1978 *People and Politics*. Collins, pp 345–55; Kissinger H 1982 *Years of Upheaval*. Weidenfeld and Nicolson, pp 228–35
39. Spaak P H 1971 *The Continuing Battle*. Little, Brown: Boston, pp 425–32
40. Talbott S (ed) 1974 *op. cit.*, p 290
41. Brandt W 1978 *op. cit.*, pp 328, 408
42. Weit E 1973 *op. cit.*, pp 142–3; Dedijer V 1953 *op. cit.*, p 285
43. Parrott C 1977 *op. cit.*, p 123
44. Barghoorn F C 1960 *The Soviet Cultural Offensive*. Princeton: Princeton University Press, p 67; Hayter W 1966 *op. cit.*, pp 41–2; Bohlen C E 1973 *op. cit.*, p 364
45. Micunovic V 1980 *op. cit.*, p 113
46. *Ibid.* pp 188, 229, 230–1, 412
47. *The Times* 19 Dec. 1981

Chapter nine
SYMBOL AND RITUAL IN SOVIET DIPLOMACY

In the late 1940s a team of American explorers was reported in the press to have gone in search of the remains of Noah's ark on the upper slopes of Mount Ararat, located in north-eastern Turkey on the border with Soviet Armenia. Nothing, one might think, very remarkable about that, at least not from a political point of view. Not so to the Soviet official mind. In Soviet eyes the expedition was seen as a sinister and subtle threat to border security – a warning of possible American infiltration and subversion in the turbulent southern republics of the USSR.[1]

This curious episode is more than just evidence of Soviet paranoia and a tendency to project on to others their own doubtful practices. It is a demonstration of a 'total view' of politics which holds that nothing occurs by accident and that the power of the state extends into every area of life. In fact, that there is no distinction between public and private acts. Time and again in relations with the West, the Soviet Union and other Communist states have assumed that the kind of pervasive control they exercise over their own societies is duplicated elsewhere.

Their error is understandable. In Communist states there are no 'checks and balances' on the power of the party; no independent legislature or judiciary; no watchdog media. All are appointed by and accountable to the party. The Western concept of the freedom of the individual is quite alien. Production and distribution are under state and therefore ultimately party control. In short the Communist party is uncontestably supreme in all major sectors of social activity.

Unfortunately, the very difficulty Communist leaders have in understanding the limits on state power in the West is reflected in our difficulty in grasping the inclusiveness of state power in the Communist system. However, unless this basic reality is accepted, it will be impossible to decipher the Communist code of communication.

The supremacy of the Communist party throughout society naturally extends to the conduct of foreign policy. The real decisions are not made by the ministry of foreign affairs or even the 'government', but by the politburo of the Communist party. As one expert explains,

> Moreover the Politburo is not only the supreme deciding body; it also has its subordinate departments dealing with foreign affairs, which are at all levels more powerful than the corresponding levels of the Ministry of Foreign Affairs. The Communist Party, as the Soviet Constitution puts it, is 'the leading core of all the organizations of the working people, both public and state', and this is true for foreign policy as for any other field of public activity. The state apparatus is there to carry into effect the policy and the orders of the party, and the Ministry of Foreign Affairs, being an organ of the state, does just that. Even its execution of these orders is at all times subject to party control, exercised by officials of the party located in the Ministry and the missions abroad.[2]

Now since the Communist party is also the supreme arbiter of activity in all other branches of government, society and economic life, it automatically has at its disposal all these selfsame organs as instruments of foreign policy. Little wonder then that the Soviet leadership should have assumed in 1949 that an American expedition close to its frontier regions was more than the whim of a group of private citizens. The 'assumption of intentionality' which underlies government behaviour in the fields of diplomacy and defence extends in the Communist system to *all* public behaviour accessible to foreign observers. Since the party is known to exert pervasive control, observers must assume that behind every public act there lies a political intention. Circularily, this obliges the regime to pay redoubled attention to its public acts. In a nutshell: since everything is staged and known to be staged, everything has to be staged.

At the beck and call of the regime, therefore, in the conduct of its foreign policy is the full gamut of public and what would in many cases in the West be 'private' activity. This includes:

- all legal publications, namely the press, journals and books;
- all public performances, whether of news, current affairs or the performing arts, on stage, screen, television and radio;
- all acts of government involving communication or contact with foreign governments, organizations or private citizens, whether in the fields of trade, technical and scientific cooperation, sport or culture;

- all articulations and gestures made by party or government officials directed at a foreign audience, either public or private.

One word of reservation: bureaucratic politics is certainly not absent from the Communist system. Although there is nothing like the cacophony of contending voices characteristic of government in the West, this does not mean that the expert will be unable to detect differences in emphasis and discrepancies between the organs of, say, the party, government and army. At moments of internal crisis these may be highly significant. But this is still the exception rather than the rule.

Of all the means of communication within a Communist society the most important are the media, which are under the direct or indirect control of the party. Since nothing can appear without official sanction, everything that is published or broadcast will be assumed to indicate official thinking. Strict censorship is imposed to ensure that nothing offensive to the party line slips through the net. An idea of how this works can be obtained from material brought over to the West by a former Polish censor, Tomasz Strzyzowski. While an employee of the Cracow branch of the central office for control of the press, publications and performances (COCPPP) he accumulated around 700 pages of confidential instructions and circulars. Strzyzowski's book of rules covers every possible area of concern. Of interest to us is its detailed treatment of international affairs. For instance, the following directives were circulated to censors at the beginning of 1977:

> No information should be published concerning possible trade with Rhodesia and South Africa, or contacts between Polish institutions and South Africa; States with which Poland maintains diplomatic relations should not be referred to as military dictatorships, or called other names such as guerrillas or military juntas. This does not apply to Chile, Paraguay, Guatemala and the Dominican Republic.[3]

Thus a great effort is made to try to ensure that anything that appears in print reflects party policy. Where different views do exist within the party, they will be carefully obscured – though this does not mean that tell-tale discrepancies may not remain to be detected by the trained observer. Even such points of detail as the wording, length and position of a text will have been carefully vetted. On major issues control is exercised at the very highest levels of the party. While on a visit to Peking Nixon's secretary of state, William Rogers, was allowed to witness – presumably intentionally –Chou En-lai going over the text of the following day's *People's Daily*. Yugoslav ambassador Micunovic has also described the extreme seriousness with which the Soviet leadership perused the press of other fraternal parties. On one occasion Yugoslav reporting of a Khrushchev speech was raised at a meeting of the presidium of the Soviet Communist Party.[4]

It is because nothing appearing in the Communist press does so by chance that the outside analyst can painstakingly build up a picture of trends and developments within the otherwise hermetically sealed citadels of power. Working on the basis of certain principles of exegesis – the juxtaposition and ordering of names in a list, the reported presence or absence of a leader at some official occasion, the frequency with which a particular name is mentioned – the expert can piece together the political jigsaw. It is far from an exact science, but more is revealed than is at first apparent.

Foreign affairs coverage has its own rules. The publication of a foreign news item, report or diplomatic text can be taken as agreement for the position expressed. Anything unacceptable is simply not printed. The title by which a fraternal party leader is referred to is of great significance. Withholding the designation 'comrade' or, worse still, his party function, is a clear sign of disapproval or even his impending political demise. An *ad hominen* attack on the leadership of another state is a sure sign of a severe deterioration in relations and suggests that little hope of improvement is possible with that given leadership. Conversely, a change in attitude to a head of state signals the possibility or imminence of a substantive change in relations. The position and wording of all press reports of whatever kind concerning other states may be of significance. Any kind of report reflecting sympathy, credit, respect or honour for another nation is intended to express a *political* attitude towards it. Even the length, position and text of obituary notices reflect political calculation.

Exactly the same principles of purposiveness apply to the publication of visual information, whether photographs, films or TV reports. One of Strzyzowski's directives required any photographs of Iran, past and present, the Shah, his family and associates to be cleared with COCPPP.[5]

As an instrument of diplomatic communication pictures can be seen to perform several supplementary functions in the Communist world.

The first of these is *legitimation*. The cult of personality which has enveloped every Communist leader since Lenin to a greater or lesser extent invests that leader with myth-like properties of excellence and infallibility. Proximity to that leader is an unerring sign of political favour. Internally, in the absence of established constitutional procedures of succession, the cult of personality can be explained as a vital mechanism for the bestowal or transfer of authority – a sort of 'transmission belt of legitimacy'.[6] Externally, the sight of the party leader with a foreign guest, on photograph or film, communicates a definitive statement about party policy towards the state represented.

Use of this device was particularly salient during the period of Sino–American reconciliation at the beginning of the 1970s. On Henry Kissinger's second visit to Peking, once the breakthrough had already occurred and it was clear that no purely tactical manoeuvre was involved, it became necessary for the Chinese authorities to establish in the public mind the acceptability of the American relationship. In the first instance this was a bureaucratic necessity; the new policy could not be implemented by hesitant, recalcitrant, officials. But it was also needed to convince American observers that China was genuinely committed to a *rapprochement*.

Accordingly, on the day of the Kissinger party's arrival, 'the official Party newspaper listed the welcoming committee; its high rank underlined the importance attached to the visit'. During the further course of the visit the *People's Daily* carried two photographs of Kissinger together with Chou En-lai – the first time in twenty years that an American official had been pictured with a Chinese leader. The ultimate accolade and demonstration of the revolutionary reversal in relations came later during the Nixon visit when the president was brought into the presence of Mao Tse-tung. Again photographic proof of the occasion appeared in the *People's Daily*.[7]

A second use to which photographs have been put by the Communist media is as a device for creating a better atmosphere in relations with another country. The presence of cameras on a diplomatic occasion indicates that an effort is being made to project an image of cordiality and friendship. Where words would be dry and formal, a photo of the leaders smiling in apparent enjoyment of each other's company demonstrates in a tangible way the 'warmth' of their political relations.

Photo diplomacy has been used with great skill by both the USSR and the People's Republic of China at different times. One of the turning-points in Soviet–Western relations in the postwar period was the improvement in atmosphere known as the 'spirit of Geneva' after the genial big four summit conference of July 1955. Ingenious Soviet manipulation of photo journalism contributed to this atmosphere. It started two weeks before the projected conference when the Soviet leadership attended, in hitherto unknown force, the fourth of July celebrations at the US embassy. Photographers were on hand to record the remarkable scenes of joviality. Soviet leaders, the Western public was being informed, were not the grim, ruthless figures one had supposed. Here was a group of gregarious, cheerful men with whom one could demonstrably crack a joke and share a drink. How could they possibly be dangerous?

In the same issue of *Life* magazine an equally unusual series of photos was published of the warm welcome given by Moscow citizens to a visiting US chess team. The *Life* photographer, it was stressed, had been given free rein, in an unprecedented manner, to photograph whatever he wished. A series of studies of life on the streets of Moscow appeared – ordinary, friendly people going about their everyday business. Everywhere, it was made clear, Americans had been greeted with warmth and hospitality.[8]

At the Geneva summit itself the Russians made every effort to ensure that their show of geniality was covered in the most graphic way possible. To their many official lunches and dinners the hordes of press photographers and reporters were given easy access. As *Life* reported at the time:

> This policy made them the most publicized of all the delegations and furthered the new Russian strategy of trying to convince the world that they are actually convivial and conciliatory fellows. Relations between the Western press and the Reds reached a friendly peak when Nikita Khrushchev accosted *Life* Photographer Carl Mydans at a party and asked whom he represented. When Mydans told him, Khrushchev threw an arm around him and declared: 'It is a good magazine. It has the best pictures.'[9]

Demonstrating the remarkable consistency of Soviet technique, thirty years later the new foreign policy leadership of Mikhail Gorbachev and Edward Shevardnadze was launched with virtually the same public relations methods. Alongside the disarmament proposals and selective cultivation of America's European allies went a skilful manipulation of the Western media. At the 1985 review conference to discuss implementation of the Helsinki final act (on security and cooperation in Europe), Foreign Minister Shevardnadze succeeded in distracting attention from the USSR's violations of its commitments on human rights and freedom of movement and information, by a sustained display of joviality. In Paris, New York and at the Geneva summit Gorbachev showed himself off to great advantage. Where Khrushchev had made use of photo journalism, Gorbachev now revealed his grasp of television. No opportunity was lost to appear before the electronic media. The innovation – for a Soviet leader – of the televised press conference enabled the new first secretary to project an image of relative youth, moderation and affability. Urbane, dapper and relaxed, it was clear that Gorbachev was out to 'out-Reagan Reagan' as a 'great communicator'. Mrs Gorbachev, in a classic ploy of the electronic statesman, was also brought into play. Attractive and well-heeled, she naturally generated sympathetic interest. In Paris, the capital of *haute couture*, she was certainly not out of place. Lest anybody miss the point, it became known that 'one of Mrs Gorbachev's favourite perfumes' was Yves Saint-Laurent's *Opium*.

A third use of photo diplomacy is to fabricate or alter the meaning of an event that may not have occurred or occurred in a different way from that portrayed. Originally, paintings and photographs were manipulated under Stalin either to present Stalin as a closer associate of Lenin than he actually was or to remove from the visual record individuals who had subsequently been discredited and purged. The practice of retouching and photo montage continued under his successors. One famous instance of this was the publication in *Pravda* of 10 March 1953 of a photograph which purported to show Malenkov with Stalin and Mao Tse-tung. Actually it was a retouched version of a photograph which had originally appeared in *Pravda* of 14 February 1950 and included a number of other people separating Malenkov and Mao. In the 1953 reproduction this section of the picture was erased and Malenkov moved next to Mao in order to reinforce the former's political stature.[10]

Several variations of this technique in the diplomatic sphere are cited by Micunovic. In June 1957 a Yugoslav military delegation arrived in Moscow for a largely ceremonial tour of the USSR. Substantive negotiations were not on the agenda for the plain reason that the Yugoslav government had no intention whatsoever of setting up a military relationship with the Warsaw Pact that could only compromise their hard-won independence. For the reverse reason the Soviets were very interested indeed in such a development. When they failed to achieve it in reality, they determined to contrive its appearance.

On 9 June 1957, for example, the Soviet press published a special communiqué and illustration supposedly of 'talks' between the Soviet and Yugoslav defence ministers, when what had occurred was simply an exchange of courtesies. Then on 25 June the Soviet authorities went one better. This time ambassador Micunovic and Defence Minister Gosnjak were scheduled to be received by Khrushchev and Bulganin. Also present, though this had not been scheduled, were journalists and photographers.

'The room in the Kremlin', Micunovic noted ruefully, 'looked as though it had been specially prepared for formal talks between the two delegations. Apart from Khrushchev and Bulganin there were Marshals Zhukov, Konev and Sokolovsky, General Antonov and Ambassador [to Yugoslavia] Firyubin. No talks in fact took place.' After chatting for fifteen minutes, everyone sat down for lunch. However, the impression outside observers would receive from the photographs was that serious negotiations had been conducted.[11]

For a society that supposedly rejects the spiritual in favour of a materialist view of human existence, the prominent role of myth and ritual in the USSR is quite remarkable. Many writers have noted the religious-like character of Russian Marxism. A considerable debt is clearly owed to the doctrines and practices of the Russian orthodox church. The idea of Moscow as a Third Rome was not invented by Stalin but appeared as early as the sixteenth century. Mary-Barbara Zeldin has argued that Marxism, as modified by Lenin and Stalin, can actually be studied as a religious phenomenon:

> Marxism has a doctrine of an *originally integrated context*, when man was not alienated from man or nature; of a *Fall*, when private property was instituted; of *salvation*, when the revolution of the proletariat brings about the classless, stateless utopia through the birth of the *new* 'socialist' man. The achievement of this utopia is arrived at through *practical action*.
>
> The principle of socialist practice is given in a body of belief, dialectical materialism, *revealed* by Marx. The citing of Marxian scripture as authority is proper usage. There are teachers and prophets, martyrs and saints of Marxism. In Russian Marxism there is a *body of believers* in communism and a priesthood in the Communist Party and its structure. There are heresies – revisions, idealist and mechanist deviations. There is the demand for *complete* dedication to the point of successful Inquisition, as seen in the Moscow purges of the Thirties. There is, as we well know, fervent *missionary* zeal. Further, as in any absolute system, there is *paradox* – the paradox, e.g. of free will and determinism. But there is in Russian Marxism a height of paradox, since all progress is due to recognized contradictions, to the negation of negation. ...
>
> Finally, there is a god, self-moving matter, making and acting in history. Matter rises, through the dialectic, to become not only conscious, but ... as seen in the role of the proletariat, divine. Matter is eternal; infinite in space and potency. It has genuine creative power, the power of bringing forth the higher from the lower by its own self movement. This matter is recognized as the ultimate and only power and reality. Thus it is *worshipped*.[12]

At the level of social control Communist regimes have introduced the whole paraphernalia of organized religion. From their earliest days in power the Bolsheviks under Lenin made use of the classic devices of symbol, image, ritual and ceremonial. Christopher Binns stresses the legitimating role of ceremonial in Soviet Russia. It has provided a geneology of the regime, solemnified its values and beliefs and drawn it and its ideology into the rhythm of life in town and country.[13]

Another function of religious forms and practices has been to redirect the inherent religiosity of the people which, left undisturbed, might seriously threaten the survival of the new faith. Traditions of the orthodox church were accordingly carried over almost intact. The Lenin cult, which bears many of the marks of saints worship, has reached extraordinary proportions. Sites associated with Lenin's life have become places of pilgrimage. The manor house outside Moscow where he died has been recreated to appear as it is presumed to have been on the day of his death. A symbolic new party membership card, No. 00000001, issued in Lenin's name in 1973, is on display. Details of his age and place of birth and his photograph are all in proper order, 'just as though he were, as propagandists religiously assert, still alive'.[14] His mausoleum, containing his embalmed corpse in the orthodox manner, is the most sacred shrine in the Communist world.

None of these developments were spontaneous. Trotsky, for one, was well aware of the important, indeed indispensable, role played by relic and rite in the indoctrination and control of the Russian people.[15]

To understand the esoteric code of communication which was developed in the USSR by the Communist leadership requires an appreciation of the role of ritual in the Russian Marxist phenomenon.

The display of icons and statues of the leader, sometimes of gigantic dimensions, is in the first instance an instrument of the cult of personality and is intended to build him up to god-like proportions. Originating in the USSR, the practice has spread throughout the Communist world. On May Day and the national holiday – in the Soviet case the anniversary of the October revolution – portraits of Lenin, Marx, Engels and the living leaders are carried aloft through the main square. In the same way, Hedrick Smith remarks, 'the icons of saints were borne aloft in religious processions through Red Square in centuries past'.[16]

Ideological schism in the Communist world is fully reflected at the iconographic level. At the 20th congress of the Communist party of the Soviet Union in February 1956 Khrushchev, at the centre of a vigorous political and ideological struggle, denounced the cult and methods of Stalin. In consequence the image of the dead tyrant became an ideogram for the whole corpus of policies and doctrines associated with his name. Within the USSR Stalin's portrait was virtually withdrawn from circulation (not always without local resistance). His massive icons, once displayed in their hundreds on Red square on 1 May and 7 November each year disappeared from view.

Outside the USSR the rejection of a man Communists had been taught was infallible caused profound misgivings. If Stalin's achievements were to be so curtly disposed of, what of the system he had built and Mao and others still directed? To discredit the Stalin myth called into question the legitimacy of all Communist regimes.

In China Khrushchev's denunciation was received with a cold and disapproving silence; the seeds of schism had been sown. In glaring contrast to Soviet practice, Stalin's image continued to be displayed everywhere, often at least as prominently as that of Lenin, if not more so. When Khrushchev arrived in Peking at the end of September 1959 on his forlorn mission to rescue something from the wreckage of Communist unity, he found a city bedecked with massive portraits of Marx, Engels, Lenin, Stalin and Mao – but not of Khrushchev. The writing was literally on the wall.[17]

Iconography has also been put at the disposal of constructive foreign policy initiatives. Both the Russians and the Chinese are skilled at canonizing some prominent historical figure as the embodiment of a desired policy line. For the launching of its peace offensive against Taiwan in 1981, based on the offer of local autonomy, the Peking leadership evoked the name and reputation of Sun Yat-sen, the father of the Chinese revolutionary movement and equally cherished by Communists and nationalists alike. During the festivities marking the 60th anniversary of the Chinese Communist party Dr Sun's giant portrait was displayed on Tienanmen square, facing that of Mao himself. At the same time his revolutionary teachings were held up for emulation and the 70th anniversary of the uprising led by Sun Yat-sen, which toppled the Manchu dynasty in 1911, was elaborately commemorated with mass rallies held in Peking and at other historical sites. The Communist party, it was repeatedly affirmed, had triumphantly fulfilled Dr Sun's wishes to establish a democratic, strong and prosperous China.

All this homage was not necessarily as ingenuous and disinterested as it might have appeared to outside observers. For by evoking the memory of the founding father the Peking leadership was also implicitly undermining the *Kuomintang's* claims to be the true repository of Dr Sun's ideas while simultaneously reinforcing its own legitimacy.[18]

Curiously enough, the use of portraiture for political and

propaganda purposes achieves its fullest expression in the miniature form of the postage stamp. Only television and the mint can rival the humble envelope as a medium for diffusing images to the masses. After all stamps are circulated in their tens and even hundreds of millions; they can be issued as appropriate; and, uniquely, they can be used to carry a visual message beyond the limits of one's frontiers virtually without hindrance. The world of postage stamps, therefore, provides a rich source of material for the study of the domestic and foreign policies of the Communist states.

Stamps can and clearly do carry propaganda messages; the recurrent Soviet peace campaigns are cases in point. But something that is reproduced in vast numbers for universal distribution both at home and abroad must express something more than empty rhetoric intended to win propaganda points. Moreover, unlike media propaganda, postal issues cannot easily be repudiated. Once a new design enters circulation it cannot be reclaimed from the wallets and albums of the public. It may not have quite the weighty distinction of a coin or a bank note, reflecting permanent values, but a stamp must be a carefully considered, authoritative statement of official policy. In a wider sense postage stamps provide an invaluable insight into the way in which a nation perceives its past and the goals it sets for the future.

Soviet stamps have historically provided an early indication of important policy initiatives and changes. For example, Soviet claims on Turkish territory were first put forward at the Potsdam conference of July 1945. However, hostility to Turkey first took pictorial and therefore public form much earlier. One postal issue, published after the outbreak of war in 1941, shows the hero Alexander Suvorov at the capture of the Turkish fortress of Ismail. Now it is true that the authorities were evoking historical heroes at this time to encourage the nation in its war effort. What is noteworthy is the depiction of a Turkish enemy. A similarly hostile finger was pointed at Turkey in November 1944 when the Soviet Union, this time exploiting the birth centenary of the painter I. E. Repin, issued a stamp on a famous Russian historical theme – the reply of the Zaporozhie cossacks to Sultan Mohamed IV's demand for their surrender. As every Russian schoolboy knows, their reply was very abusive indeed. (Although the Turks were successful at the beginning of the war their subsequent losses were so great that they were obliged to sign a treaty at Radzin in 1621 ceding territory to Russia.)

An early hint of Khrushchev's Berlin campaign, which got under way in a September 1958 speech in which he threatened to sign a separate peace treaty with East Germany, appeared in postal form. An issue of February 1958 depicted a favourite theme of Soviet historiography – the capture of Berlin in 1945. All Soviet postal designs are meticulously vetted; but it is a general rule that scenes of military action are absolutely avoided unless the Kremlin has deliberately chosen to strike a bellicose note. When policy dictates restraint and the orchestration of a peace campaign, no dissonant, militaristic tone is permitted to spoil the overall effect.

As long as Stalin was alive, Soviet foreign policy remained hidebound and inflexible. Explicit foreign symbols appear only twice on postage stamps during his long dictatorship: in November 1943 and May 1944 when the flags of the three major allies are depicted together. After the war the USSR returned to its old habits of self-segregation. One sign of a new megalomania was a 1947 postal design showing the hammer and sickle superimposed on a red globe of the world. North America is not visible in the picture.

Stalin's successors replaced seclusion by a great turning outwards. New initiatives were set in train towards the newly independent countries of Asia and, increasingly, Africa. The old Leninist idea of 'peaceful coexistence' was resurrected; open war was no longer an acceptable instrument of policy between the great powers. Negotiations and contacts with the West were the order of the day. Suddenly the depiction of foreign themes and symbols proliferated.

At this point iconography and foreign policy coincided. One way to signal to audiences, at home and abroad, that a particular state was an acceptable interlocutor was to depict its cultural heroes in a favourable light. From 1956 to about 1960 when, with the U-2 crisis and the failure of the Paris summit, the cold winds began to blow again, a whole series of great foreign writers, artists and scientists, all of them European, was depicted in stamp form.

The first foreigner so honoured was Robert Burns, with a commemorative issue on the *160th* anniversary of his death. Since Soviet practice is usually to commemorate anniversaries in units of fifty years it is clear that a deliberate gesture of good will was being made towards Britain. Indeed London was the first Western European city (apart from neutral Geneva) visited by Soviet leaders Bulganin and Khrushchev in April 1956.

But the most noteworthy development was the issue on 17 October 1956 of a stamp to commemorate the 250th anniversary of the birth of Benjamin Franklin, 'the great American statesman and scientist'. Franklin was also praised in the Soviet press along with other such 'progressive' figures as Lincoln and Walt Whitman.[19] Clearly the United States was no longer anathema.

A number of significant issues followed. In 1957 a 'defence of peace' stamp depicted a dove of peace flying over North America. A 1958 design, on the theme of Russian civil aviation, shows a Tu-104 over New York. (Moscow is shown at the focus of a global flight network taking in various domestic destinations and also New York, London, Paris, Prague, Cairo and Delhi.) At one level the stamp is a record of Soviet technological achievement, particularly in the favoured field of aerospace. At another level the very image of the world shown is in marked contrast to the projection of Soviet hegemony portrayed on the 1947 postal issue mentioned above. And this time the United States is clearly visible. Finally it should be noted that the cities marked on the map virtually define the scope of Soviet foreign policy at this period.

One further stamp on the peaceful coexistence theme is of interest. It was issued to mark Khrushchev's September 1959 visit to the United States and was the first commemorative of its kind. The stamp depicts the cupola of the Washington capitol and the tower of the Moscow state university, separated from each other by the curvature of the earth. Obviously the Soviet authorities considered the visit to be of first-rate importance. The stamp design tells us something more about the underlying meaning of the occasion in Soviet eyes: both buildings are shown as of precisely equal height and volume, and are geometrically equidistant from the centre of the picture. It is a perfect expression of the Soviet desire for equality of status with America.

Just a few days before the American issue the USSR released its first – and last – set on the theme of Sino–Soviet friendship. The official occasion was the tenth anniversary of the Chinese revolution; the motive was Moscow's frantic desire to emphasize its sincere intentions and prevent a rupture with its great Asian neighbour. Again the skyscraper tower of the Moscow state university appears, but this time as a backdrop to a tranquil scene of Russian and Chinese students studying together.

As it turned out, the stamp marked the end of an era in Sino–Soviet relations. Ironically, one of the last straws for the increasingly strained partnership was precisely that Khrushchev visit to the USA commemorated so proudly by the Soviet authorities. It was following his return from Washington that Khrushchev travelled on to Peking, only to be met by the unconcealed animosity of the Chinese leadership.

I have referred several times in this book to the role of festive parades in the Communist ceremonial system. Internally these mass displays have three separate functions: cultic, political and social. First and foremost parades are a showcase of Communist mythology and an instrument of regime legitimation. The slogans, the icons, the themes – of labour, proletarian solidarity, peace and so on – embody the myths of the system and its transcendental right to continue in existence. The parade, in fact, is an idealized enactment which makes use of artistic devices including floats, athletic displays and pictures to project an image of how Communist society is *supposed to be* rather than what it actually is. It is, in a real sense, a great charade.[20]

Moreover as an event involving mass public participation the parade reflects the central legitimating myth of the regime – that it is based on the popular will. For a system that so insistently emphasizes the idea of solidarity, its concrete manifestations cannot be too frequently demonstrated.

As political demonstrations May Day and the anniversary of the revolution serve to proclaim the commitment of the population to the party and its leadership. The 'loyalty' of the masses is very graphically conveyed by the choreography and setting of the occasion. Positioned on a central podium high above the parade ground, the party leadership looks out over and accepts the salutations of the passing multitude as it pledges its allegiance and submission.[21]

However, the display is reciprocal: the population is not only on parade for the leadership; the leadership is also on show to the people. Hence the presence or absence, indeed the very position, of the leaders on the reviewing stand acts as a guide, a barometer, to changing fortunes within the party hierarchy.

Finally the show of massed might by participants in the parade is a mechanism of social control, intended to overawe observers with the power and discipline of the regime and the loyalty of its people.

Most parades are not principally intended for the benefit of foreign audiences. Over the years they have, however, acquired this supplementary role, as one of the few occasions, in a rigidly regimented society, on which outsiders might observe the life and institutions of the country. Precisely because the event is an idealization, a performance staged by the party, it has acquired a role as a shop-window for current foreign policy and propaganda themes.

Among the means used in the parade to convey messages to foreign audiences are the slogans and pictures carried by the marchers, the identity of guests on the podium and adjacent stands, and the composition of the review itself, especially the relative weight given to military and civilian motifs.

Moscow-based diplomats, both Western and Communist, have long subjected Soviet parades to intensive scrutiny. Micunovic has well described the interest aroused by these affairs:

Long before the first of May all the embassies in Moscow were sending people scurrying round the city gathering information about the decorations, the portraits of the leaders, the order in which they are put up, the number of portraits of Lenin and Stalin, the slogans, the size of them and what they say. Some foreigners here appear to be very experienced at this business. Some of them have assured me that it is of significance for assessing Soviet policy toward a country to see whether the slogan relating to that country is displayed across a whole street or only attached to the facade of a building. As for the order in which portraits of the present Soviet leadership are displayed in the city, they say that there can be no mistakes here – it is all 'pure mathematics'. If someone's portrait is missing, that person is finished. Political relationships in the Presidium of the Central Committee can be established precisely by noting whose portraits are closer and whose farther away from that of the First Secretary, Khrushchev.[22]

Over the years significant foreign policy departures have been signalled by holiday slogans. Immediately on the death of Stalin marked shifts were noted by one American diplomat. The slogans for May Day 1953 'showed a striking contrast to those published for the anniversary of the Bolshevik Revolution the preceding November, when Stalin was still living. Instead of "down with the warmongers" and references to "imperialist aggressors" and "foreign usurpers", there were expressions of confidence in the ability to resolve all differences between nations'.

What Bohlen does not mention was that none of the by-then customary anti-Yugoslav slogans were displayed, with their exhortations to fight against Tito's 'fascist' regime. So two of the central themes of Soviet foreign policy over the next few years – the *démarches* towards Yugoslavia and the West – were already presaged in May 1953.[23]

In 1959, when Soviet–Egyptian relations were passing through a period of tension, the fact was fully reflected at the May Day parade. Where in previous years Nasser had been warmly referred to, his name was now conspicuous by its absence in slogans and speeches. The only reference to Egypt was the slogan 'Long live friendship with the *people* of the UAR [United Arab Republic]'.[24]

In the frigid atmosphere of East–West relations which followed the Christmas 1979 Soviet invasion of Afghanistan May Day slogans pointedly ceased to make any reference to the 'peace programme' of the 24th congress of the Communist party of the Soviet Union which served as the doctrinal foundation of Brezhnev's policy of detente. Nor was there any call to Western Europe, Canada and the United States to implement the final act of the 1975 Helsinki agreement and to transform Europe into a 'continent of peace', as there had been in May and November 1979. Instead the first shots were fired in the Soviet campaign to persuade Europeans to oppose the installation of American missiles on European soil. By November 1981 the parade had acquired a strongly anti-American flavour, with slogans and placards condemning the neutron bomb, missile deployment and 'the aggressive course of the Reagan Administration'.[25]

Given the aura of absolute authority and the cultic mystique surrounding the Communist leader it has long been considered an exceptional honour for a foreign visitor to appear by his side on the reviewing stand either of Tienanmen or Red Square. I have already mentioned the 1970 incident, when the Nixon administration overlooked the significance of the presence of the American writer Edgar Snow at Mao Tse-tung's side on China's national day, 1 October. The oversight is all the more unusual because General Eisenhower had been honoured by Stalin in the same way in the November 1945 Moscow victory parade.

Since that remote moment of allied unity I can find no record of any Western non-Communist figure receiving this accolade. Several Third World figures have received it though, including Nasser (1958), Fidel Castro (1963) and Algerian President Ahmed Ben Bella (1964).

Just after the Bolshevik revolution Soviet festivities seem to have had a genuinely celebratory air of optimism. Civil war and economic disruption changed this. Demonstrations of strength and protests against threats from inside and outside Russia acquired a prominent role. Stalin and his successors used the projection of an external threat, real or imagined, to strengthen internal cohesion. After the Great Patriotic (Second World) War there is no doubt that the Soviet armed forces were a genuine focus of pride and affection. Under Brezhnev glorification of the army, its achievements and sacrifices, reached new heights. Local memorials and ceremonies proliferated.

The domestic significance of this development is open to conjecture. In foreign policy terms the ceremonial display of armed force has served several purposes. During periods of relative weakness it has encouraged foreign observers to obtain an exaggerated impression of Soviet strength, discipline and preparedness for battle. Stories of dummy equipment and tanks being driven several times round the parade route belong to this tradition of deception. Second, military parades have been used to show off new equipment with a deterrent or minatory effect. Finally, the overall tone of the parade, and especially the ratio of civilian to military items, can be manipulated to create a bellicose or peaceful impression.

Since the death of Stalin successive phases of thaw and freeze in Soviet relations with the West have been reflected in these various ways. Because 7 November, the anniversary of the October revolution, is traditionally more of a military occasion than the workers' holiday of 1 May, it is the latter parade that has provided the more sensitive evidence of the direction of official thinking.

May Day 1954 was the first occasion on which both the Soviet and Chinese authorities chose to play up civilian festivities rather than the troops and tanks that had featured in past parades. However, the inaugural appearance of a new Soviet long-range bomber underlined the steady emergence of a global strike capability.[26]

By the end of the 1950s disarmament and peace campaigns were in full swing, despite Soviet pressure over Berlin. May Day 1958 was notable for its lighthearted atmosphere. An ingenious feature had divers plunging into a canvas safety net. Farm groups carrying sprays of spring blossom were showered with cascades of confetti from the roof of the GUM department store. Other floats featured sporting and hobbyist themes.[27]

While the USSR was affirming by word and gesture the need for peaceful coexistence and the non-inevitability of war, China had taken a totally contrary view. Basing itself on photo-analysis, *Life* magazine fully grasped the far-reaching ideological and political implications of China's national day of 1 October 1959. Where recent Moscow parades had de-emphasized the role of the military, Peking staged an immense display of troops and equipment. Included were hundreds of tanks and motorized artillery pieces and, in a gesture of self-sufficiency, 155 jets claimed to be of Chinese manufacture. Nine massive columns of militiamen, coming after a march-past of 100,000 soldiers, sailors and airmen, made the Maoist point, ridiculed by the USSR, of the key role allotted to people's war in national defence.[28]

Renewed tension in the early 1960s brought the tanks and, by now, ranks of missiles of all kinds, back to the festive streets of Moscow. But, as it turned out, this was a passing interlude in a continuing tendency to downplay the military content of May Day in the context of a general policy of peaceful coexistence. For ten years, from 1969 to 1978, no military contingent whatsoever was included in the parade. Even the November parade, at which the minister of defence traditionally reviews his forces and delivers the keynote speech, was celebrated quietly. Inter-continental ballistic missiles, a feature of the parades of the middle 1960s, were not in evidence. Usually the only rockets on display were 'defensive' SAM anti-aircraft missiles. The emphasis, in short, was on the pursuit of detente.

Significantly, one of the few new weapons shown during the 1970s (on May Day 1974) was the shoulder-held SAM-7 anti-aircraft missile soon to be used by guerrilla fighters around the world. It was Soviet support for 'national resistance movements' in places like Africa, the Middle East and Central America, which was to strain detente to breaking-point. The inclusion of a small military contingent in the May Day 1979 parade was an augury of things to come. On Christmas day of that year Soviet forces moved into Afghanistan. . . . [29]

Together with the accumulation of armed might the other great success story of Soviet society, and therefore showpiece for the regime, is the field of culture and sport. Its ideological significance in a materialist philosophy of life is considerable. After all, if Communist youth is not stronger and fitter than the youth of the 'degenerate' West, nor better able to cultivate its physical and artistic talents, what could be the justification of Communism? Mystical, patriotic and social undertones are also present in the cult of the body.

As with all other areas of society which come under the control of the state, culture has been extensively put at the disposal of Soviet foreign policy. Aleksandr Kaznacheev, a Soviet diplomat who defected to the West, has described the mechanics of the Soviet cultural offensive from his perspective in the Rangoon embassy: 'Great importance', he writes, was attached to cultural matters. 'Responsible for the effort was the Cultural Mission, headed by the cultural attaché, under the State Committee for Cultural Relations with Foreign Countries (until 1958 called VOKS, since then GKKSZ) in Moscow. Its function included the organization of theatrical, musical and ballet performances and sports events; the supply of Soviet literature, films and projectors to political, student, Trade Union and other groups; and the organization of cultural exhibitions.'[30]

An idea of the degree of control exercised by the state over cultural activities is given by the following anecdote. At a world youth festival held in Moscow in the late 1950s the leader of the Yugoslav youth delegation complained to the Soviet organizer that his choir had only been awarded a bronze medal. The organizer immediately got on the phone to the minister of culture and demanded that a gold medal be awarded to the Yugoslavs. The minister, who well knew of the emphasis then being placed on cultivating good relations with Yugoslavia, quashed the verdict of the Soviet jury on the spot and awarded the choir its gold medal![31]

'Cultural diplomacy' performs a vital role in Soviet foreign policy.[32] Introduced on a large scale in the mid-1950s to promote the aims of peaceful coexistence and penetration into the newly-independent states of Asia and Africa, cultural diplomacy proved itself an eloquent medium of nonverbal communication. It worked at various levels. By its very existence, after years of self-imposed isolation, it created the impression that the USSR was in favour of freedom of exchange and international contact as a path to peace and coexistence. Visits by Soviet artists could only undermine the demonic image of Soviet society which had become prevalent in the West. These were human beings just like us!

The choice of medium was ingenious. Ballet, music and art are the antithesis of the martial skills. Such dedication to culture seemed incontestable proof of Soviet peaceful intentions. Even sport was competition of a desirable, peaceful kind. As the Indian ambassador told the Soviet minister of culture on the occasion of an artistic exchange: 'In art, as in politics, India and the Soviet Union might follow different methods but in both spheres our goals were identical. In art our goal was beauty; and in politics, peace. And in the pursuit of beauty and peace India and the Soviet Union would stand together.'[33]

For all its exploitation of culture and sport for political purposes few would disagree that many of the performers sent abroad by the USSR – musicians, dancers, athletes – were of the very highest quality. And, as a credit to their country, they could not fail to excite admiration for the society that produced them: there is no quarrelling with success. Thus the campaign was also effective in projecting an image of the USSR as a world centre of progress, enlightenment and humanitarianism.

Perhaps the major achievement of cultural diplomacy came in Soviet relations with the developing world. Here the encouragement of cultural dialogue played a key role both in creating a positive image of Soviet society and in demonstrating that the USSR was prepared to respect native art on its own terms. Visits by Asian and African troupes were welcomed with open arms. If American cultural facilities might arouse envy, Soviet diplomats were under strict instructions to avoid creating any impression of superiority. 'Here in this underdeveloped country', Kaznacheev was briefed on his arrival in Burma, 'we must show ourselves so modestly, like a dog's life. We must not do anything to appear that we are better than the Asians.'[34] This approach was certainly to pay off.

Among the many fine performers sent abroad by the Soviet Union over the years, the Bolshoi ballet company has acquired a very special reputation for excellence. The tradition of Russian ballet was well-established by the time of the revolution and recruitment and training have been assiduously maintained ever since. With the launching of the Soviet cultural offensive the Bolshoi ballet was immediately thrust into the forefront of the campaign. 'We do not need the Red Army to conquer the world', UN ambassador Andrei Vishinsky once blurted out in the heat of a fierce debate. 'We will sweep it with a white cloud of dancing ballerinas.'[35]

As an instrument of diplomacy the Bolshoi ballet is reserved for only the most privileged objects of Soviet attention. In fact whether it or some other troupe is sent on a cultural mission is a good index of the target country's standing in Soviet eyes. It was not until 1975 that the Bolshoi visited the United States for the first time, for an extended three-month season. In the 1950s the superb Moiseyev company did visit the United States, but it still did not possess the same cachet as the Bolshoi. On the other hand at the same time two of the Bolshoi's legendary ballerinas, Plisetskaya and Ulanova, were sent on missions to India and Egypt. In recent years the very special status acquired by West Germany in Soviet diplomacy since the time of Willy Brandt was amply demonstrated by three visits of the Bolshoi ballet in a single decade – an unmatched record. In October 1985 the Bolshoi ballet visited the People's Republic of China for the first time in twenty years.

The West is well aware of the role and significance of cultural diplomacy for the USSR. The United States very unwisely condemned a 1954 visit by a mixed Soviet troupe to India as a form of invasion – to which the Indians not surprisingly retorted that they preferred that kind of invasion to any other. After the invasion of Afghanistan the British government let it be known that it did not favour helping to bring large Soviet ballet or theatre groups to London as this 'would probably be taken by the Russians as a signal of the end of British disapproval of Soviet policies in the political arena'.[36] French diplomacy has also been sensitive to this factor.

Sport, like culture (of which it is seen as an integral part in the USSR), is fully at the disposal of society and the state. If anything, sport possesses certain advantages over the performing and plastic arts, since it is ideologically non-controversial and enjoys wide popularity. From a domestic perspective sport can be seen to contribute to fitness and health and to channel the energies of youth in a harmless direction.[37]

Sport as a spectacle can be accommodated to other Soviet uses of ceremony which serve to legitimize the political order, vindicate ideology and foster social control. Sporting events, broadcast to millions of Soviet homes by television, provide a perfect vehicle for the enactment of the myth of the 'new' Soviet man, with its pagan undertones of youth, strength and beauty. The victories of Soviet sportsmen, as *Pravda* did not fail to point out after the 1972 Olympic games, 'convincingly demonstrate that socialism opens up the greatest opportunities for man's physical and spiritual perfection'.[38]

For spectators sport provides a unique fusion of cohesion, solidarity, integration, discipline and emotional euphoria. Moreover it is an ideal tool for arousing patriotic fervour. 'It is no accident', Hedrick Smith writes, 'that the Soviets are often the ones who seize every opportunity at the Olympic Games or other international competitions to insist on playing national anthems, displaying national flags, or performing marches past and other rituals that cater to national feelings.'[39]

But international competitions and sporting exchanges have also proved a valuable aid to Soviet diplomacy. James Riordan, in his definitive account of Soviet sport, shows that sport at the international level has been subordinate to the overall goals of foreign policy since the 1920s. Until 1939, however, Soviet sportsmen had only limited opportunities for travel. With the signing of the Nazi–Soviet pact in August 1939, they could come into their own. As part of the campaign to reinforce and project the 'friendship' between the two countries the USSR engaged in more sporting contests with Nazi Germany in 1940 than it had with all the 'bourgeois' states in all the preceding years since 1917 put together.

Another characteristic use of sport in this period was to pave the way for wider political accord. Two soccer matches took place between Moscow *Spartak* and Sofia at a time when Soviet diplomacy was attempting to conclude non-aggression pacts with Balkan states including Bulgaria.

After 1945 and the defeat of Nazi Germany Soviet sport became a focus of nationalist fervour – a vehicle for enhancing the status of the USSR and Communist ideology. Winning, not just taking part, was all important. 'The increasing number of successes achieved by Soviet sportsmen in sport', claimed a 1951 publication, 'has particular political significance today. Each new victory is a victory for the Soviet form of society and the socialist sports system; it provides irrefutable proof of the superiority of socialist culture over the decaying culture of the capitalist states.'[40]

Over the entire post-war period sport has been the medium for a variety of specific political messages beyond this general assertion of ideological superiority. The first excursion of a Soviet sports team, after the war had ended, was that of the soccer club Moscow *Dinamo* to

Western Europe. In fact the team was not a club side at all but contained international-level players borrowed from other soccer clubs for the trip. To all intents and purposes it was the Soviet national team. Not surprisingly it won all four matches played against British first division sides, creating an excellent impression. Riordan sees the tour 'as part of the effort to show that, despite the war losses, the USSR was still strong and that conditions were reasonably normal'.[41]

Then, beginning in the mid-1950s, sport, alongside other cultural activities, was thrown into the twin campaigns, for peaceful coexistence with the West and to promote Soviet friendship with the developing countries. If, in 1948, 12 foreign sports groups had visited the USSR and 23 Soviet groups gone abroad, by 1954 the figures had risen to 131 and 142 respectively. By 1967, the peak year, the numbers were 699 and 806.[42]

Soviet tactics have been shrewdly varied to suit the occasion and the audience. To encourage detente the girl gymnasts Olga Korbut and Ludmilla Turishcheva were sent on a display tour of the United States in 1972. Olga Korbut in particular had acquired great popularity in the West for her fresh, gamine performance at the Olympic games earlier in the year. Such youthful, feminine stars were well calculated to touch the hearts of American audiences. Later a USSR–USA athletics match was held. When it was over the new relationship between the superpowers, based on peaceful rather than hostile competition, was 'symbolically represented on the track by Soviet and American athletes linking arms, doing a lap of honor together and waving to spectators'.[43]

Soviet athletes had, one need hardly add, bettered their American rivals, a lesson not lost on domestic audiences. Against teams from the Third World the Soviet Union, in contrast, is careful to pit sportsmen of roughly the same level. On visits to Africa and Asia sportsmen from the USSR's outlying republics are used to show what socialism can achieve. All these contacts are conducted with the utmost seriousness, for the Soviet Union understands the importance of status and prestige to a developing country.

Soviet support for the Third World campaign to exclude South Africa from international sporting contests has provided low-cost diplomatic successes. Since the beginning of the 1960s Soviet delegates have been frequent proposers of South Africa's suspension from international sports organizations, including the Olympics committee and the bodies responsible for canoeing, cycling, wrestling, swimming, athletics and gymnastics.[44]

On the one hand this campaign has won great sympathy for the

USSR, which could appear as a champion of the fight against racial discrimination. On the other hand it has certainly contributed to South Africa's isolation.

Freed from the restraints of public opinion, the Soviet Union can afford to be absolutely pragmatic in its own sporting contacts. Just ten days after the invasion of the Falkland Islands in April 1982 by Argentina, the Soviet world cup soccer team arrived in Buenos Aires for a 'warmup match'.[45] Knowing full well the local enthusiasm for the sport, the Soviet authorities had chosen a shrewd and non-committal way to express their support for Argentina in its 'struggle against British imperialism'. The nature of the Argentine military regime was simply not a relevant consideration.

In its relations with other Communist countries the USSR has used sport to reinforce the unity of the Soviet bloc and its 'vanguard' position within it. 'Few opportunities are lost', according to Riordan, 'to associate sporting events with a political occasion or to employ sport to cement loyalties within the bloc.' To celebrate the fiftieth anniversary of the USSR in 1967, for example, climbers from the USSR and other Communist countries participated in a mass assault on peak Stalin (7,495 m) and planted their national flags on the summit. *Pravda* heralded the feat as 'a symbol of unshakable friendship inspired by the ideals of proletarian internationalism, peace and friendship between peoples'.[46]

When China and the Soviet Union resolved on an effort to improve their relations it was natural for them to turn to the sports arena. One of the first signs of the thaw between them was an announcement in June 1982 that the USSR was to send an athletics team to an international meeting in Peking 'at the invitation of the Chinese track and field association'. Three months later President Brezhnev, speaking in Baku on the Caspian sea, confirmed that normalization of relations with China was the main priority of Soviet policy in Asia.[47]

REFERENCES AND NOTES

1. Talbott S (ed) 1974, *Khrushchev Remembers: the last testament.* Little, Brown: Boston, p 296
2. Hayter W 1970 *Russia and the World.* Secker and Warburg, pp 16–7
3. Hirszowicz M 1978 Poland's black book, *Index on Censorship* 7: 28–34
4. Nixon R M 1982 *Leaders.* Sidgwick and Jackson, p 223;

Micunovic V 1980 *Moscow Diary*. Chatto and Windus, p 82; Weit E 1973, *Eyewitness*. André Deutsch, pp 125–8

5. Hirszowicz M, *op. cit.*, 1978
6. Gill G 1980 The Soviet leader cult: reflections on the structure of leadership in the Soviet Union, *British Journal of Political Science* **10**,: 167–86
7. Kissinger H 1979 *The White House Years*. Little, Brown: Boston, pp 779, 1060
8. *Life* 18 July 1955
9. *Ibid.* 1 Aug. 1955
10. Conquest R 1967 *Power and Policy in the USSR*. Harper Torchbooks: New York, pp 202–3; MacFarquhar R 1971 On photographs, *The China Quarterly* **46**: 289–306
11. Micunovic V, *op. cit.*, pp 247, 254
12. Zeldin M B 1969 The religious nature of Russian Marxism, *Journal for the Scientific Study of Religion* **8**: 108–9. Emphasis in original
13. Binns C A P 1979/80 The changing face of power, *Man* **14**: 585–606, **15**: 170–87
14. *The Times* 3 May 1981
15. Binns C A P 1979, *op. cit.*, pp 594–5
16. Smith H 1976 *The Russians*. Sphere, p 348
17. Fraser J 1980 *The Chinese*. Fontana, p 54; Menon K P S 1963 *The Flying Troika*. Oxford University Press, p 210; *Newsweek* 12 Oct. 1959; *Life* 19 Oct. 1959
18. *The Times* 13 Sept. 1981, 15 Sept. 1981; Yee H S 1982 China's reunification offensive and Taiwan's policy options, *The World Today* **38**: 33
19. Barghoorn F C 1960 *The Soviet Cultural Offensive*. Princeton University Press: Princeton, p 185
20. Lane C 1981 *The Rites of Rulers*. Cambridge University Press, ch 10
21. Binns C A P 1979, *op. cit.*, pp 597–8
22. Micunovic V 1980, *op. cit.*, p 41
23. Bohlen C E 1973, *Witness to History*. W. W. Norton: New York, p 371; Wolfgang L 1962 *The Kremlin Since Stalin*. Oxford University Press
24. Heikal M H 1978, *The Sphinx and the Commissar*. Harper and Row: New York, p 108
25. *Newsweek* 5 May 1980; *The Times* 9 Nov. 1981
26. *Newsweek* 31 May 1954
27. *Life* 12 May 1958

28. *Ibid*. 19 Oct. 1959; *Time* 12 Oct. 1959
29. Research based on the *New York Times* 1969–79
30. Kaznacheev A 1962, *Inside a Soviet Embassy*. Lippincott: Philadelphia, p 99
31. Micunovic V 1980, *op. cit.*, p 293
32. Barghoorn F C 1960, *op. cit.* is the source of many ideas in this section
33. Menon K P S 1963, *op. cit.*, p 65
34. Kaznacheev A 1962, *op. cit.*, pp 49–50
35. Rafael G 1981, *Destination Peace*. Weidenfeld and Nicolson, p 347
36. *The Times* 24 Mar. 1981
37. The following section is based on Riordan J 1977 *Sport in Soviet Society*. Cambridge University Press, pp 348–95
38. 17 Sept. 1972 quoted in *ibid.*, p 369
39. Smith H 1976, *op. cit.*, p 372
40. Quoted in Riordan J 1977, *op. cit.*, p 364
41. *Ibid.* pp 366–7
42. *Ibid.*
43. *Ibid.* p 374
44. *The Times* 19 Apr. 1982
45. *Ibid.* 14 Apr. 1982
46. Riordan J 1977, *op. cit.*, pp 379–81
47. *The Times* 10 June 1982, 24 Sept. 1982, 9 Mar. 1983

Chapter ten

THEATRE OF POWER: AN OVERVIEW

Nonverbal communication in diplomacy is not a new phenomenon but the electronic revolution has made it particularly salient. The same exigencies that require electoral candidates to pay painstaking attention to their visual image now apply, with equal force, to the self-presentation of national figures in the international arena. Reference, therefore, to a 'theatre of power' is not meant flippantly. The moment the nonverbal aspect of one's behaviour acquires prominence, as it does for someone in the public eye, then willy-nilly one becomes a performer of sorts.

Underlying diplomatic signalling is an *assumption of intentionality*. When an individual fills a representative political role his every word and gesture are assumed to possess significance. Even slips of the tongue and unconscious mannerisms are scanned for meaning. It is true that this principle may be repellent, even invidious. But this is the reality of the age of television.

Besides the ubiquity of television, other factors amplifying the role of nonverbal communication between states are, among other things: the extension of the international community to cultures not necessarily sharing the old Eurocentric assumptions of language and conduct and possessing rich nonverbal cultural traditions; the involvement of mass audiences in political activity almost irrespective of the constitutional complexion of the regime; and last, but not least, the greatly increased scope of international activity – implying that action that is not dramatic may simply be overlooked.

For the routine burden of diplomacy the written and spoken word is irreplaceable. But language has its limitations. At critical moments it may fail to attract attention or lack credibility. In a crisis verbal warnings may be mistaken for rhetoric, conciliatory tones may be drowned in the surrounding noise. The professional diplomat lives and breathes the carefully-drafted text and the exegesis of slight shades of emphasis are his stock-in-trade. But mass publics and politicians alike are less impressed by such nuances. It is the human touch, the direct visual message, the appeal to the senses, which they notice and remember. Equally, gestures may be preferred because they are ambiguous and lack the definitiveness of the written record.

There is also a bureaucratic reason for the resort to symbolic action. Collective entities, whether they be the unwieldy apparatuses that now manage diplomacy and defence, or mass publics, can best be reached by dramatic acts of leadership. This is true for both domestic and foreign audiences. Resonant nonverbal gestures can be unparalleled in their economy and diffusion. First of all, they have the capacity to attract general attention where words might be overlooked. Abstractions such as alliance, prestige and power are hard to evoke verbally. Put in concrete form they become intelligible. There is also the point that acts carry more conviction than words. People tend to be sceptical of what politicians say. Furthermore, words are further removed than acts from the realities they are intended to convey. Demonstrative action has an unmediated effect not often possessed by sounds or signs on a page.

Then there is the mobilization factor. To move a community to endeavour requires an appeal to collective symbols – motifs that reach beyond the private experience of individuals to the myths of the group. By manipulating such signs, leaders are able to evoke powerful group associations. In time a leader may become, in his own person, an object of group pride and unity.

Lastly there is the unusual ability of nonverbal signs to evoke contradictory appeals which encapsulate at one and the same time affection and loyalty to the home country and hatred and fear of the enemy; or that appeal to instincts of sacrifice while simultaneously arousing a sense of continuing life. In doctrinal-based regimes ritual is particularly useful in maintaining an appearance of continuity during periods of ideological upheaval. Externally, nonverbal messages can suggest contrary things to different target groups.

Taking the metaphor of international communication as a form of theatre one step further, one can say that diplomacy involves a performer – the statesman or diplomat; props – including costume and other effects; a repertoire of stage gestures; and a setting – a backdrop against which the drama is enacted. There must also be a dramatic theme infusing the whole production with meaning; a *metteur-en-scène* to conceive this design; an audience to which the message is directed; and a written script.

Television has greatly extended the exemplary role of the national leader. By enacting and reflecting otherwise abstract political forces he renders them comprehensible. He communicates in four ways: by personal example, guiding the community in its conduct and attitudes; by signalling the position of his government to foreign observers; by personifying the commitment of his government to an ally or policy; by elevating political acts from the level of the profane to that of the sacred.

However, the crucial dramaturgical task of leadership is to put the various constituent elements of theatre together into an integrated whole – in short, to choreograph the performance. All items of communication must serve the ends of policy. The overall design may reflect the inspired vision of a de Gaulle, the sacred universe of a Shi'ite Iran, the ideology cum fabricated cult of a Nazi Germany or Soviet Russia, or the cultural pride of an ancient civilization such as an Egypt, India or China.

When a political choreographer sets about designing a piece of political theatre, whether a great formal occasion such as a state visit, a *coup de théâtre* or a more modest diplomatic or military set-piece, he must first define – not necessarily explicitly – the point of the performance. Is it intended to show off to the world the splendour and antiquity of one's heritage, the continuity of one's institutions, and therefore to put into perspective the comparatively trivial importance of some current preoccupation? Is it to be a display of military or technological power, intended to overawe one's guest and declare one's status? Or, if it is to win over the visitor, what theme can be chosen to reflect the parties' mutual interests while suggesting a more transcendental dimension?

Having decided upon his purpose and underlying message the details of the performance have to be painstakingly stitched together. The smallest touch may draw comment and the most outstanding political choreographers have been meticulously perfectionist. Former President Nixon notes that Chou En-lai personally picked the individual soldiers who were to make up the honour guard for the 1972 American presidential visit.[1]

If genius is attention to detail, the choreographer must, however, first consider the impression he himself will make on observers. Costume usage, while reflecting national orientation, can be subtly used to make a very precise political point. De Gaulle reverted to military uniform whenever he wished to invoke his aura of wartime national saviour. President Sadat of Egypt alternated between the simple man of the people, dressed like countless millions of his countrymen in the peasant's *jalabiyya*; the sophisticated international statesman, suave in his immaculately-tailored western-style suit; and the resolute war leader, smartly turned-out in the uniform of commander-in-chief of the Egyptian armed forces. (Somewhat maliciously Mohamed Heikal claims that Sadat's military wardrobe was actually designed by Pierre Cardin.[2]) Certainly the cut and colour of clothing can be artfully varied to create a desired audience response. A particular role may be defined or a broad palette of moods painted, from the sombre, via the formally correct, to the familiar or festive. Nor need idiosyncrasy be necessarily disadvantageous. Leaders such as Qaddafi, Idi Amin, Bokassa and Tito dressed extravagantly to seize the limelight and project their own self-importance and authority.

Bodily gesture is another device of political theatre. Here the effect of television has been pervasive. Since he is the focus of incessant scrutiny the public figure can hardly allow his own true feelings to leak through. Evidence of pleasure, anger, friendship, concern and so on, as expressed through gesture and facial expression, must as far as possible be regulated for political ends. Self-indulgence may have damaging political results. Equally, a well-judged performance may make the desired point unmistakably and economically. Again, it personalizes and hence renders comprehensible otherwise abtruse aspects of state policy.

Between strangers from different cultures the repertoire of gesture that can be effectively drawn upon is limited. Nevertheless much can be said. Variants of the handshake suggest quite precisely the state of a relationship. The embrace, though less common in the West, has come to signify doctrinal fraternity in many parts of the world. Henry Kissinger was a rare Western statesman to grasp the utility of such touches. His sensitivity in this regard contributed to the restoration of American influence in Egypt after 1973.

Other bodily gestures at the disposal of the diplomatic performer are the many small marks of courtesy – or displeasure – current in personal relationships, facial expression and hand movement. There is nothing original in the observation that we communicate extensively in this way. It is just that television has transformed formerly intimate mannerisms into signals of public import.

The props of political theatre include personal effects of all kinds such as pipes – usefully avuncular – weapons and batons of authority; gifts – always carefully chosen; and items of decor, such as furnishings, ornaments and paintings. All will be noticed and commented upon. Put together with flair, the scene is set, the stage prepared for political action.

Not all diplomatic activity, of course, is staged for the benefit of television. Much of the real business is conducted behind closed doors by the professionals. But even here nonverbal communication comes into play. Signals may be aimed at a more select audience, but this does not mean that theatrical principles cease to apply. Nonverbal messages are likely to be of as much interest to present participants and absent principals as any verbal exchange. What is implied is the use of a more specialized and low-key set of dramatic conventions. Some of these come under the rubric of diplomatic protocol; others are implicit and acquired by experience and insight.

Diplomatic cues may stand by themselves, as tactful substitutes for words, or accompany a verbal message in order to enlarge upon its precise meaning, whether to reinforce its credibility, regulate its gravity or emphasize its urgency. Changes in the status of diplomatic relations are a common way to communicate approbation and support – or their absence. The granting of protocol privileges beyond those strictly called for can make similar points, though blatant infringements of convention tend to be avoided. On the other hand the warmth of ceremonial and the hospitality extended at diplomatic meetings can be manipulated to make political points without violating basic courtesy. The choreography of official and state visits constitutes an art-form in its own right in the enactment of diplomatic sentiments.

At a less historic level the routine treatment of resident diplomats, including the promptness with which their requests are met and their access to top personnel, provides a sound guide to the standing of their government. In general, great attention is paid by guest and host to the nuances of diplomatic courtesy. Comparisons tend to be made with the reception and treatment of other visitors or envoys. Though few states are indifferent on this issue, it should be noted that the post-colonial states of Asia and Africa, with the trauma of subjugation to overcome and the acute sensitivity of group-oriented cultures to face and personal relationships, may well put form at the same level as substance.

The medium through which verbal messages are transmitted has to be carefully considered in diplomacy, an illustration of the symbolic link between word and act. Different forms of presentation convey varying degrees of urgency and commitment. The seniority of the bearer is another indication of the saliency of the messsage. The rank of an envoy or delegation establishes the importance of the information being carried.

In its dealings with the outside world the Communist bloc conforms with international practice. Its envoys assiduously maintain the conventions, formal and informal, of their non-Communist hosts. But as far as intra-bloc relations are concerned, and in its internal treatment of foreign diplomats, a supplementary protocol spread after the Second World War from the USSR to its satellites.

Fraternal parties and governments ground their relations in a special protocol that is intended to convey a sense of partnership in a universal movement. At the same time the Russian obsession with hierarchy has profoundly influenced Communist choreography. Nuances of status find expression in numerous ways.

A characteristic tool of Communist *mise-en-scène* is the degree of access one is granted to the party leadership (since the party, not the government, is the true repository of power) and the presence of top figures on both formal occasions and in substantive talks. Welcoming ceremonies are graded with great precision and provide another indubitable index of the standing of a guest in Soviet eyes. For privileged visitors unparalleled festivity and sumptuousness are the order of the day.

Communism, as a classic 'civil religion', is also replete with quasi-sacred occasions and ritual events which provide many opportunities for subtle political signalling. Party congresses, May Day and the anniversary of the revolution (or the national day, as may be the case) draw upon a broad range of expedients for conveying arcane points of ideology, foreign policy and political standing. Alongside the more familiar devices of slogan, etiquette and personal gesture, current preoccupations are reflected in portraiture, decoration and mass displays. The development of Soviet and Chinese foreign policy over the years can be accurately plotted through the themes of their great festive parades.

Given the pervasiveness of party control in the Communist system, many otherwise innocuous areas of activity acquire political significance. All public articulations, in whatever medium, are assumed to be purposive. Press photographs, news films and even postage stamps have long been used to signal foreign policy positions. Since the accession of Mikhail Gorbachev to power there is evidence of an increasingly sophisticated use of television.

Finally, culture and sport, considered in the West to be eminently non-political spheres of activity, are highly politicized in the Communist world. Artistes and sportsmen are sent abroad as ambassadors of the system. The visit of a top performer is a sure index of approval or political support. Cultural diplomacy has been especially effective in the Third World. Able to act without the constraints of public opinion or moral compunction, Soviet policy-makers have long grasped that for the post-colonial leadership arms may be more welcome than grain, form as valued as substance, face as important as truth.

Having said all this the reader may still feel that there remain a number of serious objections to devoting a monograph to the nonverbal dimension of diplomacy. One is that nonverbal communication is merely a peripheral phenomenon, at the most an appendage of language. Another is that a work of this kind falls into the trap of over-analysis, of reading too much into innocent happenings. A third is that symbolic politics is about appearances and not substance.

In the first place it should be reiterated that this account does not challenge the role of language. Word and gesture are two sides of the same semantic coin. But a distinction is valid, both to facilitate analysis and to point up the special features of nonverbal communication. Moreover as long as diplomatic gesture is considered incidental to language its real salience tends to be obscured. As to the argument to over-analysis, one can only plead that this is indeed how things are. The problem with American and even British diplomacy over the years has certainly not been one of over-sensitivity to nonverbal subtleties. 'Pragmatism' or 'realism' are admirable doctrines in so far as they go, emphasizing the primacy of objective interests and relative power over 'sentimental' and transient considerations. Now no one would dispute that in a competitive world states should and will seek to achieve advantage with such means as they have at their disposal. Empty posturing and moralizing are certainly to be avoided. Consequences and not wishful thinking are of the essence. However, the point is surely that the subjective and symbolic side of international relationships can have objective consequences. Attitudes, beliefs, perceptions and memories may be as momentous in their effects as tanks and trade figures. And to the extent that such subjective factors are modified by dramatic artifice, then symbolic action cannot be overlooked.

The 'theatre of power', in short, is as much about substance as about appearance. One way to demonstrate this is to examine the diplomacy of such successful statesmen as Charles de Gaulle, Chou En-lai and Anwar Sadat. It is no coincidence that each of these men was a master of diplomatic theatre. Moreover for all the differences in the circumstances and situation of their countries their conduct of foreign policy clearly displayed certain common dramaturgical features.

All three began their careers in utterly inauspicious circumstances. De Gaulle came to power (for a second time) with a France on the brink of civil war, her influence at a low point and a demoralized army.

Chou presided over the foreign affairs of a poverty-stricken, backward power which was ostracized by the Western world. Sadat inherited a deeply humiliated country, part of its territory under military occupation, held in open contempt by both friend and foe. Yet as a result of their skilful direction each one achieved great prestige for his country, restoring its position and influence in the international community. Nor was the achievement superficial but entailed a genuine amelioration in national power and status.

Obviously the dramaturgical dimension was only one facet of a complex picture, but it was no less decisive for that. The first characteristic possessed in common by these men was great personal dignity and stature accompanied by quite remarkable dramatic ability. They were accomplished performers in their own right, totally in their element when on stage, attentive to the fine detail of a performance, skilful at the technical preparation of a diplomatic appearance. No one seeing them in their public role could doubt for a moment that here were national leaders, displaying total poise and control. A second trait was their ability to radiate, in unequivocal terms, an immense pride in the antiquity and moral elevation of their civilizations. In time they came to personify for outsiders the essence of their cultures, perhaps because they had succeeded so well in enacting its innate qualities. Partly this personification derived from a sincere personal sense of destiny linking their own fate with that of the nation. It also surely derived from an adept manipulation of ritual, setting and props. Each leader was able to use the cultural resources of the state to great effect in the staging of diplomatic set-pieces.

In the substance of their diplomacies these leaders also shared a conviction of their own national centrality bordering on the arrogant. The international role they conceived for themselves was as ambitious as it was daring. Each insisted, in his own way, that his state be treated as a great power. Not for them a resignation to secondary status. They dealt in the big league as equals alongside other great powers. An utter refusal to accept either the appearance let alone substance of subordinacy went along with a stubborn nurturing of national autonomy. Independence was a value treasured above material benefit. All three leaders, in fact, demonstrated a willingness to pay a real price for seemingly insubstantial symbolic assets. Denied equal footing in NATO with the United States and Britain, de Gaulle simply left the organization. Chou refused to play second fiddle to the USSR and was prepared to take principle to the point of rupture. Sadat, in the throes of preparation for a fateful war, preferred to expel Soviet advisers rather than have them obstruct his freedom of manoeuvre. In purely strategic terms these actions were perceived at the time as bordering on the foolhardy. Seen in 'pragmatic' terms they did not make sense; they were magnificent, but not war. In fact the risks in each case were carefully calculated and any inconvenience gladly borne as a price well worth paying for the subsequent gain in self-respect, wider international standing and the demonstration that these powers would never reconcile themselves to supplicant status. The lesson is worth pausing over. These were not petty acts of petulance but immensely successful *coups de théâtre* which drew the attention and admiration of the world, put a superpower in its place at low cost and proved the leader's ability to make tough, crucial decisions. Whatever the consequences, they seemed to be saying, we are not to be taken for granted. If loyal compliance does not earn your respect and consideration, then you will have to witness the damage we can do when we choose not to cooperate.

Lastly, none of these leaders was ever deterred by unpopularity or painful isolation. On the contrary, they appeared to relish being out of step. Leadership in their view, both at the domestic and international levels, demanded a willingness 'to go it alone'. A state content with a diffident, self-effacing diplomacy, reconciling itself to the role of subordinate, can hardly expect the respect and influence that accrue only to the great. France under de Gaulle, China under Chou and the Egypt of Sadat, all saw themselves in leadership roles. In Europe de Gaulle accepted only the USSR as an equal and ruthlessly excluded Britain from the EEC to avoid any challenge to French domination of that body. Outside Europe he received the respect due to a leading world statesman representing a very great power. This was not the least because de Gaulle consciously demanded nothing less than treatment 'fit for a king'. On trips to places like Mexico, Canada and the Soviet Union the tangible achievement was secondary to the appearance of international stature. But de Gaulle understood that prestige is in itself an asset to be assiduously cultivated. It translates into real influence, military credibility and respect for the products of one's industries. Moreover it has constructive domestic implications, fostering internal pride, unity and purpose.

Like de Gaulle, Chou single-mindedly conducted himself as the trustee of a state of the very highest rank. Transient circumstances may have momentarily weakened China's material resources. However, in historical terms the elevation of her role was unquestioned. Excluded from the United Nations, where as a permanent member of the security council China would have acquired great power status as of right, Chou brilliantly engineered the nonaligned movement of

African and Asian countries as a fitting forum for the exercise of Chinese influence and the consolidation of her legitimacy. For his part Sadat saw Egypt – as, indeed, had Nasser – as a regional and Third World great power, and himself as an international statesman of the first order. In Mohamed Heikal's words: 'By going to Jerusalem Sadat achieved a world-wide constituency.' He was 'one of the Third World leaders who realized the implications of the communications revolution'.[3] Unfortunately the very achievement of the peace treaty with Israel which regained the Sinai for Egypt and placed the resources of the West at his disposal, also cut Sadat off from the Arab world. His expectation that others would be bound to follow in his footsteps proved, in the short run at least, to be a serious miscalculation.

It would be foolish to claim that these giant figures were without their shortcomings. Their faults were on the same scale as their successes. What they displayed was an acute sensitivity not only to the substance and reality of power but also to its intangible dimension. For them theatre and symbolism were vital elements in the equation. One would be hard put to find examples of these men submitting to such humiliations as the Hills affair. (To secure the release of a British lecturer sentenced to death in Idi Amin's Uganda in 1975, the Wilson government agreed to send two senior officers bearing a letter from the Queen. 'I am only fierce to the British because I want these people to kneel down at my feet', Amin was quoted as saying. After having kept the officers waiting Amin received them in a traditional African thatched house with a low door. To get in the two men had to bend over. Uganda radio actually reported that they went down on their knees, but the Foreign Office insisted that they merely had to 'stoop'. When this gesture proved insufficient Her Majesty's Foreign Secretary, James Callaghan, went out to Uganda to receive Hills. Despite the evident indignity of the whole affair, there was almost unanimous support in parliament for the government's approach. Enoch Powell's accusation that the Crown had been humiliated was dismissed as 'idiosyncratic' by the foreign secretary.)[4]

The Hills case demonstrates that the implications of diplomatic theatre cannot always be taken as read. Politicians are clearly not like Molière's *bourgeois gentilhomme* who effortlessly spoke prose as well as any scholar. Nonverbal communication requires every bit as much tact and painstaking attention as the drafting of a legal text. Just as a lack of basic technical expertise would not be pardoned in any other field of public service, so is it equally intolerable for the conduct of a state's foreign policy to be jeopardized by the 'illiteracy' of practitioners.

However, it is one thing for British policy-makers to neglect the intangible dimension of power, quite another when the culprit is a superpower. Yet for all its awesome responsibility and experience since 1945, the United States has displayed a remarkable lack of dramaturgical self-consciousness. The most recent administration for which we have first-hand evidence is that of President Carter. The picture one obtains is of serious and continuous diplomatic mis-signalling and a failure to grasp the meaning of symbolic factors. The most grotesque example was the Iran hostages affair, seen as a humanitarian issue when at stake was the prestige and credibility of the main pillar of Western civilization. But let us restrict ourselves to a brief glance at the United States' relations with the Soviet Union and the People's Republic of China – relations upon which the central balance of power and therefore world peace ultimately rest.

It has already been pointed out how President Carter incorrectly resorted to the 'Hot Line' to communicate with President Brezhnev. A typical instance of Carter's obtuseness on these matters is revealed by his own account of a meeting with Soviet Foreign Minister Gromyko to discuss the momentous question of disarmament. On Carter's desk in the White House was a small wooden display showing all the American and Soviet missiles known to exist. At the end of their meeting the President decided, 'on the spur of the moment', to present it to Gromyko. Not surprisingly the foreign minister was 'taken aback' at the gesture: 'the set of models showed the gigantic size and many types of Soviet missiles contrasted with the few and relatively compact American ICBMs'.[5]

The significance of his action or indeed that it might be seen as a meaningful gesture at all seems to have escaped the president. Yet here was the leader of a superpower, engaged in a tough and crucial negotiation, giving a gift. And not just any gift, but a model of his missile force contrasted unfavourably with that of his rival. It must have seemed to Gromyko like an astonishing acknowledgement of American inferiority. At the best it was naive and confused. To the argument that one is reading too much into a generous and spontaneous action of little importance one can only make the rejoinder that superpower relations hardly provide a fitting context for generous and spontaneous actions. The point is that gift-giving is of its very essence symbolic, the investment of some minor artefact with significance in order to make a statement about a relationship. Furthermore a Soviet foreign minister, of all people, would be acutely sensitive to anything redolent of the symbolism of hierarchy.

Should there be any doubt, though, of the effect of these errors, let us consider another lapse that occurred during the Afghanistan crisis. Only two months after the Soviet invasion of that country President Carter decided, at the suggestion of Secretary of State Vance, to send a senior aide with a message for President Brezhnev. It was bad enough that the initiative was to be taken at all. Vice-President Mondale rightly saw that it could be taken as a 'sign of weakness'. However, worse was in store. When the state department applied for a visa for the envoy – Marshall Shulman – they were humiliatingly snubbed. The Soviet ambassador told Brzezinski that 'somebody at Shulman's level might be able to see the Soviet Deputy Foreign Minister but certainly not Brezhnev'. Turning the knife in the wound, Dobrynin added: 'We want to talk to someone who shapes policy, not to a messenger. This is not serious. Did the President actually approve it? I really thought the whole idea was an effort by you, Zbig, to indicate to us that you are not serious about negotiating.'[6] So the Soviet Union had pocketed America's admission that the invasion of Afghanistan was negotiable and now contemptuously rubbed in American powerlessness and irrelevance by declining even to receive the envoy.

In the light of the erosion of American credibility effected by the Carter administration a simultaneous impression of collusion with the anti-Soviet policies of the People's Republic of China was not only ill-considered but also positively dangerous. We have already mentioned the way in which Carter was manipulated by Deng Xiaoping during the latter's visit to the United States in January–February 1979 on the very eve of the Chinese offensive against Vietnam. It is therefore somewhat alarming to read Carter's own pained and self-righteous version of events: 'When the Chinese military forces crossed the northern Vietnam border in February 1979, the Soviet leaders immediately accused us of complicity in the act – although this was, of course, untrue.'[7] Note the 'of course'; it was incomprehensible to Carter that Deng's visit to Washington two weeks before the attack and the elaborate choreography of alliance that pervaded public appearances of the American and Chinese leaders could have such an effect on outside observers.

At the risk of labouring the point, it should be reiterated in conclusion that the impressions and messages one conveys nonverbally are read every bit as assiduously and are as politically consequential as what one communicates in so many words. Because a humiliation is unspoken and implicit makes it no less damaging in terms both of domestic morale and international reputation. Misleading or confusing information can be conveyed equally well by gesture as by word of mouth. Thus nonverbal communication is not a mere footnote to a basically linguistic agenda, but a crucial instrument of diplomacy in its own right. International politics is being increasingly conducted on a great stage, as it were, under the eyes of a watchful audience. Better to be oversensitive to nuance than obtuse. Considering the issues at stake in international comprehension, one neglects the theatre of power only at one's peril.

REFERENCES AND NOTES

1. Nixon R M 1982 *Leaders*. Sidgwick and Jackson, p 224
2. Heikal M 1983 *Autumn of Fury*. André Deutsch, photo between pp 66 and 67
3. *Ibid.*, p 5
4. *The Times* 14 June 1975, 21 June 1975, 22 June 1975; Great Britain House of Commons, *Parliamentary Debates* 1974–75, vol 893 col 962, vol 894, col 166
5. Carter J 1982 *Keeping Faith*. Bantam Books: New York, pp 221–2
6. Brzezinski Z 1983 *Power and Principle*. Weidenfeld and Nicolson, pp 435–6
7. Carter J 1982, *op. cit.*, p 237

INDEX